This book is the first to investigate the problems that committed Catholics allegedly faced if they sought careers in state employment under the Third Republic in France.

Using ministerial and Masonic archives, the book explores the broad divergence of practice between individual ministries and between particular governments, depending on the current climate of Church–State relations. It also examines the factors that underlay these discriminatory attitudes – notably the accusations of Catholic involvement in the right-wing subversive activities of the late 1890s at the time of the Dreyfus affair. This assessment draws extensively on evidence in the Jesuit and Assumptionist archives, as well as in the Archivio Segreto Vaticano and the personal papers of the monarchist pretenders. It likewise investigates the increased difficulties that French Catholics faced after the change of pope in 1903. The autonomous archives of the papal Segretaria di Stato confirm the view that if the Austrian intervention had not then prevented Cardinal Rampolla from becoming pope, Church–State relations might have evolved very differently in France. Later chapters explore the degree to which wariness towards committed Catholics in the public services evaporated under later regimes, despite the traumas of the Vichy years.

The Wiles Lectures given at The Queen's University of Belfast

Religion, politics and preferment in France
since 1890

Religion, politics and preferment in France since 1890

La Belle Epoque and its legacy

Maurice Larkin

Richard Pares Professor of History, University of Edinburgh

CAMBRIDGE
UNIVERSITY PRESS

Published by the Press Syndicate of the University of Cambridge
The Pitt Building, Trumpington Street, Cambridge CB2 1RP
40 West 20th Street, New York, NY 10011–4211, USA
10 Stamford Road, Oakleigh, Melbourne 3166, Australia

First published 1995

Printed in Great Britain by Redwood Books, Kennet House, Kennet

A catalogue record for this book is available from the British Library

Library of Congress cataloguing in publication data
Larkin, Maurice.
Religion, politics, and preferment in France since 1890: la Belle
Epoque and its legacy / Maurice Larkin.
    p.   cm. – (The Wiles lectures)
Includes bibliographical references and index.
ISBN 0 521 41916 6 (hc)
1. Catholics – France – History – 20th century. 2. Civil servants –
France – History – 20th century. 3. Church and state – France –
History – 20th century. 4. France – Church history – 20th century.
5. France – Politics and government – 20th century. I. Title.
II. Series.
BX1530.2.L37   1995
282'.44'0902–dc20   94–20600 CIP

ISBN 0 521 41916 6 hardback

WD

Contents

Preface

Lord Halifax wrote in 1690 that 'the struggle for knowledge hath a pleasure in it like that of wrestling with a fine woman'. While French scholars can seldom be accused of faint-heartedness in fighting the good fight, they also have a shrewd eye for assessing opponents with whom it is wiser not to tangle. This presumably explains why the main theme of this book has not been previously addressed by any of the numerous French historians who would be far better placed to attempt it than I have been.

The greater part of this text is based on the Wiles lectures which I was privileged to give in 1986. The Wiles Trustees specify that the lectures should be 'broad in character and of a pioneering nature'. This is not an easy combination, since innovatory research by an individual tends necessarily to take place on a fairly narrow front – while any attempt at innovation on a broad scale inevitably invites accusations of being merely speculative. I hoped that my subject, spanning a century of change, would meet the criterion of breadth, and that the untried nature of my theme would provide the pioneering spirit that the Trustees were seeking to stimulate.

Readers should therefore not expect a general survey of religious issues in French politics, even if the intelligibility of the book's main theme has required a fair amount of this background to be sketched in. Its prime aim is to examine the problems that committed Catholics allegedly faced if they sought careers in state employment in France – more particularly in the branches that were regarded as politically sensitive. The larger part of the book concerns 'la Belle Epoque' – the period 1890 to 1914, when the issue was at its most contentious. But the later chapters investigate the degree to which these problems evaporated in the years that followed.

Current discussion of the matter – insofar as it exists – tends at times to be little more than an exchange of assertions and denials, reminiscent of the Devonshire debating society's 'It be!', 'It bain't!', 'It be!', 'It bain't!', etc. One side claims that during the anticlerical years of the Belle Epoque, there were wide categories of public service in which regular church-going was regarded as a disqualification not only for positions of trust but also for quite modest employment in many regions. 'My grandfather remembers seeing the mayor's secretary outside church on Sunday mornings, mentally noting those who went to Mass' is a frequent refrain in such discussions – as is 'my great-uncle gave up going to church when he became a revenue collector [or prefecture clerk, etc, etc]'. On a more exalted level, there are many who claim that it was only in the armed services and the diplomatic corps that committed Catholics felt welcome; elsewhere it was a matter of keeping a low profile and counting on the tolerance or indifference of superiors and promotion committees. Others respond that these claims are not only grossly exaggerated, but insofar as anticlerical discrimination took place in the public sector it was as a result of the anti-Republican milieux from which the rejected applicants came; Catholics who professed their faith unobtrusively and who were clearly loyal to the Republic could enter any branch of the *fonctions publiques* – except the *corps préfectoral* which was the main instrument of government policy in the provinces, including its anticlerical legislation.

Neglect of the matter by historians has stemmed from three major difficulties. The official obstacles to obtaining access to the personal dossiers of civil servants for this period prevent large-scale sampling over a wide spectrum of ministries; and it is significant that the few existing prosopographical studies of state employees for these years are generally limited to small samples in individual branches of the public service. Moreover these studies are largely concerned with the socio-economic origins of *fonctionnaires* and make little attempt to ascertain their attitudes and personal convictions. To do so is difficult, not only because of the restricted access to dossiers, but also because of the reticence of these dossiers in such matters. Present-day arbitration bodies, investigating claims of racial or gender discrimination, are well aware that selection boards are unlikely to commit their prejudices to paper when justifying their decisions; so departmental dossiers may give very little idea of the real motives of selectors in rejecting candidates. But at least the investigators of such cases have a fair idea of the colour and gender of the rejected applicants, whereas the historian, investigating anticlerical discrimination, is often hard put to it to distinguish the committed Catholic from the bulk of French applicants – whose forms indicate that they were baptised Catholics, but who in fact had long since ceased to have any significant religious commitment.

As explained in the central part of this book, these archival and methodological difficulties are not insuperable; and I eventually obtained access to sufficient samples of *fonctionnaires'* dossiers for certain patterns to emerge. There also exist additional ways of approaching the issue –

notably through the use of secondary-school records, although these too present serious problems of interpretation. Yet the resulting evidence is inevitably tenuous, making it hard to come to firm conclusions – let alone conclusions that could be pithily summarised in a brief preface such as this.

It is nevertheless clear that even in the quarter-century of the Belle Epoque there were marked fluctuations in the fortunes of committed Catholics seeking state employment. It is likewise clear that even in the most virulent years of anticlerical government, Catholics had little difficulty in entering and rising in the more technical ministries where professional skill rather than political commitment was the principal requirement. The contentious areas were those ministries and *grands corps d'état* where the government felt the need to be assured of the complete loyalty of its servants, especially in the implementation of policies that some *fonctionnaires* might personally find uncongenial; and there was endless debate as to which branches of the public service should be classified in this way. On the one hand, Catholics objected to the inclusion of the judiciary, whose role, they argued, should be that of complete impartiality; while, on the other, the Masonic Grand Orient argued for the inclusion of all forms of public employment – given the need to protect the young Republic from clerical subversion. The book makes substantial use of Masonic archives to examine the role of the Grand Orient in this matter – and also to assess its highly organised system of soliciting employment and promotion for Masons in the public services. While its attempts to 'declericalise' the Army are well known, its parallel if more diffuse activities in civil service matters have hitherto received little attention.

If the main part of the book seeks to assess the extent to which committed Catholics were kept out of public positions of trust, the opening chapters examine whether Catholics deserved the suspicion they encountered. The personal papers of the Orleanist and Bonapartist pretenders reveal the involvement of several Catholic figures with the abortive schemes for overthrowing the regime in the 1890s, as well as disclosing the cautious interest of a number of Catholic generals. The more ambivalent attitudes and involvement of members of the clergy are also looked at in these pages with the help of the Assumptionist and Jesuit archives in Rome, supplemented by the Archivio Segreto Vaticano. The Vatican itself had an important if indirect effect on how French Catholics were viewed in government circles. Leo XIII (1878–1903) was anxious to be on good terms with the Republic – partly in the vain hope of obtaining French help in his chimerical bid to recover Rome from the Italian government, as the Vatican archives amply demonstrate. His

Secretary of State and close confidant, Mariano Rampolla, would undoubtedly have succeeded him as Pope, had not the Austrian government intervened to prevent his election. The book demonstrates how the very different policies of Pius X and Merry del Val exacerbated Church–State tension in France, compounding the difficulties of French Catholics in seeking public employment. The autonomous archives of the papal Secretariat of State, hitherto unused for these matters, reveal the deep divergence of views between Rampolla and the new Secretary of State – thereby underlining how very different the fortunes of the French Church might have been if Rampolla had not been deprived of the tiara by Austrian intervention. Rampolla's continued membership of the Holy Congregation for Extraordinary Ecclesiastical Affairs enables the reader of its minutes and papers to measure the extent of their differences on a wide range of issues.

The third and final section of the book investigates Catholic penetration of the *fonctions publiques* in the period since the First World War and the factors that allowed it. The historian is here deprived of the archival sources that make the Belle Epoque such a rewarding area for research. The Vatican archives are not available for the post-1922 period, while access to the personal dossiers of French civil servants requires even greater luck and ingenuity than it does for the pre-war years. This makes for thinner evidence and a thinner story. The effect on the shape of this book is to make it somewhat like Erik Satie's *Morceaux en forme de poire*: a full-bottomed base for the Belle Epoque; a tapering waist for the forty-five years that followed; and a slender stem for the period since the Debré law of 1959.

Yet this dwindling girth is not just a matter of archival short commons; it is primarily a reflection of the dwindling nature of the issue at stake. Although the inter-war years did not see as great a *rapprochement* between Church and Republic as the warm-hearted titles of some histories might suggest, animosities were undoubtedly less acute than they had been before the war. Even the unhappy record of the Catholic hierarchy during the Vichy years did not result in the massive retribution against Catholics that many had predicted – for reasons that are explained in the penultimate chapter. Moreover the Fourth and Fifth Republics saw the inclusion of a substantial number of Catholic ministers in government, thereby making the *cordon sanitaire* around the last bastions of Republican purity in the civil service increasingly anachronistic. Even so, the *droits acquis* and hard-won promotion procedures of the various ministries ensured that there would be no substantial change of personnel until the eligible survivors of earlier, less tolerant regimes had reached the age of retirement. By the late 1960s, however, the religious issue itself had lost much of its political significance. The concessions to Catholic education in the Debré law of 1959 had largely removed the *raison d'être* of the principal Catholic lobby in parliament, while the rapid decline in formal religious practice during the 1960s helped to soothe the fears of surviving old-style anticlericals. These and other adjacent issues are discussed in the final chapter.

Readers may well wonder whether any place in this book has been devoted to members of other religions. Although the title speaks of 'religion', the contents page refers continually to 'Catholics'. At the turn of the century nine-tenths of the population were baptised as Catholics – whatever their personal convictions in adult life – and the politico-religious issues that divided Church and Republic had much less significance for Protestants and Jews – as is explained in the opening chapter. Indeed Protestants were an intrinsic part of the Republican establishment; and the barriers that Jews encountered in some of the elite branches of state employment during the Belle Epoque stemmed from racial prejudice rather than specific politico-religious factors. The same might be said of the problems faced by Muslims and other immigrant groups in more recent decades. This is not to deny the existence of important religious factors in these situations, but their complexity lies beyond what can be effectively examined in a book of this length.

The pursuit of a complicated subject through a century of its development and decline has inevitably left me with many debts of gratitude. In the field of religious and political issues, Françoise and Jean-Marie Mayeur have long been a source of help, advice and encouragement, as have Ralph Gibson and Emile Poulat. Before embarking on this book, I knew very little of the chequered world of the French civil service, and I owe much to the early comments and suggestions of Vincent Wright, Marie-Christine Kessler and the late Louis Fougère. I have also benefited from the knowledge, expertise and benign scepticism of many others, notably Jacques Aubert, René Bargeton, Bernard Bergerot, Paul Bouteiller, Michel Brisacier, Christophe Charle, Jacques Delors, André Encrevé, Danièle Hervieu-Léger, Yves-Marie Hilaire, Bertrand Joly, Jean-Pierre Machelon, René Rémond, Pierre Sorlin and Guy Thuillier. I should also like to thank the many archivists, public and private, whose interest and goodwill eased my access to information that would otherwise have eluded me. In this respect, the school-records staff of the Collège Stanislas and the Ecole Ste Geneviève were outstandingly helpful.

I am especially indebted to Mrs Austen Boyd whose generosity resulted in the foundation of the Wiles Lectures in memory of her father,

Thomas S. Wiles. I must also express my gratitude to Lewis Warren, Denys Hay, Geoffrey Elton and David Harkness for their preliminary work in arranging my delivery of these lectures. Lewis Warren and his fellow Wiles Trustees and departmental colleagues made my stay in the Queen's University, Belfast, a particularly happy one. I gained enormously from their contributions to the discussion sessions that followed each lecture; and I would especially thank those participants who came from other universities to give us the benefit of their expertise: Christopher Andrew, Roger Austen, Geoffrey Cubitt, Brian Fitzpatrick, Ralph Gibson, Hugh Gough, Douglas Johnson and James McMillan. The metamorphosis of the lectures into the present book has been heavily dependent on the patience of William Davies of Cambridge University Press, while the preparation of the text for publication has been greatly eased by the vigilant eye and swift thinking of Virginia Catmur.

My greatest debt, as always, is to my wife, Enid. Not only did she participate in much of the research, but she typed the entirety of the text, and, together with my daughter, Katie, prepared the Index.

Part 1

As it was: Catholics and the Republic, 1890–1914

1   Ralliés and *dérailleurs*: Catholics and subversion

'Les deux France'

When Disraeli spoke of Britain as 'two nations', the division he saw was primarily socio-economic. When French writers spoke of 'les deux France', the division they had in mind was primarily political. On the one side there was democratic France, heir to the Revolution and optimistic in its faith in the power of reason and knowledge to create a better future. On the other there was conservative France, sceptical about mankind's capacity for progress unless guided by its tried-and-true mentors – the ruling elites whose experience, education and material stake in the country guaranteed stability and common sense, and whose entitlement to lead the nation was buttressed by the legacy of Church and monarchy. If French Socialists were more inclined to share Disraeli's socio-economic vision of the divided nation, even they frequently resorted to the political imagery of 'les deux France'. For them, as for Clemenceau, 'la Révolution est un bloc' – with the Church squarely placed in the tradition of repression and distrust of human nature. For these reasons the governments of the Third Republic felt the need to be wary about placing committed Catholics in positions of power and influence. Catholics for their part riposted that the Third Republic was indeed 'deux France' – 'la république des camarades', where favour and advancement went to the supporters of the ruling Republican parties, and an outer wilderness where committed Catholics were condemned to keep company with other pariahs of the regime, deprived of public outlets for their talents, other than the armed services and the diplomatic corps. Polemicists described them, in Tertullian's phrase, as 'exiles in their own country'.[1]

The prime purpose of this book is to investigate the truth of such a claim. But a major problem for contemporaries – and for present-day historians – was how to define a Catholic. There were *catholiques avant tout* whose personal lives were strongly influenced by their religious beliefs, and whose political choices were strongly influenced by what they thought to be in the best interests of the Church – even if it was at the expense of their own ambitions or the material interests of their own particular social group. There were others whose Catholicism was essentially a product of their social background – part of a package of upbringing and group loyalties. They would defend Church interests as part of this package, but the Church could not necessarily rely on them if group and Church interests parted company on political issues. And between these two categories there was an infinitude of intermediary positions, which the occupants themselves would have been hard put to define or fully comprehend. There was also much overlap and shifting of positions. Many 'social-package' Catholics became *catholiques avant tout* and periodically found themselves at odds with their social peers on specific matters. And in a country where the vast majority of people were christened as Catholics and counted on a religious marriage and burial, there was the great amorphous mass of 'don't really know or care' whose religious allegiance was as vague and marginal as the appellation 'C. of E.' in British army records – which covered anyone who did not specifically claim to be something else. The breadth of meaning to 'Catholic' in France often surprised self-professed Catholics in pre-dominantly Protestant cultures, for whom Catholicism meant allegiance to a distinctive minority with an uncompromising code of beliefs and practices which one accepted or rejected as a whole rather than in parts. Indeed the easy-going uncertainty of many self-styled Catholics in France was much more comprehensible to an English 'C. of E.' or similar adherant to a majority faith, whose nominal membership entailed little personal inconvenience and was apparently compatible with a wide range of life-styles and political options.

A study of this kind has to limit itself to the problems of 'practising Catholics' – those with some degree of commitment to the Church – even if this epithet embraced not only *catholiques avant tout* but a sizeable slice of the 'social-package' variety as well. But it was precisely this bunching together of elements from both categories as 'practising Catholics' that gave rise to many of the difficulties and injustices of Republican govern-ments in their dealings with the Church. France was spared the tagging of rival ethnic groups as 'Catholic' and 'Protestant' that bedevils the pol-itics of Ulster. Yet there was an analogous tagging of conservative and anti-Republican groups in France as 'Catholic', because, as with Irish Republicans, many of their members were self-professedly Catholic. The exclusion of such groups from certain branches of the public services took in its wake the exclusion of committed Catholics who were of no particular political persuasion and were not necessarily ill disposed towards the governments of the Republic, despite the anticlerical record of a fair number of them. Yet it would be a distortion of the facts to see the exclusion of these Catholics as merely a crude failure to discriminate between Catholics *tout court* and Catholics who were opponents of the government and its policies. There was unquestionably much intrinsic matter that set Church and Republic against each other.

The importance and stridency of religious issues in French politics partly reflected the fact that the dominant spokesman of religious interests in France was the highly disciplined and doctrinally monolithic Catholic Church, with its world-wide commitments and complex diplomatic concerns. France lacked the religious pluralism of several of her neighbours, where denominational diversity tended to blur and soften the confrontations of Church and State. The limited headway made by the Reformation in sixteenth-century France had left Protestantism vulnerable to persecution by Catholic monarchs, with the result that it had only a small numerical base. Even in the 1890s baptised Protestants were well under a million, perhaps 800,000, of whom the bulk belonged to the Calvinist Eglise Réformée and most of the others to the Lutheran Eglise de la Confession d'Augsbourg. Jews probably numbered about 80,000. The fact that Protestantism lacked the administrative and doctrinal unity of the Catholic Church allowed a greater diversity of opinion within it, which rendered it less intransigent towards the ideas and attitudes of secular Republicanism; and this allowed it to cohabit reasonably comfortably with the militant secularism of the late nineteenth century. Much of the conflict between Church and State under the Third Republic was for intellectual control of the rising generation. During the early years of the Third Republic, the Church had openly sympathised with the monarchists – seeing them as a bulwark against the secular ideals of the more militant Republicans. For the Republicans it was a matter of deep concern that a large minority of the children of France were educated in Catholic schools, where they were subjected to irrational Christian concepts such as Revelation and imbued with hostile attitudes towards the Republican establishment. The result was a long struggle, culminating at the turn of the century in the dispersal of thousands of monks, friars and nuns, the closure of many of their schools, and the disestablishment of the Church in 1905.

In France as a whole in the 1890s, well over 90 per cent of the population had been baptised as Catholics. Yet on reaching adolescence, the great majority ceased to go to Mass; and their subsequent visits to Church were largely restricted to the *rites de passage* of marriage, christenings, *communions solennelles* and burial. This was a situation which had its reflection in other denominations, but which was arguably more significant and disturbing for Catholics, in that they had been traditionally taught that deliberate non-attendance at Sunday Mass was a matter of grave sin. The reasons for this decline are familiar enough. In much of western Europe the traditional social compulsions to church-going were eroded by the massive socio-economic changes of the nineteenth century; but these were compounded in France by the experience and legacy of the French Revolution, which inaugurated periods of government hostility. At the same time the Revolutionary and Napoleonic inheritance laws, with their equal division of property among heirs, created for the peasantry a tension between traditional Church teaching on sexual morality on the one hand, and, on the other, the growing economic imperatives in France to limit family size. By the turn of the century only a fifth or a quarter of the adult French population could be regarded as practising Catholics, in that they went to Mass regularly on Sundays and outwardly conformed to the other prescriptions of the Church, such as Eastertide communion. And of these, the majority were women. Observance was highest in the remote pastoral areas of France, such as the Breton peninsula, the Massif Central, and the eastern uplands, where there was less sustained contact with the changing patterns of secular behaviour and attitudes, and where traditions lasted longer. But it was also high in those areas of France that bordered on the parts of Belgium and the German Rhineland where Catholicism was traditionally strong-rooted, and which had not been subject to anticlerical programmes on the scale of those of Republican France, except during their brief period of annexation to France during the French Revolution. Catholic observance was likewise strong in those parts of France where there had traditionally been confrontation between Catholics and Protestants – and where regular church-going was an assertion of tribal loyalty (see map on p. 206).

L'Esprit Nouveau

By the late 1880s it was evident to many percipient Catholics that the Republic was there to stay – and that until the bulk of French Catholics accepted the fact, the Church could not expect better treatment from the politicians who ruled France. The collapse of Boulangism in 1889 confirmed Pope Leo XIII in this view and resulted in the encyclical of February 1892 advising French Catholics to accept the Republican regime. Concern for their well-being, however, was not the only reason for this eminently sensible step. As demonstrated in later pages (pp. 54–8), he and his Secretary of State, Cardinal Mariano Rampolla, entertained vain hopes that this conciliatory move towards the French government might induce it to support the Pope in his various attempts to recover Rome which the Papacy had lost to the Italian government in 1870. While this hope was to remain a pathetic illusion, the papal policy of a *ralliement* to the Republic was undoubtedly of unqualified benefit to the Church in France. The move was welcomed by disillusioned monarchists who were looking for an occasion to drop old loyalties which had become an embarrassment, and join forces with conservative Republicans against left-wing demands for social reform. At the same time the moderate Republicans who were in office in the mid 1890s were glad enough to have the support of Catholics against the Left – and were prepared to resist the demands of militant secularists for further anticlerical legislation. This was notably true of the ministries of Charles Dupuy (May 1894–January 1895), Alexandre Ribot (January–October 1895) and Jules Méline (April 1896–June 1898). The Catholic Ralliés had some thirty to forty seats in the Chamber of Deputies which, when added to the two hundred and fifty-odd moderate Republicans, gave these governments a comfortable majority against the Radicals and Socialists, as well as marginalising still further the fifty or so members of the dissident Right. Until ill-health weakened his voice, their most effective speaker was the widely respected if often mistaken Albert de Mun, who had abandoned royalism in obedience to papal policy. Ironically their most representative figures, the committed Republicans, Etienne Lamy and Jacques Piou, were both outside parliament in the mid-'nineties, although playing major roles in the 1898 electoral campaign. Indeed by the middle of the decade it seemed that Catholics were well placed to become part of the conservative Republican establishment, with the more fashionable Catholic schools attracting a growing clientele from staunch Republican families who were seduced by their social distinction and conscious emphasis on character-building. While Catholics with a social conscience might regret that the Church was being welcomed into the Republican fold for the wrong reasons, this so-called 'esprit nouveau' between Church and government had the merit of removing the religious issue and the constitutional issue from the forefront of French politics and clearing the parliamentary decks for the discussion of the basic social and economic issues that dominated politics in most advanced parliamentary democracies.

The significance of these developments for the main theme of this book was that entry into the more political branches of the Civil Service was likely to become easier for those committed Catholics who had hitherto been regarded with suspicion. Indeed, as later chapters will demonstrate, the Méline ministry (April 1896–June 1898) was already seeing a softening of the situation.

Yet there were unquestionably a large number of Catholics who resented the Pope's advice to accept the Republic; and of those who ostensibly followed it, many did so merely to stand on firmer ground in their fight against Republican ideals. The explosion of the Dreyfus Affair in the late 1890s seemed to offer them – and their opponents – the opportunity to snuff out the *esprit nouveau* and realign the nation's politics along the old fault lines of the religious and constitutional issues. It was this that called into question once more the fitness of committed Catholics for employment in positions of public trust and gave rise to demands that all members of the *fonctions publiques*, including officers of the armed services, be products of the state school system (see pp. 79–81). More tangibly, it led to a sustained attack on the counter-system of Catholic private schools – where so many Catholic officers and civil servants were educated – and ultimately resulted in the closure of over nearly a third of them (see pp. 43–4).

It is arguable that the Dreyfus Affair itself brought nothing fundamentally new to French politics, but merely revealed with startling clarity the division that still existed between 'les deux France'. It gave militant secularists the opportunity to recreate the old Republican concentration of the pre-Ralliement period. Radicals and Socialists were able to reinflate the clerical spectre; and many Socialists saw the Affair as a chance for their party to come in out of the cold – while the more sanguine among them hoped that the generous Republican *élan*, engendered by the Affair, would gather a momentum that would eventually carry government activity into the sphere of social reform.

Although the courtmartialling of Dreyfus for allegedly supplying military secrets to Germany dated back to 1894, it needed the suicide in August 1898 of one of Dreyfus's principal accusers, Colonel Hubert Henry, to multiply public misgivings about the conviction and make a retrial inescapable. Anti-Republicans now feared that public opinion would sway in favour of Dreyfus and destroy the image they had created of a vilified army valiantly protecting France against the traitors that the Republic had set in its midst – not only Dreyfus himself, but the Jews, Protestants and Freemasons with whom the Republic was allegedly colonising the public services. This campaign to use the Affair as a stick to beat the Republic was in danger of collapse; and it was in a mood of desperation that the more militant among them turned their minds to a *coup de main*. Such action might also benefit from the current wave of industrial unrest in Paris and from the government's embarrassment over its recent capitulation to Britain over the Fashoda episode of September 1898.

The historian is confronted with two problems. In the first place, there is still disagreement as to whether this subversive activity amounted to a

serious threat to the Republic. And, secondly, it is still debated whether
the degree of Catholic involvement justified the subsequent reprisals
against Catholic schools and against the Catholic presence in certain
branches of the public services. This chapter seeks to clarify both issues
in the light of little-used archival evidence.

The events of 1898–9

Any examination of these problems inevitably starts with Paul
Déroulède, leader of the Ligue des Patriotes; but other elements among
the Right-wing opponents of the regime sought to profit from his
activities. Speculation has surrounded the degree of involvement of the
Army, the monarchist pretenders and the Church; and all of them
were caught in varying degrees in the retribution that followed – with
the Church arguably the prime victim of the retaliatory action of the
successive governments that came to power with a mandate to root out
the sources of subversion. Clarification of these issues has been aided by
the release of three major sets of documents at the Archives Nationales
in Paris and by the growing range of papers now available in various
ecclesiastical archives in Rome – particularly those of the Jesuit and
Assumptionist orders, and of the Vatican and papal Secretariat of State.[2]
Of the three French collections, the papers of Paul Déroulède are the
least illuminating in that they reveal disappointingly little about his
activities in 1898–9. They largely consist of letters addressed to him; and
it would appear that the more revealing ones were ultimately destroyed,
following the non-fulfilment of his intention to write a personal account
of his political activities. The surviving letters confirm the impression
that public esteem for his patriotism was much more widely felt than
sympathy for the plebiscitary republicanism which he and his Ligue des
Patriotes had also come to represent. But they leave no doubt about
the resplendent cult-image he enjoyed among the *sociétés de tir et de
gymnastique* and in the café-concerts of the artisan belt and elsewhere.
The headed notepaper of his correspondents gives tantalising glimpses of
the widely entrenched demi-culture of popular patriotism. 'Georges
Lenique. Le Turco Virtuose. Dans ses Chansons et Scènes Militaires
avec sonneries de clairon' or 'Le Zouave Leprince. Le Barde Militaire.
Scènes d'Afrique. Chansons Vécues'.[3] And on a more exalted thespian
level, Déroulède's admirers included international celebrities such as the
indomitable Sarah Bernhardt – who, when he returned from political
exile in 1906, was to send him an enthusiastic telegram, regretting that
the recent injury to her leg prevented her coming to kiss him in person
'for I am nailed to my bed by order of the surgeon'.[4]

Déroulède was not a practising Catholic in any meaningful sense of the word, but claimed to be a 'Christian republican'. 'I have fought the clergy, although I am a believer. I am a man of no sect, because I hate all types of intolerance.'[5] But he was opposed to disestablishing or weakening the Church since this would imperil 'the fund of moral force that we all sooner or later need in the restoration of *la patrie*'.[6] There was a similar ambivalence about the beliefs of his principal lieutenant, Marcel Habert: 'I am a Catholic but a Gallican Catholic; I am a Catholic in the French fashion, not the Roman.'[7] And he blamed the Third Republic for bringing about an increased intervention of the Pope in French affairs – presumably a reference both to its persecuting policies and to the Ralliement. Déroulède's sincerity, generosity and flamboyance gained him the liking – often an amused admiration – of many Catholics who disagreed with his politics; Pierre Veuillot of *L'Univers* was a typical example. After Déroulède's abortive coup of 1899, Veuillot was among those who urged that he be punished with five years' exile, rather than imprisoned – a solution that eventually became a reality.[8] And his many admirers among the senior clergy were to include Archbishop Ricard of Auch.[9] Indeed the formal tribute at his funeral in 1914 was given by Bishop Henri Chapon of Nice, a man whose political sympathies were poles apart from Déroulède's (see pp. 64–6) but who admired in him his patriotism and generosity of character.[10]

Affectionate esteem was one thing – political collaboration another. Several prominent laymen and ecclesiastics played an ambivalent role in the events of 1898–9. The laymen included political associates of Déroulède, who were thought of primarily as anti-Republican politicians rather than spokesmen of Catholic interests – although in periods of anticlerical government the distinction was not always easy to make. Edouard Archdeacon was to be at Déroulède's side during his ill-fated attempt in 1899 to deflect the Army against the Elysée (see pp. 20–4); and when he subsequently slid into parliament with the Nationalist landslide in the Paris elections of 1902, he came to be popularly regarded as a paladin of the Church during the anticlerical onslaught of the years that followed. Archdeacon was a financial buttress of *Le Drapeau*, the daily newspaper of the Ligue des Patriotes, which Maurice Barrès edited. The same crusader's cross was popularly accorded to another financial pillar of *Le Drapeau*, the immaculate Comte Boni de Castellane. Although Castellane was on close personal terms with the Orleanist pretender – and later enjoyed affable relations with the Bonapartist claimant – he increasingly regarded a plebiscitary republic as the only realistic alternative to the existing regime.[11] A product of both the Marianist Collège Stanislas (see pp. 38–9), and more briefly the Jesuit Ecole Ste

Geneviève, he had at one time considered studying theology, before the attractions of *la vie mondaine* and the opposite sex diverted his energies to becoming France's best-dressed man and leader of fashion – 'pourri de chic', as a wistful admirer once remarked. His marriage to the American heiress, Anna Gould, multiplied his material means for pursuing this role, as well as giving him the wherewithal to help his political friends, including the Ligue des Patriotes. But he described his wealthy wife as 'a shrew'; and it was claimed that, when conducting guests around the Palais Rose that he had built with her money in the Avenue du Bois, he referred to the conjugal bedroom as 'la chapelle expiatoire'.[12] His subsequent defence of the Church in parliament led to his being widely if undiscerningly viewed as one of the leaders of the Catholic cause in France – especially by foreigners, including several major Vatican figures. The Catholics *avant tout* were only too glad to have support from anywhere, and were consequently happy to let the illusion stand. The price was paid in 1906, when Castellane's divorce from Anna Gould scandalised foreign opinion, especially in America, where Catholics had been lavish in their promises of financial aid to the French Church.[13] Even so, he took his Catholicism sufficiently seriously not to marry again, following the Vatican's refusal to grant him an annulment; and he modestly prefaced his memoirs with the declaration, 'j'ai conscience de demeurer fidèle à ce que j'ai voulu être: un catholique, un Français, un Castellane'.

Among Déroulède's ecclesiastical sympathisers, the Assumptionists and their daily newspaper, *La Croix*, had consistently given Déroulède a good press since the reconstitution of his league in September 1898; but *La Croix*'s respect for papal directives had inhibited it making a direct demand for a stronger regime. The Assumptionists had already incurred the displeasure of the Pope by their virulent antisemitism and their half-hearted reaction to the papal injunction to form tactical alliances with Méline's moderate Republicans in the 1898 elections. In a highly ambiguous article of 19 January 1899, *La Croix* declared, 'On all sides people are demanding a strong-fisted man, determined to devote his life to liberating France from the traitors, *sectaires*, and imbeciles who are betraying her to the foreigner.' But it went on to say that the nation's infidelity to God had yet to be expiated; and until that time 'Christ must inflict on the Eldest Daughter of the Church a punishment reminiscent of his own passion. That is why he has allowed her to be betrayed, sold, jeered at, beaten, covered with spittle, and crucified by the Jews.' Even so, the Assumptionists were to take a close interest in Déroulède's preparations for a coup in February 1899.[14]

As did the Orleanists – whose papers in the Archives Nationales have much to say on the events of 1898–9.[15] Despite the Pope's encyclical of 1892, many Catholics remained sympathetic to Orleanism, especially since it had shed the last vestiges of the Voltairian liberal image that it had inherited from the first half of the century. This metamorphosis arose from two factors. The death of the Comte de Chambord in 1883 had made Orleanism heir to the Legitimist as well as to the Orleanist branches of French Royalism, while the defection of so many of the *haute bourgeoisie* and the liberal intelligentsia to the Republic had deprived Orleanism of many of its ablest and most percipient supporters. The influx of Legitimists and the departure of commerce and industry gave conservative landed wealth a proportionally stronger voice in the counsels of the movement in the short run – even if this was offset by the long-term decline of agriculture as a source of wealth and political influence. At the same time the growth of a Right-wing lower-middle class in some cities provided anti-Republican movements with new followers who sought protection against loss of identity in a changing society; and those of them who chose Royalism tended to strengthen its illiberal wing. Then came the cruellest blow of all, Pope Leo XIII's exhortation to French Catholics to desert the monarchists and accept the Republic. The obvious attractions of joining forces with conservative Republicans against the rising strength of the French Left were now even harder to resist, with the result that Royalism was increasingly left with hard-core loyalists, less amenable to arguments of common sense and compromise.

To compound their problems, the death of the Comte de Paris in 1894 left the party in the hands of Philippe, Duc d'Orléans, who, while favoured with youth and good looks, was impetuous and lacking in political acumen. Moreover his inclination for a life of pleasure meant that at crucial political junctures he was usually far from where he could take advantage of the crisis. This was true of each of the critical months of October 1898 and February, July and August 1899.

January and February 1898 had seen a wave of antisemitic riots in France and Algeria, incited by antisemitic leagues but having their roots in the combined effects of the economic malaise of the winter of 1897–8 and the animosities stirred up by the Dreyfus Affair. There existed a traditional antisemitism among many members of the Catholic landed aristocracy, aggravated by the agricultural depression of the late nineteenth century. But the 1890s saw the growth of a strong urban petit-bourgeois antisemitism whose potentiality for violence was startlingly revealed in these recent riots. Among the Pretender's advisers, the Comte Eugène de Lur-Saluces and André Buffet saw antisemitism as a means of broadening the social base of Royalism and providing it with a rank and file that was prepared to use physical intimidation to achieve its ends: 'which of course is not to say that the Jews will be pillaged or expelled'.[16] July 1898 had already found Buffet establishing contact between the Pretender and Jules Guérin's Ligue Antisémitique. The league prided itself on the enthusiasm of its members: some of its central figures genially signed their letters 'Bien antisémitiquement à vous'.[17] The prime attraction of the league to the Royalists was its exaggerated claim to command the services of a sizeable contingent of strong-arm men, mainly recruited from the butchers and slaughterhouse-men of La Villette. The Ligue also contained a considerable number of committed Catholics – notably in the eleventh *arrondissement*.[18] Even the Rallié deputy, the Abbé Hippolyte Gayraud, had expressed an interest in the Ligue, writing to Guérin in April 1897, 'a true Christian democrat can only be a fervent antisemite'.[19] Guérin, an unsavoury swindler, sought to instruct the Duke on what he should do in the present political situation. 'This movement is Caesarian; but Monseigneur is in a position to take it over – by loudly affirming his readiness to enter the fray, *if necessary*. If a crack appears, *everything is possible*!!! It is up to us to make sure that the crack appears *in the right place*.'[20] Just such a crack seemed offered by Déroulède's attempted coup in the following month.

The Duke had been a pupil in the early 1880s at the Marianist Collège Stanislas in Paris; but he was subsequently transferred to St Mary's College, an exiled French Jesuit school near Canterbury, at a time when the popularly portrayed *éminence noire* of clerical intrigue and influence, Father Stanislas du Lac, was rector. The Duke was generally regarded in ecclesiastical circles as feckless and lacking the qualities of his father. Leo XIII – who as father of the faithful continued to be on courtesy terms with the Duke, despite the Ralliement – would ask visiting members of his entourage, 'The Duc d'Orléans, has he settled down yet – is he calmer?' And the Papal Secretary of State, Cardinal Rampolla: 'your prince, has he become a little more sensible?'[21] If Leo was prepared to show the Orléans family a benign if conditional courtesy, he regarded them as politically finished; in the words of the Papal Nuncio in Paris, Mgr. Benedetto Lorenzelli, 'The Duc d'Orléans has no chance; he has leaders but no army.'[22]

Yet a number of the senior French clergy continued to see in him the only hope for France. Bishop de Cabrières of Montpellier wrote to the exiled Pretender at the end of December 1898, advising a clandestine pilgrimage to Lourdes or Fourvières so that he might be blessed with a son.[23] The suggestion was not without a certain unconscious piquancy, since the Pyrenees were one of the agreed secret entry points for the Duke in the event of an impending coup.[24] The Assumptionists, while sticking to the letter if not the spirit of the Ralliement, had established amiable relationships with the Royalist election committees in the 1898 elections. Much to the Pope's annoyance, the Assumptionist electoral organisation, Justice-Egalité, had preferred to do deals with Catholic candidates of any provenance, Royalists included, rather than follow his strategy of supporting Méline's ministerial moderates in the interests of keeping out anticlericals.[25]

As for the Jesuits, one of the four provincial heads in France reported to the General of the order in 1896 and 1898 that 'the Pope's political instructions [i.e. the Ralliement] are still meeting with the strong repugnance of several members'.[26] The General for his part questioned the French Jesuits on accusations that they were anti-Republican, partly because their schools were supposedly dependent on the money of the aristocracy. The respondents were quick to point out that the aristocracy represented only a small minority of their school clientele, and that in these circumstances 'we could not express monarchical sentiments without *ipso facto* affronting a large number of families and losing their confidence. While such sentiments could be expressed at other times, this has long since become impossible.'[27] In any case, when it came to donations as distinct from fees,

Most of the nobility who have their fortune in land are now hard up. The donations that come to us are given by the commercial and industrial bourgeoisie . . . [Aristocratic] families, by contrast, give little because they are impoverished by the legal system of divided inheritance, by the long-standing agricultural crisis and much else. Those who are rich have too many financial responsibilities and needs. For example, I have long-standing relations with the Duc de Rohan and the Duc de Larochefoucauld Doudeauville, but have they ever given me a centime?[28]

Prudence, or perhaps ignorance, prevented him adding that the Duc de Doudeauville's finances were too heavily committed to helping the Royalists for there to be much to spare for the Jesuits.[29]

The Jesuit who was most widely accused by the popular press of complicity with anti-Republican sentiment in the 1890s was Father Stanislas du Lac, who had been responsible for the Pretender's education during his Canterbury schooling. Yet the anticlerical *Lanterne* perciupiently and prophetically wrote of du Lac in 1913, 'He understood that despite everything, the people were going over to the Republic, and that the Church had only one way of keeping its power: it would be to put the Republic in the hands of a soldier whom the Company [of Jesus] had shaped. This dream preoccupied him for thirty years.'[30] This dream – if indeed he had it – was to become a reality in 1958 when General de Gaulle took over France and then reshaped the regime in a semi-presidential, semi-plebiscitary fashion. De Gaulle had been a pupil at two Jesuit schools – notably the Collège de l'Immaculée Conception in the Rue de Vaugirard in Paris, where his father was prefect of studies (see p. 44), and the Collège du Sacré Cœur in Belgium – before moving on to the Marianist Collège Stanislas in 1908 (see pp. 38–9). Given du Lac's close dealings with the Jesuit schools in the Paris region, du Lac and de Gaulle *père* must have known each other; but whether du Lac ever set eyes on the posthumous incarnation of what *La Lanterne* believed to be his dreams can be savoured only as a possibility. Du Lac had earlier been headmaster of the Jesuits' most prestigious French school, the Ecole Ste Geneviève, in the 1870s; and in the 1890s he was often consulted by the school's governors – at a time when the school was providing more entrants to the military academy of St Cyr than any other school in France. He was likewise widely accused of involvement in the murkier aspects of the Dreyfus Affair. Not untypical of the more sensational reports that appeared abroad was an article in the American *Evening Telegraph*:

If the truth could be known, it seems not unlikely that Father du Lac would prove to be the one person of all others on whom the greatest responsibility would rest for the present miscarriage of justice . . . All these forgeries, veiled ladies, false telegrams, suicides, the misleading of public opinion, etc., are in strict keeping with the Jesuitical tradition, and altogether beyond the capacity of dunder-headed, absinthe-drinking, commonplace military officers. Judge Bertulus, in his evidence, shows that the forgers of the 'Blanche' telegram could only have been inspired by Father du Lac, who was the confessor of the lady who was known to Colonel Picquart as Blanche. This is a terrible indictment, for if substantiated, it shows that the secrets of the confessional were utilised for political purposes.[31]

Certainly du Lac's strength of personality had won him a considerable reputation as a confessor and spiritual adviser in senior Army circles. Among his penitents was General Raoul de Boisdeffre, the anti-Dreyfusard Chief of Staff, who had resigned after the suicide of Colonel Henry. Like other embittered casualties of the Affair, Boisdeffre was viewed by many as a potential instrument of insurrection. The agents of the Duc d'Orléans attempted to sound out Boisdeffre's fellow officers to discover whether he would be prepared to lend his support to a royalist coup d'état; but the letters preserved among the Duc d'Orléans's papers present a discouraging view of its likelihood.[32] Du Lac admitted to being Boisdeffre's confessor, their acquaintance dating back to a chance meeting at Le Mans in 1870, where Boisdeffre had landed in a balloon at the time of the siege of Paris.[33] Needless to say, du Lac's spiritual encounters with the Army's top brass were popularly seen as an occasion for pushing the career prospects of the Jesuit schools' choice pupils (see pp. 36–8). *La Lanterne* was later to write of Boisdeffre 'in charge of the general staff, in charge of the Army, and bending them to the orders which he, as a humble and submissive penitent, received from his confessor, Father du Lac'.[34]

Another penitent was the long-suffering Monsieur Monnier, whose wife was accused of being the celebrated 'veiled lady' in the Dreyfus Affair. It was supposedly Monsieur Monnier who had given Major Esterhazy the equally celebrated 'ce canaille de D' letter which had helped to convict Dreyfus. Given the mystery surrounding the case – and given the highly charged atmosphere of the time – it was inevitable that du Lac should be denounced as an occult influence. Among much else he was reputed to have acquired extensive knowledge of the nation's mobilisation plans. There was even the smell of insurrection about him, since he was accused of being on close terms with General de Pellieux, Déroulède's great white hope for 23 February (see pp. 21–3). Indeed it was to General de Pellieux that du Lac had supposedly revealed the secret of 'the veiled lady' – despite du Lac's denials that he was personally acquainted with Pellieux.[35]

On the other hand du Lac admitted to having had 'very intimate relations' with the leading antisemite, Edouard Drumont, whom he had encouraged to become a committed Catholic, and whose marriage he had helped to bring about. Du Lac claimed, however, to have persuaded Drumont to moderate much of the text of his notorious book, *La France Juive* (1886), and to have reproved him for the violence of his anti-semitism. Du Lac asserted that no Catholic would legitimately oppose the Jews as Jews – only on the grounds of their alleged shady financial dealings and their part in the anticlerical policies of the Third Republic. Du Lac specifically distinguished the role of the Jesuits from that of the Assumptionists, 'who in this matter sometimes sound a false note in *La Croix*' – a delicate understatement that perhaps owed something to the traditional Jesuit abstention from paying back other religious orders in their own coin, when recrimination was in the air.[36]

If the Papal Nuncio, Lorenzelli, was dismissive of the Orleanists, he was even more so of the Bonapartists. 'Prince Victor could only come to power by a *coup de force*, which has been out of the question for a long time. And in any case Napoleon signifies the Revolution with a crown on – despotic caesarism, the persecutor of the Church, scheming to enslave it.'[37] In fact Prince Victor's papers in the Archives Nationales clearly show that he had little taste for uncertain undertakings such as coups – a cautious attitude that was encouraged by Bonapartism's last prime minister, Emile Ollivier, a liberal deist who was later to enjoy the benevolent respect of Pius X and his Secretary of State, Merry del Val.[38] Ollivier had long since ceased to play an active part in Bonapartist politics, and his letters to the Pretender in the 1893–1911 period are those of a friendly spectator, leisurely in tone and completely belying Royalist fears that Ollivier was at the centre of a Bonapartist plot to take over the Republic in 1899.[39] In the early years of the Ralliement, Ollivier's belief was that Bonapartism's best chance of coming to power was on the back of a popular reaction against a conservative Republican government 'of narrow and clerical bourgeois'.[40] Such a government failed to materialise, and Ollivier felt that 'the Napoleons have no hope in face of a popular republic', which the leftward swing of politics in the late 1890s made a more likely prospect.[41]

The most active subversive in 1898–9, Paul Déroulède was as much opposed to a Bonapartist empire as to an Orleanist monarchy. Yet his political package had much closer affinities with Bonapartism. French patriotism could not ignore the Napoleonic legend, despite the counter-vailing memories of Napoleon III's disasters in foreign policy; and the popular plebiscite was an important Napoleonic device. As for Déroulède's proposal that the head of state be elected by universal suffrage, this had been the ladder by which Louis Napoleon had indirectly re-established the Empire half a century earlier. These common elements between Bonapartism and Déroulède's movement had ambivalent implications for the Bonapartists. Pessimists might argue that Déroulède's republicanism had pre-empted all that was attractive in Bonapartism, and had freed it from the ball and chain of the hereditary principle, with all its hazardous dependence on the personality of the heir. Optimists, on the other hand, could point to the lessons of half a century earlier, and groom the Pretender or his brother for the presidential election. Indeed Déroulède himself admitted to Victor's brother, Louis Bonaparte, who had recently been promoted general in the Russian Army,

it is open to anyone to be a presidential candidate, and universal suffrage decides the outcome . . . Many good republicans like and respect in you the deployment of your moral and physical strengths. That does not mean that any of us would hand over the Republic to you or restore a dynasty, but we willingly envisage . . . that a day will come when General Louis Bonaparte could very well be . . . one of the faithful servants of republican democracy.[42]

Not all Bonapartists were content with Victor's circumspect policy. Cuneo d'Ornano and a number of other belligerents became increasingly impatient with what they saw as the feeble inactivity of the prince and his advisers – notably his secretary, Edmond Blanc, and the Comte de Laborde.[43] Like Archdeacon and Boni de Castellane, Cuneo d'Ornano was yet another figure of the anti-Republican Right whom events were to cast in the role of defender of the Church. Victor's disinclination to take advantage of the Dreyfus crisis may also have been influenced by family considerations. Not only did the Bonapartes share the suspicion of many royal families that Dreyfus was probably innocent, but the Princess Mathilde was a widely respected ornament of Paris society and had no desire to have her position as such jeopardised by illegal activity on the part of her nephews' supporters.[44] It was likewise suspected that the Empress Eugénie did not want her British hosts and her freedom of movement embarrassed by Bonapartist activism against the French government.[45] Cuneo d'Ornano sourly referred to the women as 'hostages' in the hands of the Republic and not only expressed relief at Princess Mathilde's death but added the wish that the Empress Eugénie should rapidly join her.[46]

Victor could draw solace from the fact that his cautious policies had the approval of the Duc de Morny, heritor of the architect of Louis Napoleon's coup d'état of 1851.[47] Morny believed that the Bonapartists should adopt an attitude of 'conciliation rassurante' towards Republican politicians and avoid all suggestion of revolution in the Bonapartist press – given the fact that the bulk of the nation was currently Republican. But in the event of the Republic collapsing, it was vital that the issue of a new regime be put to a plebiscite not to a parliament since 'a vote of the chambers would be favourable to the Duc d'Orléans, but a popular vote would go your way'. As far as money was concerned, Morny thought that there was a strong case for gently wooing Jewish and Protestant financiers, and reminding them that it was the founder of the Napoleonic dynasty who had securely integrated Jews and Protestants into French national life. Indeed Prince Victor's disinclination towards antisemitism incurred the strictures of Edouard Drumont – who personally had Bonapartist sympathies – and of the Nationalist deputy, Joseph Lasies, who was later to join the Church's Swiss Guard of circumstantial defenders in the Chamber of Deputies.[48] As for his fellow combatant, Cuneo d'Ornano, he vainly attempted to persuade a Bonapartist meeting in February 1899 to seize the opportunities created by President Faure's death – and in effect do what Déroulède himself was planning (see pp. 20–3) – but these proved as fruitless as the vigil kept by the police inspectors at the Gare du Nord to intercept the prince, should he awake from circumspection and decide to take the plunge.[49] Six months later the exasperated Cuneo was writing to Déroulède's sister, announcing that he was 'at your orders, and at the complete disposal of your brother'.[50] Indeed Victor's secretary was warned that many Bonapartists felt that if Victor was not prepared to take advantage of the existing political situation, then he should abdicate in favour of Louis.[51] According to General Jules de Sancy, 'the position of Prince Louis Bonaparte in the Russian Army inspires confidence' in military circles, and was a substantial factor in Bonapartism's growing appeal in the Army.[52]

Despite Rome's suspicion of Bonapartism as 'the Revolution with a crown on', many churchmen in their time had shown it sympathy, notably Archbishop Lavigerie of Algiers, Leo XIII's chosen instrument for reconciling the Church with Republican institutions.[53] It might have surprised many leading members of Church and State to know that Bishop Geay of Laval was a warm supporter of Prince Victor in the late 'nineties. Given the bishop's subsequent notoriety as a supporter of Combes's government – and his involuntary role in the rupture of diplomatic relations between Paris and Rome in 1904 – his penchant for the prince is not without piquancy. Not that he made any secret of the matter to the Pope, to whom he presented the idea of a plebiscitary empire as an apotheosis of the democratic aspirations of many Republicans. His eulogy of the Bonapartist cause to the Pope of the Ralliement might seem extraordinarily risky – even when presented as a transcendent form of Republican democracy. But Geay slyly offered it as a solution to the Roman Question: 'Yes, Holy Father, it is the Plebiscitary Empire which is preparing to emerge at some point in the future . . . which will bring about in Europe the restoration of the independence of the Holy See!'[54] Other episcopal advocates of a return to the Empire included Bishops Henry of Grenoble and Herscher of Langres (see pp. 25–6), while the Catholic press and its fellow-travellers had several Imperial sympathisers among their editors, notably Father Vincent Bailly of *La Croix* and his fellow antisemite, Edouard Drumont of *La Libre Parole*.[55] Among laymen, the Catholic Deputy for the Tarn, Baron Xavier de Reille, and General François Thomassin, were sympathisers who tried to put pressure on Prince Victor to have a higher profile in defence of the Church, particularly in the matter of Catholic schools and the retention of the Concordat.[56] But Bonapartism's most favoured representative in Roman eyes – especially after Leo XIII's death in 1903 – was Emile Ollivier, whose increasing caution and remoteness from the politicking of the Pretender's entourage posed no problems for a papacy committed in principle to the Ralliement. Pius X and Merry del Val were to find his austere pessimism on French religious issues particularly congenial.

These were the groups that in varying degrees were prepared to exploit the government's embarrassment over the Dreyfus Affair – and which now feared that the prospect of a retrial might result in the Affair petering out before they could draw the maximum advantage from it. It was Déroulède who took the initiative in striking while there was still iron to be struck; and the events of February 1899 owed most to his activity – even if there was a circle of rival conspirators poised ready to rob him of whatever spoils he managed to secure. Affinities with the situation in Algiers in the second week of May 1958 spring to mind – with the opposing forces of Delbecque and Lagaillarde vying for advantage. It has become fashionable to minimise the importance of these events – and even to claim that they were in part fabricated by Premier Waldeck-Rousseau to obtain exemplary government convictions. The latter claim is largely based on documents in Waldeck-Rousseau's papers, which were seen by his leading biographer as an attempt by the prime minister to provide additional buttressing to the evidence against the accused; and this view has been inflated by several subsequent writers into the charge that the subversive events of 1899 were largely manufactured by Waldeck-Rousseau.[57] Whatever the extent of Waldeck-Rousseau's interference, it does not invalidate the wealth of evidence from other archival sources, indicating the subversive intent of the participants in these events.

The Royalists were hoping for trouble in February 1899. The principal manager of the Paris Exhibition expected a renewal of strike-action by the Exhibition-site workers and its expansion elsewhere. Thuret had discussed the likely repercussions with General M. L. de Garnier des Garets, commander of the 2nd Corps, based at Amiens, who shared his hopes that it would necessitate the strengthening of the Paris garrison and thereby provide a Right-wing coup with potential military support.[58] Garnier des Garets was esteemed by the Jesuits as the first old boy of Ste Geneviève to reach general's rank; and he was proud of being a Chevalier de l'Ordre Pontifical de Pie Neuf.[59]

It was perhaps a similar calculation that led Déroulède and his lieutenant, Marcel Habert, to contemplate a coup for 24 February or thereabouts, which, according to a police report, would seize the Chamber of Deputies or the Elysée.[60] Whatever the truth of the matter, the unexpected death of the President of the Republic on 16 February provided a much sharper focus for such an enterprise. The President's mysterious death gave rise to immediate speculation – which has continued to this day, as reflected in the title of a recent book, L'Assassinat de Félix Faure.[61] His well-known opposition to a retrial of Dreyfus encouraged the anti-Republican press to claim that he had been murdered by Jews or Freemasons; but society gossip preferred a more *boulevardier* explanation of his demise. Mistinguett's memoirs typified its more colourful variants:

Among the ladies of the President's choice a certain Madame Steinheil had a distinguished place. When she came to visit him at the Elysée Palace she used a private door, and the President would be informed of her arrival by a particular ring of the bell. He would then rapidly swallow a pill [that was currently esteemed as a potent rejuvenator]. One day there was some misunderstanding, and the Archbishop of Paris walked in instead. The President had heard the bell, and was forced to listen to the Archbishop while endeavouring to control his growing excitement. The bell rang again. This time it was indeed Madame Steinheil. The President rapidly took more pills but the dose must have proved too much for him, for he was subsequently found [in a state of apoplexy], clutching the hair of his unfortunate friend who was screaming for help.[62]

The Vatican Archives contain a letter from the Archbishop to the Papal Secretary of State, giving a more sober account of the occasion, in which he retailed the President's appreciative remarks to him on the Vatican's friendly and helpful attitude towards France. 'Nothing in our interview gave me to suppose that the President was going to die a few hours later.' He confirmed, however, that two priests were successively called to the Elysée to give spiritual succour to the ailing President; and the French ambassador informed the Vatican that his death was the result of an 'apoplexie foudroyante'.[63]

Déroulède imagined that Faure's funeral procession on 23 February would be an emotionally charged occasion, in which a denigrated army would be paying homage to a conservative president who, unlike his successor, had put his trust in their integrity over the Dreyfus Affair. Déroulède's comic-opera attempt to deflect part of the homecoming procession into a march on the Elysée is too well known to require recapitulation. Defendants, prosecution and observers are agreed on the broad outline of what happened between Déroulède's seizure of General Roget's bridle near the Place de la Nation and his ultimate self-inflicted arrest in the Reuilly barracks, after vainly exhorting the general and his men to change direction and occupy the presidential palace.

The Royalists' hopes on 23 February were contingent on Guérin being able to dispossess Déroulède of the fruits of his enterprise. There was little love lost between Guérin and Déroulède. Apart from the issue of Guérin's recent links with Royalism, Déroulède was not personally an enthusiastic antisemite, even if many of his followers were. Fernand de Ramel had written to the Pretender on 21 February, urging him to make a secret entry into France before the funeral and await events at one of two hiding-places prepared for him in Versailles and Paris. The Pretender would have to be ready for a Royalist intervention in the crucial interval between Déroulède's overthrow of the regime and the setting-up of a provisional government – otherwise Prince Louis Bonaparte who was rumoured to be in Paris might snatch the prize.[64] The main problem would be gauging the moment when utilising Déroulède should turn to displacing him. Déroulède's declarations and the police reports concur on his hostility to any monarchical solution to France's problems, and they clearly reveal his subsequent contempt for the Royalists' schemes to reap the rewards of his activity. Guérin and his men kept close to Déroulède throughout the afternoon of 23 February, even to the point of rushing forward with him when he made his vain appeal to General Roget to turn his troops on the Elysée. According to a police spy who was shadowing Guérin, Guérin and his men had close at hand a cab-load of fire-arms ready to 'kill [Déroulède], that is the word one must use', should the coup succeed and Déroulède refuse to hand over power to Guérin.[65]

Guérin's apparent readiness to go to these extremes on behalf of the Royalists was strengthened by the antisemitic stance recently adopted by the Pretender. Perhaps in response to Lur-Saluces's advice of 6 February, the Duke had committed himself to a widely reported declaration on 'the Jewish question'. According to his subsequent notes of 22 February, it was an economic rather than a racial problem: French landed wealth needed to be protected against the crushing weight of 'anonymous, roaming wealth' with no national loyalties; and he attributed the recent flare-up of antisemitism to the Jews' initial 'slitting of the throat of the Union Générale', a Catholic bank, in 1882.[66] Highly alarmed by this new tack, one of the Pretender's wiser advisers, the Comte Alfred de Gramont, wrote 'I beg Monseigneur to speak no more . . . of the Jews.'[67] While de Luynes warned him against alienating the 'big industrialists' who 'will be very necessary to you and form the future of France and the undoubted foundation of any new government', Gramont made no secret of his contempt for the disreputable Guérin – and even Lur-Saluces was later to concede that a number of senior army officers regarded Guérin as a political liability to the Pretender.[68] Others, however, recognised his utility – including, it would seem, the Comte Boni de Castellane.

Unfortunately the Orleanist papers have no light to shed on the role attributed to Castellane by Joseph Reinach and less explicitly by Maurice Barrès.[69] Police reports to Waldeck-Rousseau later claimed that Castellane gave Guérin 200,000 francs, and was likewise helping Déroulède.[70] Reinach alleged that Castellane visited Déroulède on the night before the *tentative* in order to sound him out on his plans for the morrow. Déroulède apparently revealed to him his hopes of obtaining the support of General Georges de Pellieux (see pp. 31–2 below), but also made it clear that he would physically resist any attempt by the Pretender to profit from the coup. Castellane then supposedly appraised Guérin of this information, thereby enabling Guérin to keep a close eye on Déroulède on the day itself. A police report to Waldeck-Rousseau quoted Castellane as subsequently saying, 'In my opinion, Guérin would have killed Déroulède.'[71] But on the day of the funeral the unenthusiastic Pellieux arranged for his contingent to peel off from the main column before it reached the Place de la Nation, thereby leaving the expectant Déroulède to be confronted by the unforeseen and utterly bewildered General Gaudérique Roget. Déroulède subsequently blamed an unnamed Orleanist, in whom he had confided, as having betrayed his plans – the implication being that Castellane was responsible for General de Pellieux losing his nerve and absenting himself from the scene (see p. 31).[72] Whatever the truth of the matter, the police authorities' report to Waldeck-Rousseau denied receiving any information of this kind.

If it was only 'political' Catholics of the plebiscitary Right who were directly conversant with what was happening, there were nonetheless clergy who indirectly knew more than was good for them. The day after the President's death, the head of the Assumptionist order, Father François Picard, was already asking Father Vincent Bailly, editor of the Assumptionist newspaper, *La Croix*, whether General de Pellieux would make a good President.[73] Given Pellieux's remoteness from the parliamentary world, it suggests that the Assumptionists were well aware of the drift of Déroulède's scheming. Three days later they were secretly asked to give financial help. Vincent Bailly responded to the request in exemplary fashion: 'Whatever may happen on that night, I would sooner have nothing to do with an insurrectionary movement. I wish to be faithful to the spirit of Leo XIII's directions.' But, with engaging indecision, he added that if he changed his mind he would let the conspirators know by four o'clock that afternoon. In fact Bailly decided to refuse – although not without several hours' agonised reflection.[74]

Whatever temptation Bailly may have experienced, his eventual stance was an energetic one. On the day of the funeral, *La Croix*'s leading article was a strong warning against violence. 'This day, zealous men, indignant at the triumph of Jewry in the presidential election, wish to resort to armed force. We reply to them as Christ did to Peter – and the comparison should flatter them – "Whoever lives by the sword shall die by the sword." . . . Only moral force will prevail.'[75] Even so, a certain wistfulness may be detected in Bailly's subsequent comment to his brother, 'Déroulède has spoilt everything by launching the adventure in the Rue Reuilly, while [the Royalists] were gathered in the Place de la Bastille.'[76]

Déroulède's acquittal of conspiracy by a sympathetic jury in the Cour d'assises de la Seine left him free to prepare a second coup. But as it happened, it was Guérin rather than Déroulède who was to become the focus of Royalist hopes in the following months. The police raids, which gathered in Déroulède and Buffet on 11–12 August, failed to catch Guérin, who had spent the night with one of his mistresses. He thereupon managed to make his way to the fortified headquarters of the Ligue Antisémitique in the Rue de Chabrol, where he and a number of colleagues resisted arrest until 20 September.[77] The Pretender's papers confirm the claims of the police that the Royalists continued to gather funds for Guérin throughout the siege, while among the Nationalists with Catholic connections, Boni de Castellane and Archdeacon were both said to have contributed to the original purchase of 'Fort Chabrol'.[78] As for those Bonapartists associated with protecting the Church, Joseph Lasies acted as an intermediary between the government and Guérin, in a vain attempt to bring the episode to an end.[79]

The Assumptionist La Croix gave Guérin sympathetic coverage during the siege – so much so that Cardinal Rampolla asked its editor, Father Vincent Bailly, if the Assumptionists were involved 'in the plot', while the Pope asked him point-blank if he had been giving money to Guérin.[80] When Bailly vigorously denied the allegation, the Pope then asked him whether the Jesuits had been giving money to the extreme Right – to which Bailly replied that he did not know, but thought it unlikely.

Aftermath

The High Court eventually sentenced Guérin, Déroulède and various of their associates to modest terms of exile and imprisonment; and, given that the semi-farcical incidents of February and August 1899 had brought more ridicule than glory to the Republic's enemies, violent subversion lost much of its appeal as a short-term strategy in the years that followed. Even so, public unease at these apparent threats to the regime brought to power a broad-bottomed ministry under René Waldeck-Rousseau (June 1899–June 1902) with a mandate to suppress right-wing subversion and restore public confidence. His successor, 'le petit père' Emile Combes (June 1902–January 1905), took the clean sweep much further; and his obsessive anticlericalism saw draconian reprisals against those elements in the Army and Church suspected of anti-Republican sympathies. These developments are examined more closely in the following chapter. The government's punitive onslaught encouraged the disparate elements of the anti-Republican Right to reassemble their forces on the terrain of defending the Church – partly in the hope of widening their circle of friends, while demonstrating to committed Catholics that the Ralliement had been an expensive mistake. The expulsion of the religious orders, the closure of many Catholic schools, the rupture of diplomatic relations with the Vatican (1904), and the disestablishment of the Church (1905) enabled them to play the role of the forgiving wife to the errant Ralliés – and follow this up with generous offers to the Church of closer domesticity.

The Bonapartists were to commission the future Cardinal Alfred Baudrillart in April 1906 to convey to the Vatican Prince Victor's views on how Church–State relations should be governed in the event of an Imperial restoration.[81] Baudrillart – who was later to be a leading advocate of collaboration with Nazi Germany against Bolshevism in the 1940s – was regarded by the prince's advisers as 'a Bonapartist for many years . . . has a horror of parliamentarianism, Action Libérale, Piou, and the Piou underlings' (i.e. the Rallié party and its leader).[82] These proposals envisaged a new concordat which would also cover the authorised religious orders – and it also guaranteed their right to open schools. By 1911, however, Prince Victor's inclinations were in favour of 'an honest regime of separation', rather than a new concordat – 'if one day I should be called to power by the will of the French people'. And he asked the Vicar-General of Paris, Mgr. Odelin, to outline his views to Rome on his next visit there.[83] As will be apparent in later pages, Mgr. Odelin was a discreet but important link between the extreme Right and the Catholics *avant tout* (see pp. 49–51). The prince's proposals included the resumption of diplomatic relations between France and the Vatican, and 'new statutes for the Catholic Church in France'. He likewise pledged himself to freedom of education – all of which Odelin conveyed to the Holy See.[84]

The Vatican remained courteous but circumspect in its dealings with Bonapartism. Thus Pope Pius X happily sent his apostolic blessing to the newly born Prince Imperial, Louis Napoleon, in 1914; but his Secretary of State, Merry del Val, insisted that it would be inadvisable for a French bishop to baptise him. There would however, be no objection to a non-episcopal prelate, such as the Rector of the Institut Catholique of Paris – the ever-ready Baudrillart – from doing so, provided that the Archbishop of Paris agreed. The Archbishop, however, did not agree, predicting trouble from several bishops on the one hand, and from the Royalist movement, Action Française, on the other.[85] Prince Victor had to settle for the retired Bishop of Langres, Mgr. Herscher, known for his 'respectful attachment' to Prince Victor, 'hope of so many Frenchmen', and to his new-born son, 'the august infant'.[86] Even so, the ranks of the self-professed Ralliés contained many closet Bonapartists – notably Jules Dansette, wealthy textile manufacturer and pillar of the Rallié party, Action Libérale.[87]

There were considerably more whose inward inclinations favoured Orleanism. Like the Bonapartists, the Orleanists lost little time in outlining a plan for Church–State relations in the event of a Royalist restoration. In November 1909 the French Benedictine, Dom J.-M. Besse, submitted to the Pretender a memorandum on 'the position of the Churches in France after the return of the king', outlining a quasi-concordatory regime for the Catholic Church and simple common-law status for the rest, with guarantees for their religious freedom.[88] Although Besse did not use the word 'concordat', he spoke of the organisation of diocesan government in France as 'regulated by common agreement between the Pope and the King'. The bishops and parish priests would receive salaries as under Napoleon's concordat, and bishops would likewise be 'appointed by the Sovereign Pontiff, after nomination by the King', as in Concordatory times. On the other hand, there was to be no recrudescence of State restrictions on the freedom of the Papacy and French Catholics to communicate directly with each other, as had happened with the Organic Articles that Napoleon had unilaterally appended to the Concordat.

Besse's principal departure from the Napoleonic Concordat was the provision of a 'Grand Chaplain', who would provide something of a central focus to Church organisation within France. He would not only occupy a political place at the royal court but he would be president of 'an ecclesiastical Chamber or Council of State' which would broadly take over the administrative and financial functions of the Napoleonic Direction des Cultes. This chamber would consist partly of ecclesiastical lawyers, elected by the archdiocesan councils, while the others would be laymen appointed by the king. When, a decade earlier, Legitimist elements in the Royalist camp had spoken of an official 'royal chaplain', the devout but eminently sensible Comte Alfred de Gramont had warned the Pretender against throne-and-altar flummery of this kind, which 'sends a cold shiver down my back'.[89] He would surely have squirmed, had he known of Besse's proposal in 1909 to resurrect the privileged role of the Abbey of St Denis – burial place of the kings of France – with the Grand Chaplain as abbot and the ecclesiastical members of the Chamber as canons of the abbey. Nor would a good monk like Dom Besse need to suggest a candidate who would combine the requisite political sympathies and monastic experience for the post of Grand Chaplain.

The religious orders would receive no state salary and would be free from diocesan control. On the other hand the ecclesiastical Chamber would have a vetting role on the establishment and financial viability of new monasteries and convents. Needless to say Besse's scheme envisaged the resumption of diplomatic relations between France and the Vatican on the traditional basis of ambassador and nuncio.

The optimism that Besse's memorandum revealed was also reflected in his comments on 'Rome's termination of its constitutional policy' (i.e. the Ralliement) – itself a major presumption on Besse's part – which he saw as responsible for the increasing readiness of several bishops to 'profess Royalist sympathies'. He likewise claimed to see an evolution in the Rallié newspaper *L'Univers* in this direction, which he thought would be followed by a similar move by *La Croix*, the former Assumptionist paper. He laid particular store on what he saw as the 'inevitable papal condemnation' of Marc Sangnier's Christian democrat movement, Le Sillon, which would bring the Catholic democrats to their senses. In the meantime he saw Action Française as principally responsible for the Royalist renaissance in France – while on the celestial level, 'I recognise there an intervention by Joan of Arc. It is she who will deliver Monseigneur to Reims and to Paris.'

Besse's comments on the role of Action Française were perhaps the only part of his missive that showed any sense of realism. Of relatively recent creation, the highly cerebral but polemically lively Action Française of Charles Maurras was just embarking on its love–hate relationship with the Orleanist leadership. The virulence of its anti-Republicanism, combined with the ambiguity of its Royalist political programme, made it an attractive travelling companion for frustrated Catholics who hated the Republic but were uncertain what road to take politically. The fact that Action Française issued slogans rather than route-maps was paradoxically consoling to people whose previous disappointments made them wary of specific proposals, requiring practical commitment rather than the venting of spleen. The inroads it made into the bewildered sensibilities of many French ecclesiastics – and briefly into the Vatican itself – were to be a source of embarrassment to the Church, as later pages will demonstrate.

It is not clear whether Rome was shown Dom Besse's proposals for a re-established Church in France. But even if it was, his suggestions were unlikely to evoke any more positive response than those of the Bonapartists. Despite Pius X's break with Leo's conciliatory policies towards France, the Vatican never departed from its formal acceptance of the Republic. As his Secretary of State, Merry del Val, said in 1910, 'When I meet monarchists, I respect their opinion which is sincere, but I say to them: "You are deluding yourselves. One cannot go against currents of opinion like the one that dominates France." '[90]

2 *Le sabre et le goupillon*: Catholics and the Army

Try as they might, the governments of Waldeck-Rousseau and Combes failed to establish conclusive links between Church figures and the anti-Republican conspiracies of the Dreyfus years. What was incontrovertible, however, was that many of the conspirators had been to Catholic private schools, as had a large proportion of their sympathisers. This could scarcely have been otherwise in a country where nearly 20 per cent of the entire male secondary-school population in 1898 were taught in schools run directly or indirectly by religious orders – while a further 22 per cent attended other Catholic schools.[1] To keep matters in perspective, only 5 per cent of French children received secondary education of any sort at that time; but these included a large proportion of the men who were to occupy positions of responsibility in the Army and Civil Service. It was alarming to Republicans that so large a minority of this elite was passing through the hands of 'celibate fanatics, brimful of political hatred and sexual frustration'. Yet the fact that the minority greatly outstripped the proportion of practising Catholics in the circles from which they came indicated that the benefits that many parents were seeking for their sons were social and 'character-forming' rather than specifically religious. Secularists reacted to this consideration in ambivalent fashion. It was reassuring on the one hand that 42 per cent of secondary schoolboys were not necessarily clerical dragon's teeth, impatiently counting the days until they could combat the government through the ballot box or stab it in the back by infiltrating the Army and the Civil Service. On the other hand it was disquieting that the appeal of the Catholic private sector was not confined to practising Catholics. The daily drip-feed of religious education into boys of impressionable age might turn the progeny of mere social climbers into committed clericals, to the embarrassment and inconvenience of parents and government alike. The Republican reprisals against Catholic schools after 1899 were therefore fuelled by much broader considerations than the rumoured connections between clericals and political subversion; and the resultant disquiet was compounded by the fact that the Catholic share of boys' secondary education had appeared to be on an upward curve, 32 per cent in 1887 to 42 per cent in 1898. Even so, what linked these wider worries with the fears of 1899 was the fact that a substantial minority of army officers had been educated in Catholic secondary schools – notably in Jesuit schools.

The geese of the Capitol

It is significant that the first serious signs of disquiet came from men who were closely involved with the Dreyfus Affair. A case in point was Auguste Scheurer-Kestner, vice-president of the Senate and an early protagonist of Dreyfus. Early in 1898 he noted in his diary, 'There are ninety-six Catholic military circles in France . . . All the Paris garrisons are clerical. Officers without patrons, or who are anticlerical, are exiled to distant garrisons. The leaders claim that in the event of a coup d'état in Paris, all the officers of the Paris region would side with it and would bring their troops with them.'[2] The Freemasons went further. When the General Assembly of the Grand Orient met in September 1898, it was urged by one of its members to create a 'commission of republican defence' against the 'long-recognised alliance between clericalism and militarism . . . to put the Army into the hands of the Jesuits and allow them to seize government by a coup d'état'. He followed this plea with what he saw as evidence of impending subversion in the provinces, notably in the Angers area.[3] The warning prefigured the flesh-creeping claims made in the press sixty years later in May 1958, when rumours that parts of the provinces were preparing to welcome paratroopers from Algiers caused widespread unease, intensified by the blank spaces that appeared in many newspapers, resulting from the government's insistence that the more alarming of these reports be withheld.

While the rumours of 1958 were given subsequent plausibility by what happened – and by what nearly happened – those of 1898 did not receive the accolade of being followed by a collapse of the regime. The result has been that they have given rise to a wide spectrum of speculation, both at the time and among later generations of historians, ranging from apprehensive concern to contemptuous dismissal. Recent releases of papers in the Archives Nationales have helped to clarify the question and put it into perspective.[4]

At the same time a perusal of other sources suggests that the generals who were periodically thought to be sympathetic to anti-Republican activity were as much the product of state schools as of the Catholic private sector – perhaps significantly more so, in that the uneven information provided by their dossiers precludes an overall numerical assessment. The schooldays of most of them went back to the Second Empire if not earlier, a time when the Catholic private sector in secondary education was much weaker; and their personal odysseys and opinions had subsequently undergone decades of weathering and challenge. The main impact of Catholic education was on the younger generations of officer who had yet to reach a rank where they became potentially interesting to political subversives.

The only senior officer to be seriously suspected of implication in the preparation for Déroulède's coup was General Georges de Pellieux, whose death in 1900 left his role in the previous year's events open to uninhibited speculation. All one can say is that Déroulède claimed subsequently that Pellieux's departure from the President's funeral procession on 23 February 1899 was the prime factor in the failure of the coup.[5] But it is impossible to gauge whether Déroulède's reliance on Pellieux stemmed from an encouraging response by the general to Déroulède's overtures, or whether it merely reflected Déroulède's ebullient optimism. What is indisputable is the encouragement that Pellieux gave to the Royalists after these events.

In 1898, an unidentified lady canvassed public opinion among generals' wives on behalf of the Royalists, and produced an annotated list of senior officers, mainly based on information supplied by the wife of General Arthur de Brye.[6] In October of the same year the Pretender commissioned Lur-Saluces – himself a former officer – to interview generals and report on their attitudes; and at much about the same time Thuret was engaged in a similar task.[7] It was to Lur-Saluces that Pellieux confided that the Royalists could 'entirely count' on him and that he was 'unreservedly devoted' to the Pretender.[8] Although the government appears not to have known of this two-hour discussion between Pellieux and Lur-Saluces, it moved the general in the following month from his command in the Paris region to garrison duty and political impotence in Quimper.[9] Pellieux had been state educated as a boy; and when the Assumptionists pondered on his suitability as a future head of state in 1899 (see p. 23), they clearly knew little about him.

Other generals whom speculation tried to link with Déroulède were the Military Governor of Paris, Emile Zurlinden – who was replaced by a more overtly Republican general in July 1899 – and Edouard Jamont, who resigned in pique from the vice-presidency of the Conseil Supérieur de Guerre in July 1900, following Waldeck-Rousseau's shake-up of military personnel. Both Lur-Saluces and his lady counterpart in investigating military attitudes considered Zurlinden 'timide'.[10] The third Royalist emissary, Thuret, had gone as far as trying to tempt him into persuading Félix Faure to exploit his presidential position to instal a new regime, but the only response Thuret got for his plan was a wistful smile.[11] As for Jamont, several generals had told Lur-Saluces that a lead from him against the regime would enjoy a wide military following, but Lur-Saluces doubted whether Jamont was prepared to give it. Lur-Saluces suspected that Jamont distrusted the parliamentary traditions of Orleanism, although he later reported that Jamont was said to prefer a Royalist solution to a Bonapartist or plebiscitary regime.[12]

Déroulède's plans for a second coup in August 1899 provoked rumours in the Ligue des Patriotes that General François Oscar de Négrier intended to lead the crowd in a march on the Elysée.[13] He had been removed a fortnight earlier from the Conseil Supérieur de Guerre for having openly criticised the government for failing to defend the honour of the Army. On the other hand the fact that he was reinstated in July 1900 would indicate that the government did not seriously connect him with Déroulède's plans; and it is also worth noting that none of the three Royalist reporters on dissident officers mentioned him as a man who might respond to Royalist advances. Like Pellieux, Négrier had been state educated.

Constitutional issues apart, there were many senior officers who admired Déroulède as a patriotic spokesman on national defence. Another state *lycée* product, General Félix Hervé, even took it upon himself to send Déroulède highly sensitive information on what he regarded as the inadequacies of frontier defence in the Nancy district.[14] Lur-Saluces claimed that Hervé was an opponent who might well have been recruited to the Pretender's cause, but for the Duke's inactivity. He cited a remark by Hervé's wife, 'since the Prince is making no move, we will have to go with Déroulède'. Lur-Saluces nevertheless suggested him to the Duke as a possible minister of the interior in a future Royalist cabinet.[15] Hervé was among the senior officers who were to be involuntarily retired in October 1899 – which arguably strengthened his availability from the Royalists' point of view. General de Brye's wife had counselled the Royalists that retired generals were likely to be the most co-operative since they no longer had a career at risk, and the prospect of ministerial office under a new regime could be an attractive alternative to enforced leisure. She listed as ministerial material Generals Henri Berge, François Thomassin, Amédée de Cools, Camille de France and Alphonse Coiffé. Of these, de Cools was state educated and Coiffé was a *divorcé*. For less exalted office she suggested Generals Charles Haillot (an 'impoverished Bonapartist' and a Chevalier de l'Ordre Pontifical de Pie Neuf), Etienne Locmaria, Herbrié, Edmond du Guiny, de Lannay and Frédéric Boussenard.[16] Both Locmaria and Boussenard had been state-educated in Versailles. None of these featured significantly in subsequent reports, except Berge and Thomassin who were feared by some informants to have Bonapartist sympathies. Even this did not deter the ever assertive Lur-Saluces from recommending General Berge to the Pretender as a future prime minister.[17]

For a coup to consolidate itself in the country as a whole, however, the benevolence of the provincial garrisons would be required; and this would largely depend on the attitude of the twenty corps commanders. A list in the Pretender's papers, dating from about January 1899, indicated seven of these commanders as favourable, two as possibly well disposed and three as hostile.[18] But supplemented by other reports, the overall situation in the Royalists' estimation would appear to be seven favourable, three possible, four hostile and six unknown.[19] The favourable included Generals F. A. Jeannerod (1st Corps, centred on Lille), M. L. Garnier des Garets (2nd, Amiens), G. E. Sonnois (4th, Le Mans), C. Kessler (6th, Châlons), G. P. Jacquemin (13th, Clermont Ferrand), L. F. H. Metzinger (15th, Marseille) and J. de Monard (20th, Nancy). Of these, Garnier des Garets was a papal knight (see p. 20) and Jeannerod and Metzinger sent their children to Catholic private schools (see p. 41). Metzinger himself had been to the secular private school, Ste Barbe of Paris, as had Monard, while Jacquemin was state educated. The possible were Generals E. Pierron (7th, Besançon), J. B. H. Caillard (8th, Bourges), and C. M. R de Sesmaisons (17th, Toulouse). Pierron was a product of the secular private school, Ste Barbe; but he had subsequently proved his credentials – and courage – by marrying the daughter of the intemperate ultramontane polemicist, Louis Veuillot, and provided him with eight grandchildren, most of them destined for Catholic private schools. The hostile were Generals C. A. Langlois (3rd, Rouen), C. J. Zédé (14th, Grenoble) and J. A. Varaigne (18th, Bordeaux), with a probable fourth, General P. V. Faure-Biguet (16th, Montpellier). But even among the favourable, only Garnier des Garets seemed actively prepared to advise on the preparations for a coup (see p. 20 above). Much more typical of the well disposed were the cautious responses of Metzinger, Jacquemin and Sonnois, who all told Thuret that the Royalists would have to get control of the Ministry for War before they could count on the generals' active participation; otherwise, as Sonnois pointed out, the unity of the Army would be imperilled. If this condition were met, however, Metzinger undertook to keep order for the Royalists in Toulon, Nice and Marseille, while Jacquemin gave a similar undertaking for St Etienne.[20]

Nor were more venturesome opinions expressed by the divisional commanders and other junior generals who were favourably disposed towards the Royalists. Edouard de Verdière, now in the reserve, warned

Lur-Saluces against expecting 'de la part de l'armée *une initiative concertée à l'avance'*, and advised the Pretender against sending a letter of appeal to the corps commanders except on the very eve of a coup. Early appeals would merely give them time to lose their nerve, as well as increasing the risks of government discovery.[21] As it was, General Auguste Mercier was already under suspicion as a result of Royalist attempts to sound him out.[22] These replies indicated all too clearly that even the most sympathetic generals were not prepared to initiate a coup; they would merely rally to a seizure of power, once it was established and enjoying support.

Cautious though the generals' replies were, it is arguable that they might still have given an inflated impression of the degree of support that the Pretender could confidently expect in the event of a call to action. Prudence and the traditional role of 'la grande muette' favoured military loyalty to the existing regime. Yet the very uncertainty of the political future of France likewise counselled that the regime's enemies for their part should be given at least a polite hearing by the generals. Otherwise the generals might find themselves out of favour in the event of a successful coup – which would be all the more galling if their personal sympathies happened to incline towards the Pretender.

Believers in a military conspiracy would doubtless have drawn strength from the fact that the personal dossiers of the supposed discontents examined in this survey reveal that five of them were enthusiastically recommending the promotion of five of the others to important posts in the command structure.[23] Sceptics might reply that this was the coincidental outcome of the pattern of annual reports at a high level, where posts were few and where a certain incestuousness among obvious military talent was only to be expected.

Yet as the events of sixty years later were to indicate, initiative and enthusiasm for active subversion were more likely to be found among the lower ranks of the officer corps. Ability, however, was not enough in a body built on disciplined reflexes like the Army: a putsch organiser needed the pull of both rank and an established reputation to guarantee a worthwhile number of followers. In practice this meant that any officer below the rank of lieutenant-colonel would have to have unusual charisma and ability to be of much interest to the political opponents of the regime. The Royalists' tripartite trawl of the military had been largely confined to generals – and the fragments of evidence for other oppositional movements suggest a similar level of search. Yet had any of the generals who indicated an interest in a Royalist restoration taken the plunge in 1899, support would very quickly have become the responsibility of colonels – just as in 1958–62, it was the colonels who were making the running in Algiers, albeit under the leadership of generals. It is at that lower level that evidence is too scanty for either historians today or the politicians of the period to hazard a guess at the degree of support that insurrection might have received.

Catholic schools and the Army

If evidence was lacking, misgivings remained; and both during and after the Dreyfus crisis, press and politicians paid close attention to the Catholic schooling and background of a large selection of the officer corps – particularly to the role of the Jesuit secondary schools. The historian, wishing to measure the grounds for the claims of a clericalised army, encounters several difficulties. As in the case of civil servants (see pp. 72–4), the personal dossiers of officers in the War Ministry archives frequently give no indication of the schools attended before entry into the military academies. Performance and pass-out grading in these academies were the prime criteria used in assessing suitability for the officers' initial military postings. On the other hand the military academies themselves usually kept a note of the secondary schools attended by their annual intake, while the old boys' associations of the secondary schools often endeavoured to keep records of the whereabouts and activities of their former pupils, even if their information was often patchy and inaccurate.

For all its imperfections, the available evidence confirms the general assumption that men of Catholic background were positively welcomed into the armed services. As always, it is difficult to disentangle the religious element from the social and political factors in this situation. Men from landed families, where horse-riding and country sports were a major part of life, were an indispensable element in the cavalry and other mounted sections of the Army, where the relevant skills took time and money to acquire. And in other branches of the Army, where 'officer qualities' of leadership and self-confidence were required, advantage lay with young men who were used to seeing their fathers giving orders to servants or to farm or factory workers. They were happily free from the embarrassment and sense of absurdity that inhibited youths from humbler backgrounds, who often found themselves obliged to play omniscient authoritarian roles before subordinates twice their age, bedecked with campaign ribbons from colonial wars. Families at ease with wielding authority were often conservative and Catholic – and sent their sons to private Catholic schools. Given the difficulty that they had in penetrating certain sections of the Civil Service, the Army was correspondingly more attractive to them as a career – thereby compounding the Catholic presence there. It was a fact, coincidental or not, that many of the officers who reached the rank of brigadier-general and above came from regions where religious observance was high.[24] The Masonic claim of a clerico-military plot to put the Army 'into the hands of the Jesuits' might seem to be a case of one band of conspirators paying over-generous tribute to the fiendish ingenuity of another. Yet taken together, the Jesuit secondary schools in the 1890s supplied about 18 per cent of the intake into the military academy of St Cyr, 13 per cent into the Polytechnique and 22 per cent into the Ecole Navale.[25] Given that the Jesuit schools accounted for only 5 per cent of the total French secondary-school population, this was an impressive achievement. The Jesuit fees were roughly equivalent to those of the *lycées* – about £40 to £65 a year for boarders in Paris and £30 to £45 in the provinces.[26] Although there were reduced fees for deserving members of the lower officer class or impoverished nobility, the Jesuit schools had tended to go increasingly upmarket in the last quarter of the nineteenth century, both socially and in academic rigour. Several of them rapidly acquired a reputation for successfully preparing boys for the 'grandes écoles' – the prestigious state institutions for training the future elites of the public services and technical professions – the Polytechnique, St Cyr, the Ecole Navale, the Ecole Centrale des Arts et Manufactures, the Ecole des Mines, the Institut Agronomique, etc. The particular requirements of the *grandes écoles* encouraged the Jesuits to develop specific preparatory classes for them in the Ecole Ste Geneviève in Paris which from its inception in 1854 was devoted exclusively to training older boys for these high hurdles – its age-group being somewhat similar to a modern English sixth-form college. Originally opened in the Rue des Postes, its products continued to be known as *postards,* even after the street was renamed the Rue Lhomond. Unlike Ste Geneviève, the other Jesuit schools offered the full secondary-school age-range of classes, with several of them also preparing boys for the *grandes écoles.* But an increasing number of ambitious parents, with their eyes sharply focused on the *grandes écoles,* transferred their sons to Ste Geneviève when they reached the appropriate age. Indeed by the 1890s, Ste Geneviève had virtually monopolised the input of successful Jesuit candidates into the Poly-technique. Even so, the Jesuit college of Caousou in Toulouse sent a sizeable contingent of its boys into the military academy of St Cyr, while that of Notre Dame des Bons Secours on the Isle of Jersey specialised in preparing pupils for the Ecole Navale.[27]

By the 1890s the Jesuit colleges had an enrolment of some 8,000 pupils – despite their ambiguous legal position. The decree of 1880, dispersing the Jesuits, was still technically in force; and legal responsibility for the schools was vested in bodies of laymen – equivalent to English school governors – who in practice largely consisted of old boys of the particular school. Ste Geneviève's chairman in the 1890s was the leading Catholic politician, Albert de Mun. Teaching was supposedly entrusted to laymen and secular priests; but there was an increasing if discreet presence of Jesuit priests in the schools, whom the civil authorities tolerated as 'chaplains', despite the wide spectrum of functions they actually filled. Indeed in Ste Geneviève – which had 530 boys in 1898, mostly aspirants for the *grandes écoles* – the Jesuits increasingly took over the running of the school by employing Jesuit teachers posing as secular clergy; and by 1895 even the rector was a Jesuit once more.[28]

During the first two decades of 'la République des républicains' (1881–1901), Ste Geneviève sent 1,515 boys to the military academy of St Cyr and 572 to the Polytechnique (two thirds of whom were adopting military careers in the early 1880s, dropping to a third by the end of the period).[29] In 1891 Ste Geneviève took over 15 per cent of the places at the Polytechnique, surpassing even the state *lycée* St Louis which had traditionally headed the list.[30] Not surprisingly, the hazardous position of the Jesuit schools, after the punitive legislation of the Waldeck-Rousseau and Combes era, lowered this percentage. Even so, despite these difficulties, Ste Geneviève continued to win an impressive number of entries into the military academies – 568 into St Cyr between 1902 and 1913, and 188 into the Polytechnique.[31]

The old boys' association records of Ste Geneviève cover about half the school's former pupils, and reveal that nearly two-thirds of them embarked on military careers in the period 1854–1916. An astonishing 219 rose to the rank of brigadier-general or higher, five of whom ultimately reached marshal's rank – Lyautey (who left the school in 1873), Fayolle (1873), Franchet d'Espérey (1874), de Lattre de Tassigny (1908) and, later, Leclerc de Hautecloque (1922). General Edouard de Castelnau, destined to be prominent in Catholic politics in the inter-war years, was also a *postard* – as were Generals André Bapst (1872), Fernand de Langle de Cary and Auguste Noguès (1897), best known as Resident General in Morocco during the Second World War. Other military alumni included General Louis Loyzeau de Grandmaison (1881), pre-war head of the Third Bureau (Operations) and the notorious architect of 'l'offensive à outrance' which sent tens of thousands to their deaths before the Dominican-educated religiously uncommitted Pétain put an end to it at Verdun.[32]

Despite the prestigious names that punctuate the lists of the Jesuit schools, they contain remarkably few of those officers who were rumoured to be associated with the subversive activities of the Dreyfus period – even if they include a disturbing number of the political figures who hoped to benefit from them, the Orleanist Pretender *en tête* (see pp. 13–14). His ablest adviser, the Comte Alfred de Gramont, had been at Ste Geneviève before entering St Cyr – as had several members of the Lur-Saluces family, including the disastrous Eugène, who played devil to Gramont's guardian angel among the Pretender's counsellors.[33] The fastidious subversive, Boni de Castellane, had likewise spent two years there, after happier times at the Marianist Collège Stanislas and the Oratorian Collège de Juilly.

> My two years in the Rue des Postes left me with appalling memories. One should not imprison young people in such a dark place, under such a severe discipline . . . I detested the idea that my letters were opened . . . On Thursdays and Sundays we were marched out on walks, in serried ranks in the Bois de Boulogne or Vincennes under the eye of a sly *surveillant* . . . These excursions were a torture. When I spotted someone I knew, I tried to hide myself behind my neighbour, for I felt humiliated that I should be seen regimented in this way and so uncomfortably clothed.[34]

But as far as officers implicated in the Dreyfus case itself were concerned, Father Stanislas du Lac pointed out to his anxious superiors that

> Our former pupils, thanks to Providence, have been in no way mixed up in it, either as judges, witnesses or authors, until the retrial when two of them were called upon, one as a judge, Major de Bréon – it is said that he voted for acquittal – the other, Major Ducros, as a witness in Dreyfus's favour. But among the main participants, Dreyfus, Picquart, du Paty de Clam, Cuignet, Esterhazy, Mercier and all the others, I see only pupils of state *lycées*.[35]

Even Boisdeffre was at a Jesuit school – the Collège de l'Immaculée-Conception, Rue de Vaugirard – for only two years before moving to the state *lycée* of Alençon. Paty de Clam had in fact been at the Marianist Collège Stanislas; but that was another order's worry, not du Lac's. Of the seven corps commanders who the Royalists hoped would support them in the event of a successful coup (see pp. 33–4), only one, Garnier des Garets, appears to have been at Ste Geneviève, or indeed at any of the other Jesuit schools.

It was a measure of the sinister pre-eminence that the Jesuits held in anticlerical mythology that the Marianist Collège Stanislas aroused much less suspicion in Royalist minds, despite the fact that its record of entry into the *grandes écoles* and alleged 'colonisation' of the armed and civil services ran close on the heels of Ste Geneviève's, and was much more impressive than that of the other Jesuit schools. Indeed its high score of entrants into the *grandes écoles* encouraged ambitious parents to transfer their boys from less distinguished secondary schools to Stanislas for their final years. Moreover, unlike Ste Geneviève, it combined preparatory classes for the *grandes écoles* with the full age-range of secondary-school classes. And, as already indicated, its old boys included some notorious names in the annals of anti-Republican sentiment and legend, including a number of those who had also spent years in Jesuit schools. Apart from the Royalist Pretender himself, his leading spokesman in parliament, Fernand de Ramel, had been there – as had his Bonapartist counterpart, Gustave Cuneo d'Ornano. Greatest irony of all, so had Father Stanislas du Lac, the archetypal Jesuit in the anticlericals' demonology – before destiny took him to a Jesuit school in Belgium for his later years of schooling. But the Collège Stanislas could boast angels as well as demons, notably Etienne Lamy, one of the architects of the Ralliement, and Denys Cochin, a Royalist by personal inclination but a born conciliator, who in 1915 was to be the first Catholic to sit in a Republican cabinet. Nor was the social conscience of French Catholicism unrepresented there – with Marc Sangnier of Sillon fame and Jean Lerolle of the Association Catholique de la Jeunesse Française among its old boys.

In the 1890s the Collège Stanislas sent on average thirty-six boys a year to St Cyr – representing about 9 per cent of the military academy's intake and about half of what Ste Geneviève was sending.[36] It also achieved an average entry of twenty-three to the Polytechnique, not far behind Ste Geneviève's average, and equivalent to about 10 per cent of the Polytechnique's total intake.[37] In common with the general trend, an increasing number of these Polytechnicians made their way into civil careers rather than the Army (see p. 81), but altogether about twelve hundred Stanislas old boys embarked on military careers between 1880 and 1900. This was a smaller number than Ste Geneviève's and included fewer of the great names of French military history. Yet Stanislas was to have Charles de Gaulle on its roll, when in 1908 he left his Jesuit school in Belgium to prepare the entrance examinations for St Cyr. Although the Stanislas teaching staff was mainly made up of laymen and several priests, it suffered like other congregationist schools from the upheavals of the Combes era, with the result that its input into St Cyr and the Polytechnique fell to a third of what it had been in the 1890s, with only a slight recovery in the immediate pre-war period.

L'Affaire des fiches – and its antecedents

A strong Catholic presence in the officer corps created a distinctive ethos in many regiments, which inclined officers to send their own children to Catholic private schools. This was a matter of concern to militant Republicans. Combes's brief tenure of the Ministry of Education during the short-lived Léon Bourgeois ministry of 1895–6 found him conducting a large-scale enquiry into the educational preferences of the officer corps. Combined with a similar enquiry into the predilections of the Civil Service, it was entrusted to the sixteen Académies, which were responsible for the administration of secondary and higher education in the various regions of mainland France. Intended as a confidential probe into reprehensible attitudes among public employees, the investigation had a somewhat furtive character.[38] Even so, the various regional reports concurred on a number of major conclusions.

The French Army was a hermetic, hierarchical society, where regiments were frequently moved from one garrison town to another. Regional factors therefore had much less influence in shaping officers' educational preferences than was the case with the Civil Service (see pp. 75–8); and the only local consideration that played a major influence was the paucity or abundance of private Catholic schools. If these were in short supply in the region, then many *bien pensant* officers, especially ill-paid junior officers, would patronise the state sector, rather than face the financial burden of sending their children to board in Catholic schools elsewhere. This apart, the main determining factors in choosing schools were the ethos of the regiment and the example set by the senior officers in the military region – not forgetting the personal convictions of the parents themselves. It was the conviction of most Académie reports that the cavalry were heavily committed to the Catholic sector – as one would expect from the social background of most of its officers (see pp. 35–6). The more technical branches of the Army, however – engineers, artillery etc. – showed a greater predilection for the state sector. Many of their officers were themselves products of the *lycées* and public colleges; and the Polytechnique, through which a lot of them had passed, took over two-thirds of its entrants from the state schools, many destined for civilian careers. Moreover their friendship and attitudes left their mark on those who had come from the private sector. Even so, officers who had their sons in state schools often sent their daughters *chez les bonnes sœurs*.

The infantry occupied an intermediate position, where predilections for the public or private sector were contingent on a mixture of factors. Although some of the more prestigious infantry regiments had a similar ethos to that of the cavalry, the bulk had fewer social pretensions, and recruited their officers from a fairly wide background, many having been to state schools. In these mixed regiments, the example given by the commanding officer was an important consideration; and his example might well be influenced by that of the generals above him.

This was strongly borne out in the heavily garrisoned *circonscription académique* of Nancy where siege-hardened towns and sullen barracks glowered at Wilhelmine Germany across the lost provinces. In these garrisons, where senior officers from aristocratic families were few, most officers sent their children to the state *lycées* and colleges – as was the case in Bar-le-Duc (Meuse), St Dié (Vosges) and Toul (Meurthe-et-Moselle). In St Mihiel (Meuse), where the general favoured the state college, 'nearly all the officers' children are at the college', whereas at Epinal (Vosges), where the general was 'hostile', 'all the clientele go to the [Holy Ghost Fathers'] school, although the [state] college is excellent'. Similarly in the *circonscription académique* of Montpellier, notably in the Aude, officers' children largely went to the school favoured by the commanding officer – the state school in the case of Narbonne, the Catholic school in the case of Castelnaudery. A change of corps commander could have far-reaching effects, as exemplified in the *circonscription académique* of Poitiers. In the days when General Villain had been commander of the 9th Corps (Tours), the *lycée* had had a number of officers' sons, though fewer than the Jesuits. His replacement by General de Kerhué saw them reduced to six. Not only did the new corps commander discourage the officers from sending their sons there, but he made disparaging remarks about the *lycée* to local *fonctionnaires*: 'they do nothing there; they have no success'.

There was a similar situation in the *circonscription académique* of Besançon, where few officers' children attended state secondary schools. The corps commander, General Pierron, and his subordinates, Generals Jeannerod and Metzinger (both to become corps commanders in the near future), sent their children to be educated by the Marists. All three were later to be regarded by the Royalists, albeit over-optimistically, as possible allies in a coup d'état (see p. 33). Pierron was son-in-law of the arch-ultramontane journalist, Louis Veuillot, and Jeannerod was brother of the *chef de cabinet* of General Cavaignac, the Minister for War. By contrast the corps commander in Bourges, General Brugère, sent his children to the *lycée*; and an increasing number of officers were starting to do the same, despite a large residue in the private sector.

Yet even the good example of superiors with boys at *lycées* was not enough to swing the balance in Dijon, where the Académie report spoke sadly of the presence of 'nearly all the sons of senior officers' at the two Catholic schools, despite the benevolent attitude to the *lycée* of two generals who were themselves products of the state system: 'it is a daily sorrow for the *lycée* teachers, obliged to go past these two large enemy institutions, to see groups of military batmen delivering and waiting to collect their officers' sons'. Not only the cavalry officers but many of the infantry officers too sent their sons 'chez les Jésuites'. Even the gendarmerie favoured the Catholic schools – 'même le lieutenant-trésorier' of Dijon, who as a numerate among blockheads should presumably have known better.

A third factor, usually operating in favour of Catholic schools, was the influence of senior officers' wives. Several Académie reports presented wives as an insidious factor. Religious commitment was more widespread among them than among their husbands; they were concerned that their children acquire social graces; and, in the provincial boredom of small garrison towns, they were vulnerable to the social example set by the wives of the higher ranks. A fund-raising bazaar, organised by a general's wife for the local Catholic schools, broke the monotony of provincial life and drew into its orbit wives who might otherwise have been less interested in Catholic education. But pressure could take a more intimidating form. In Vannes, where the majority of officers' children attended Catholic secondary schools, 'The wives of officers who have sons at the St François-Xavier Institute ostracise those who have their children with us [i.e. the state schools]. Last year at a reception one of them said, speaking of another, "she seems very nice; but one cannot mix with her; she has her boy at the [state] college".' Similarly in the Maine-et-Loire where only a third of the officers sent their children to the state lycée, newly married officers' wives were told by those welcoming them, 'People will not mix with you . . . if you send your children to the lycée. It's not done.' Yet more chilling was the situation in Epinal in the Nancy region: 'the wife of the general tells officers that they are free to send their children where they want, but she adds that the general will bear in mind their choice when writing his notes on them.'

A further factor that favoured some of the less prestigious Catholic schools was that the religious orders who ran them were often prepared to be flexible in the matter of fees, when confronted with the financial difficulties of impecunious junior officers – whereas the state sector was not, with scholarships few and highly sought after. Conversely those officers' children who were lucky enough to obtain a state scholarship would often attend the lycée during the duration of the scholarship, but revert to the private sector when it expired.

Although Combes and his colleagues did not remain in office long enough in 1896 to make use of the ammunition that this enquiry provided, his chance was to come six years later – in circumstances far more propitious to his purpose than he could possibly have imagined in 1896. In the meantime the events of 1899 brought Waldeck-Rousseau to power on 22 June with the task of eliminating Right-wing threats to the regime. Not only were the leaders of the anti-Republican leagues put on trial (see p. 24), but the Assumptionists were declared dissolved as an unauthorised order in January 1900, and General Gaston de Galliffet was appointed as Minister for War to restore faith in the political loyalty of the Army. His main concern however was efficiency; and the retirements and shiftings which he inflicted on the upper echelons were mostly the result of his administrative reforms, rather than conscious political retribution. As the former 'butcher of the Commune', he was unresponsive to Left-wing demands for a wholesale political purge; his aim was to improve morale, not jeopardise it.

One of the early moves of the Waldeck-Rousseau government was an abortive bill to make entry into the *grandes écoles* and *fonctions publiques* conditional on candidates' having spent the final years of their secondary education in a state school (see pp. 78–81). There were too many secular but socially aspirant members of parliament with their children in private schools to make this a reality; so the emphasis was increasingly put on declericalising the private sector – or at least of removing those religious orders who rightly or wrongly were regarded as installing anti-Republican attitudes in their young charges.

But the main outcome of the clean sweep was to take place under the man to whom Waldeck-Rousseau bequeathed the task of completing the mission, Emile Combes. It is still a matter of controversy why a man of Waldeck-Rousseau's common sense and relative moderation should have recommended Combes as his successor.[39] Combes took advantage of the atmosphere of crisis to indulge his own anticlerical enthusiasms; and the result was that the innocent not only suffered with the guilty, but far outnumbered the guilty. He expelled a large proportion of the religious orders, and closed down a third of the country's Catholic schools. Those that survived had mostly to be run nominally by laypeople or by clergy in the guise of laity.

France contained no fewer than 3,216 different orders, totalling nearly 200,000 men and women. Five male orders and 909 female orders had already been authorised by previous governments, and were in principle safe from attack. But in the years following their authorisation, these various orders had gradually established thousands of schools and hospitals for which they had not obtained official sanction. Despite Waldeck-Rousseau's protests, Combes ordered them all to be closed. There were, however, 11,000 houses which had thought to play safe by submitting requests for authorisation, but these too were scheduled by Combes for closure. Even so there remained the vastly greater number of orders which had never been authorised; and it had almost certainly been Waldeck-Rousseau's intention to recommend clemency for the bulk of them – though not the Jesuits. But Combes earmarked only five orders for sympathetic consideration. Eventually a law of 7 July 1904 prohibited authorised as well as unauthorised members of religious orders from teaching, and prescribed the closure of their schools within ten years.

The irony was that the schools that had supposedly posed the greatest threat to the political integrity of the Army and the Civil Service were still open, and were still supplying a substantial, if reduced, input into the *grandes écoles* and the public services they fed. In the case of the Jesuit colleges, the teaching and administrative posts were handed back once more to laymen and secular priests, while the Jesuits themselves – who were scattered in clandestine groups of two to four in the neighbourhood – confined their activities in the college to religious duties and subsidiary coaching.[40] Even this was risky, since the colleges were subjected to police raids. At the young Charles de Gaulle's boyhood school, the Collège de l'Immaculée Conception, raided by some twenty *agents*, even a visiting dentist was searched for evidence that he might be a Jesuit. A lay teacher, with his family in the room above, was interrogated by three policemen:

> Come on, own up, you're a Jesuit!
> You must be mad! Haven't you seen my wife? Haven't you heard my children yelling upstairs?
> That's neither here nor there! You could be a Jesuit just the same![41]

Legal harassment and financial problems eventually obliged the Collège de l'Immaculée Conception to close in 1908; and although its last rector, de Gaulle's father, opened a small private day school to keep alive some of its work, it did not survive the First World War.[42] Ste Geneviève and a number of the other Jesuit colleges were more fortunate; but even the ever-resourceful Ste Geneviève eventually had to move to new rented premises in Versailles in 1913.

If the entry of Ste Geneviève and Stanislas pupils into the Poly-technique was a third of the levels of the 1890s, it was real enough, and provided a sardonic comment on the legislation that had sent thousands of non-political men and women into exile. Many anticlericals would retort that it was not the intention of the legislation to close schools or create exiles, but rather to encourage timid or misguided, if mostly good-hearted, people to renounce their communal way of life – a rather harder adjustment, some might reply, than burning the pinch of incense which the equally fair-minded Romans had demanded of the early Christian martyrs.

Whatever the efficacy of these chequered attempts to eliminate con-tamination of the public services at the point of entry, there still remained the problem of reducing to a minimum the malign influence of the infected elements that were already there. As far as the Army was concerned, Waldeck-Rousseau's first War Minister, Galliffet, was not prepared to engage in a witch-hunt that would create divisions and demoralisation; and rather than move in this direction he resigned in May 1900. His successor, General L. J. N. André, claimed to have a specific mandate from the premier to investigate subversion in the Army and to prevent officers of uncertain loyalty to the Republic gaining advancement and promotion: 'the progressive and prudent, although energetic, move towards purging'.[43] During André's tenure of the War Ministry, a systematic watch on the private lives and opinions of Catholic officers was inaugurated with a view to stalling their promotion. Although it was under Emile Combes's ministry that the system came to full flower, Waldeck-Rousseau was partly though not fully aware of what was happening – and he knew, for instance, that the War Ministry was employing members of the Sûreté Générale to compile reports on those officers who went to Mass or sent their children to Catholic schools. What Waldeck-Rousseau claimed not to have known was that the Ministry was also employing the Masonic network of the Grand Orient to spy on officers and report those who were assiduous church-goers. Such officers were put on the 'Carthage' list, and ran the risk of spending the rest of their military careers on their current rungs of the ladder, deprived of opportunities of staff-work in Paris or interesting assignments abroad. When the system became publicly known in October 1904, the scandal caused a furore in parliament and led indirectly to the resignation of the.Combes government three months later. This so-called *Affaire des fiches* raised many unanswered questions at the time, and is still debated by historians.

Combes's private papers contain a report from the Directeur de la Sûreté Générale, in November 1904, which would seem to suggest that the system of delation may have originated earlier than General André's tenure of the War Ministry, perhaps even in the last days of the Dupuy ministry when Camille Krantz was War Minister.[44] Ambiguities of chronology and identity in the details.of the report restrict its utility as evidence – and its author may have been primarily concerned to minimise his own responsibility in what had now become a very unsavoury matter. But he claimed that as early as 14 June 1899 the Secretary-General of the Ministry of the Interior, Demagny, had asked him for information on the political opinions of a handful of officers, listed by the cabinet of the War Ministry.[45] Worried by the request, he had then asked for guidance from the prime minister – although the report does not make clear whether this was the outgoing Dupuy or the incoming Waldeck-Rousseau, nor does it indicate the premier's response. At a later unspecified date he repeated his plea to Waldeck-Rousseau, who advised him 'without enthusiasm' 'to satisfy General André's requests'. The Sûreté had thereupon dispatched '*commissaires spéciaux adjoints* to make enquiries in person in various towns'.

Combes's personal papers contain reports on twelve colonels compiled in June 1900 by the *commissaires spéciaux* of the departments where they were garrisoned; and they may well have been the officers envisaged in the War Ministry's approach to the Sûreté Générale.[46] These reports were noteworthy for the relatively balanced view they attempted to present of the officers concerned. Colonel Ferré, a staff-officer in Lille, was described as 'a practising Catholic . . . belongs to the conservative party. He fulfils his religious duties, but it appears that he restricts himself socially to military circles and has a very correct attitude', the report concluding with a warm tribute to the respect he enjoyed among his subordinates. A long eulogy of Colonel Lebrun, staff-officer in Montpellier, ended with the brief, almost wistful comment, 'Monsieur Lebrun is certainly not a partisan of the republican regime, for which he would not seek to hide his antipathy', and referred to the Royalist circles that he frequented. Even the less complimentary reports generally displayed an attempt to explain rather than simply denounce the deficiencies of their subjects: Colonel Lorriot, like his ornithological namesake, 'est très décoratif' and his anti-Republican diatribes sprang from a desire to show off rather than from deeply held conviction. On the other hand Combes would doubtless have been intrigued to note the close similarities between the *commissaire spécial*'s report from Lille and that of the Académie de Lille four years earlier (see pp. 39–42). The *commissaire* claimed that all except one of the 1st Corps's staff officers 'are regarded as professing conservative, clerical opinions, and that they all have their children educated in schools run by the Jesuits', including the corps commander himself, General Jeannerod, who, unknown to the *commissaire*, was regarded by the Royalists as a likely ally (see p. 33).

Le Gaulois rapidly got wind of the Sûreté's enquiries, and the War Ministry suspended the operation – on the Sûreté's entreaties, or so its director claimed.[47] Whether this mishap was a factor in deciding André to make use of the Grand Orient can only be a matter for speculation. Although deeply committed to the ideological principles of the Republic, it seems that André was not himself a Mason – despite widespread claims that he was.[48] And the initial proposal to use the Masonic network appears to have come from Frédéric Desmons – a vice-president of the Senate and several times president of the Conseil de l'Ordre of the Grand

Orient – who visited André shortly after he became Minister.[49] The attraction of the proposal may have been increased by André's decision to transfer to his office sole responsibility for all promotions of commissioned officers (decree of 9 October 1900) – not merely those to brigadier-general and above, as decreed by his predecessor (29 September 1899). This endowed him with great power, but also saddled him with an onerous burden, since it was impossible for the ministry itself to be sufficiently well informed to make sensible decisions on the Army's 27,000 officers.[50] While the candidates' dossiers were a guide to their professional competence, the repetitious, bland formulas in which many assessments were written made selection difficult, except by officers with some direct knowledge of the writer's personal hierarchy of judicious phrases. The Grand Orient's offer of help was thus both politically attractive and a lightening of a daunting task; and in March 1901 André set in motion negotiations to make it a working reality. It fell to a Masonic member of the Minister's cabinet, Captain Henri Mollin, to establish the details; and he became in due course the recipient and analyst of the information that the Masons supplied.[51] Nor was he slow to exploit the potential of the link. Within weeks of assuming the task, he was asking the Grand Orient for information on the candidates for the command of the St Cyr military academy – 'It is absolutely essential that we put an anticlerical republican there' (13 July 1901).[52] The Grand Orient, for its part, channelled this information to Mollin through its ambivalently named secretary-general, Narcisse-Amédée Vadecard. Even before the scheme became a reality, Vadecard had been bombarding the Ministry with requests for advancement for deserving Masons (see pp. 122–6). In December 1900 he had typically been seeking to obtain a transfer for a major of the gendarmerie to the Garde Républicaine – 'There is no doubt that it would be interesting for us to have in the Garde a republican senior officer' – 'republican' being the usual code-word for Mason in this type of solicitation.[53]

As a donor of information, however, Vadecard was nothing if not thorough. His network of informants were asked to describe their subjects' 'political attitude, religious opinions and practices, way of educating their children . . . Do the candidates have any family in the locality? If so, what circles do they move in?' Some of Vadecard's team, however, allowed their enthusiasm for the hunt to outrun their discretion, prompting suspicion and awkward questions from government officials whom they had imprudently quizzed on officers in the locality. Vadecard thereupon cut down his ring of spies to a semi-reliable group of three hundred. To this predominantly civilian network, he added a military counterpart, an association of Masons of all persuasions in the armed services, entitled with unconscious irony 'Solidarité des Armées de Terre et de Mer' (SOLMER).[54] Of the 230 civilian informants, whose identity emerged in the subsequent scandal, two-thirds were senior Masons, *vénérables de loge* or one-time members of the Conseil de l'Ordre. Five were members of parliament, nine were *conseillers généraux*, a number were mayors or deputy mayors; and added to these democratically elected watchdogs of the public interest were a collection of state employees – three prefects, three sub-prefects, three *procureurs de la République*, and a *conseiller de Cour d'Appel*, two *juges de paix* and a dozen or so other legal officials, twenty-six salaried dependants of the Ministry of Education and various employees of the more technical ministries.[55] But among the forty army officers involved, the network even enjoyed the co-operation of a corps commander. General Peigné, commander of the 9th Corps in Tours, was a Mason in discreet liaison with Vadecard, and boasted of his 'vigorous struggle against the clericals of the 9th Corps', exiling several to uncongenial posts elsewhere.[56] In the private sector, lawyers, doctors, journalists and other articulate recipients of gossip were prominent, as were traders and insurance agents.[57]

Six months after Waldeck-Rousseau's resignation, he was visited by one of André's aides, General Percin, who was uncomfortable with the Ministry's use of Masonic reports (24 December 1902). Waldeck-Rousseau agreed that, unlike information from accredited government officials, such material was inadmissible; and six days later he told Combes so (30 December 1902). Combes affected surprise and sympathy with Waldeck-Rousseau's opinion; but his subsequent interview with André merely advised the War Minister to accord different levels of credence to official and unofficial information.[58]

It is thought that altogether some 20,000 *fiches* were submitted to the Grand Orient – some officers being the subject of half a dozen or more.[59] The matter became public in October 1904 before all their contents could be conveyed to the War Ministry; and the bulk of them were subsequently destroyed. Of the 2,836 surviving *fiches*, 2,626 were unfavourable to their subject, and only 210 were favourable.[60] Given the number of senior posts to fill, and the predominance of hostile verdicts in the Masonic *fiches*, it was inevitable that the Ministry had to promote a fair number of officers who had been unfavourably reported upon by the Grand Orient – a fact that André subsequently emphasised in his self-defence, without indicating its real explanation. Church-going was a dominant accusation – as was sending children to private Catholic schools, and the religious activities of wives.[61] Some *fiches* imaginatively combined accusations of clericalism with immorality: 'Forces his mistress to go to Confession'; 'His wife, a clerical, appears to be a woman of very light conduct and goes to bed predominantly with clericals.'[62] As for the favourable *fiches*, Vadecard took the same precautions as he normally did when soliciting posts: he substituted 'républicain' or 'libre-penseur' for 'franc-maçon'.[63]

Despite the size of this undertaking, it was not vigorous enough in the opinion of some critics. A lengthy unsigned report, which found its way into Combes's hands, blamed André and Percin for failing to act on the information at their disposal.[64] Whether intended for Combes or merely passed on to him, the recommendation that most impressed the recipient (who marked it 'important') was the need to dilute the dangerous regiments in the Paris region. 'Break up the centres of resistance (regiments such as those of Fontainebleau, 7th Dragoons – 9th *Cuirassiers* (Noyan) – 21st *Chasseurs* (Vendôme) – 2nd Hussars (Senlis) – 7th *Chasseurs* (Rouen)) by successive changes – easy enough to do, *if one has the will*, by invoking the ministerial circular, authorising changes of officers after six months' posting in Paris.' These recommendations were remarkably similar to some of those that were to circulate in May 1958, when particular senior officers and locally based tank regiments were suspected of collusion with the Algiers-based paratroopers preparing for 'Operation Resurrection'. Like his counterpart in Toulouse in 1958, the commander of the 15th Corps in Marseille, General Metzinger was the subject of a Masonic *fiche:* 'His activity is pernicious at the head of an army corps. His opinions and the circles he frequents have not changed. He would be harmless in Paris as a member of the Conseil Supérieur de la Guerre.'[65]. Inasmuch as Metzinger was one of the Royalists' hopes for sympathetic support, the *fiche* was perhaps not as misplaced as many; and even if its recommendation of a Paris posting would seem to bring Metzinger dangerously near to the usual scene of attempted coups, it plausibly calculated that a dissident general without troops was less of a threat than one with many – albeit at a distance.

Given the expressions of disquiet that individuals in the War Office and the Sûreté had made to Waldeck-Rousseau about this unsavoury system, it is perhaps surprising that the lid should have been pulled off it by a key figure on the other side of the enterprise, the Grand Orient. Vadecard's assistant, J.-B. Bidegain, gave some two thousand of the *fiches* to a Nationalist deputy, Guyot de Villeneuve, in exchange for 40,000 francs. The transaction came about on the advice of the Vicar-General of Paris, Canon Odelin, who was Bidegain's godfather and recipient of his misgivings about the uncongenial task in which he was currently employed. Odelin's initial instinct was to suggest handing the matter over to Jacques Piou, leader of the Catholic party, Action Libérale. But deciding that Piou might be too pale and gentlemanly to exploit the explosive possibilities of the haul, they turned to the brother-in-law of Piou's daughter, Guyot de Villeneuve, with whom contact was made at a reception given by Boni de Castellane in May 1903 – albeit by an anonymous note passed by one of Boni's regiment of liveried footmen.[66] Indeed it was subsequently suggested by the police that it was Boni de Castellane and his Catholic Nationalist colleague, Edouard Archdeacon, who had come up with much of the 40,000 francs intended to compensate Bidegain for the almost certain loss of his job.[67]

The rest of the story is familiar enough. The last week of October 1904 inaugurated a daily drip-feed of *fiches* into the pages of *Le Figaro*; and Guyot de Villeneuve confronted the government with the matter in the Chamber on 28 October. The Nationalists' main aim was to detach Combes's less fervent supporters; and although Socialist deputies such as Jaurès and Francis de Pressensé eloquently reminded the Chamber that it would be playing the Nationalists' game in sacrificing Combes, the ministry was undoubtedly discredited. It was only by a handful of votes that it survived the initial indignation of the house. Further unexpected support came from Gabriel de Syveton's brutal assault on the abject War Minister, André, in the following week's debate. The spectacle of a Nationalist deputy hitting an older man momentarily swung emotion the other way. And the Nationalist cause was scarcely helped when Syveton apparently gassed himself a few weeks afterwards. Despite stories of an elaborate Masonic contrivance to lethalise the gas heating in his room, few doubted that he had taken his life to avoid legal proceedings; he was faced with the double charge of embezzling the funds of the Ligue de la Patrie Française and of entertaining sexual relations with his daughter-in-law. Jaurès, for his part, claimed that Syveton had been murdered by his outraged wife, who had then positioned the body to suggest suicide.

Whatever the truth of the matter, Boni de Castellane's role of knight errant of the Catholic cause was not enhanced by the revelation that he had been paying the disreputable Syveton to act as his part-time private secretary – a relationship that was considered improper between two elected members of parliament. The running battle between the Nationalists and Jaurès was to take physical shape several days later, when Jaurès exchanged shots with Déroulède on a wooded hillside near the Spanish border – Guyot de Villeneuve acting as second to the exiled Déroulède who had crossed the frontier in response to Jaurès's challenge. The readiness of a man of Jaurès's intelligence and principle to participate in ritual of this kind was but one instance of the persistence of duelling in French social tradition – as was the government's authorising of Déroulède's brief incursion into France for this illegal encounter, even if the government stood to benefit by the possible death of one or both of these inconvenient men. Nor was this the end of symbolic violence. An ill-judged attempt by the Catholic Right-wing deputy, the Marquis de Baudry d'Asson, to push Combes's head into a copper saucepan during a parliamentary debate on 13 January 1905 saved the ministry from being put into a minority – just as Syveton's slapping of André had saved it two months earlier. But Combes knew that rivals in his own coalition were seeking to supplant him; and so he made as gracious an exit from office as he could a few days later, while he still had a majority of sorts.

The settling of scores continued, however, albeit in unexpected ways. Guyot de Villeneuve had a road accident in the following year; and when he died in hospital, the Nationalists had no hesitation in claiming that his death had been assisted by the ministrations of a male nurse who belonged to the Brotherhood.[68] As for Bidegain, who had betrayed the *fiches* to Guyot de Villeneuve, he embarked on a career of anti-Masonic journalism, which eventually ended in suicide in 1926. It seemed that like their counterparts in popular fiction – the archaeologists who invaded Egyptian tombs in the name of unearthing truth – the violators of Masonic secrets mostly came to a sticky end. Even the enterprising Canon Odelin never became a bishop.

If the Masonic dimension to the *Affaire des fiches* was supposedly buried, the system of official reporting on the political inclinations of officers by prefects and others continued.[69] Opinion differed as to the propriety of this. Many argued that since this was routine in the case of other ministries with teeth, notably the Interior and Justice, it was equally necessary in the Army, whose capacity to subvert the regime or frustrate its policies by refusing to obey orders was, if anything, greater. The expulsion of the religious orders had indeed put the issue to the test. A small number of officers had taken the hazardous step of refusing to obey orders, including Major Leroy-Ladurie, who had in consequence lost both his livelihood and his pension.[70] Others chose to resign after carrying out the formalities of the command – including Colonel de Coubertin, entrusted with the repugnant task of expelling the Carthusians from the Grande Chartreuse.[71] Other polemicists argued that officers, like the engineers of the Ministry of Public Works, were professional experts serving the country rather than a particular party or government – and that their private political preferences were irrelevant. The new government, however, and its Minister for War, Maurice Berteaux, were insistent on the government's right to be assured of the political acceptability of senior officers – from lieutenant-colonel upwards.[72] And insofar as this was now the responsibility of the Ministry of the Interior and the prefects, they claimed to rely exclusively on local councillors, mayors and their elected aides.[73] But with the worsening international situation in 1911, and the increasing emphasis on professional competence in the officer corps, Adolphe Messimy and his successor at the War Ministry, Alexandre Millerand, scaled down the political surveillance of junior officers, until by January 1912 only senior officers were subject to political vetting.[74]

It is argued by some historians that the importance of politics in promotion in the anticlerical era impoverished the professional quality of the Army that faced Germany in 1914. Certainly in the first four months of the war, Joffre was obliged to transfer to less responsible posts 180 of the country's 425 senior officers. It may be mere coincidence that of the nineteen officers whose skill in 1914 earned them unusually rapid wartime promotion, fourteen had been the victims of unfavourable Masonic *fiches* – which suggests that their qualities had remained unrewarded in the pre-war promotion lists.[75] Thus the Comte de Maud'Huy had been described in a Masonic *fiche* as 'Monarchist, but does not show it. Correct. Practising Catholic. Philosophical and general ideas subordinated to a Catholic outlook'; and in consequence he was systematically rejected by André in the annual *tableau d'avancement* for lieutenant-colonel. More fortunate under subsequent ministers, he had become a divisional general by the outbreak of war – but within months he was commanding an army. Conversely one of André's most assiduous supporters had been Lieutenant-Colonel Sarrail, a member of his cabinet until his transfer to the headship of the Ecole Militaire de Saint-Maixent. Intransigently committed to purging the Army, he attempted to continue this policy in his various war-time posts with disastrous effects. He was successively transferred to less responsible positions and finished the war in disgrace. The advent of Edouard Herriot's anticlerical government in 1924 saw him pulled out of obscurity and made High Commissioner for Syria – but once more he created trouble and had to be removed.[76]

If political vetting in the Army was a matter of major scandal, toppling one government and creating embarrassment for others, its equivalent in the Civil Service was more discreet and more enduring. It was likewise more widely accepted as a necessary guarantee of public order. But the degree to which it happened was something of a mystery, both to contemporaries and the historians who followed – a mystery that the middle chapters of this book will attempt to address.

3 *Raison d'état, raison d'église*: the Roman dimension

A neglected source of suspicion that coloured Republican attitudes to committed Catholics was their ambivalent allegiance to a foreign figure, the Pope in Rome. The Roman dimension to the Catholic Church had been a major cause of friction in Church–State relations since the Middle Ages, leading to massive fissures in European Christianity in the eleventh and sixteenth centuries. But the French monarchy had learned to live with the situation by unilaterally inventing Gallican liberties which allowed it to regulate the communications between Rome and the faithful in France. Napoleon had continued the tradition in the Organic Articles that he had unilaterally attached to his Concordat with the Pope; and although these were never recognised by Rome, a tacit agreement to differ enabled the system to work after a fashion for much of the nineteenth century. But the loss of the Temporal Power in 1870 and the declaration of papal infallibility in matters of faith and morals tended to sharpen the spiritual allegiance of many Catholics to the See of Rome, and put new pressures on the easy-going tolerance of the Gallican *mésentente cordiale*. The advent of anticlerical secularising governments inevitably worsened matters, as did the anti-Republicanism of a large number of French Catholics. Leo XIII's Ralliement policies helped to alleviate tension in the 1890s, but, ironically, his conciliatory attitudes made French governments correspondingly aware of the dependence of tolerable Church–State relations on the personality and preoccupations of the Pope and his advisers. This awareness became more acute after 1903, when the very different attitudes of Pius X and his Secretary of State, Merry del Val, seemed to undo much of the goodwill that Leo and Rampolla had achieved, despite the aftermath of the Dreyfus Affair. This gave papal policy a somewhat arbitrary character in the eyes of anti-clericals – which by extension saddled committed Catholics with the added stigma of being manipulated, however indirectly, by a fickle, foreign theocrat, and therefore made them doubly unsuited to positions of public trust. The Roman dimension to a French Catholic's loyalties was denounced as a professional encumbrance – much as the Moscow connection, in far more dramatic fashion, compounded the difficulties of French Communists in the inter-war years. And, as in the case of Moscow, it was the switches in Rome's policy that French ministers found disconcerting; straightforward animosity could simply be taken into account in forward planning.

Leo XIII

The Vatican archives show papal policy towards France as less arbitrary than was often supposed in Paris.[1] French politicians took insufficient account of the international context and worldwide preoccupations of the Vatican in its dealings with them – as have a number of French historians. Symptomatically the benevolence of Leo XIII towards French governments has puzzled writers, just as it exasperated many Catholic contemporaries – especially during the anticlerical high tide of the Dreyfus crisis. French scholars have tended to see it largely (though by no means exclusively) in terms of his concern for the well-being of the Church in France, coupled with his recognition of the importance of France in the overseas mission field. The Vatican archives reveal, however, that until his last days Leo continued to entertain hopes of using France to recover Rome, and that even during the Waldeck-Rousseau and Combes ministries, the nuncio in Paris was actively trying to enlist French support for the removal of the Italian government from Rome and its re-establishment in Florence. Perhaps the best summary of the papal position is contained in an exchange between the Paris nuncio (Mgr. Benedetto Lorenzelli) and the French Foreign Minister in November 1901. Describing his interview with Delcassé, Lorenzelli wrote to the papal Secretary of State:

I demonstrated that the territorial sovereignty of the Holy See was necessary to the Pope so that he should not be, or seem to be, a privileged subject of the Kingdom of Italy, nor run the risk of being or appearing to be the subject of any other state, be it Austria, Germany or France. In this way his acts will be seen as the expression of his apostolic conscience and cannot be suspected of being politically dictated by this or that government and its allies . . .

Delcassé brought up the idea – not as his own – of giving the Pope an island where he would be sovereign ruler; and I replied that the Pope to be sovereign did not need a gift but a restitution. He ought to be a sovereign ruler because he is Bishop of Rome. He therefore ought to have the sovereignty of Rome and not of an island.[2]

The Vatican's principal worry was that other governments might use the Pope's alleged dependence on Italy as an excuse to ignore him when it came to dealing with the Church in their own territories. To demonstrate its independence to the rest of the world, it rejected every Italian attempt at conciliation and formally forbad Italian Catholics to participate in national elections. If the continuance of this prohibition into the twentieth century seemed to many contemporaries to be an act of self-mutilation which weakened the Church's capacity for self-defence, it contained, nevertheless, a certain element of political realism. The Italian monarchy looked to the propertied classes as its main support; and, as the papal nuncio in Bavaria pointed out in 1902, the growing challenge of the Left increased the monarchy's desire to see the forces of conservatism strengthened by the addition of Catholics to the electorate.[3] It was, therefore, very much in the monarchy's interest to bargain with the Vatican for the lifting of the prohibition. Even so, the monarchy was at no time prepared to pay a price as high as the restoration of Rome to the Pope.

Before the Franco-Italian trade treaty of 1898, the Vatican had assumed that Italy's membership of the Triple Alliance would guarantee Franco-Italian hostility; and the papacy had therefore tried to interest France in the Roman Question by presenting the Pope's claim to Rome as a means of weakening Italy.[4] But with growing Franco-Italian friendship, Lorenzelli then tried to persuade Delcassé that it was to Italy's advantage, as well as to France's, to abandon Rome to the Pope and transfer the administrative capital to Florence. This, according to Lorenzelli, would create a much stabler situation in Italy, where the Italian government would no longer have to look to Germany for military protection against any attempt by other countries to restore Rome to the Pope. Clarifying these points on 9 May 1902, Lorenzelli claimed that 'the occupation of Rome is the motive for Italy's alliance with Germany and with England in the Mediterranean; while the recreation of the papal state would set Italy free, and make possible a defensive league running from Madrid, through Paris, Florence [sic] and Vienna, and extending to St Petersburg'.[5] Delcassé's reluctance to comment was understandable; and it must have been hard for him not to betray amusement at Lorenzelli's references to Italy as 'Florence'. He had already told Lorenzelli on 2 April 1902 that the restoration of the Temporal Power would fatally destroy Italian unity.[6] And France was scarcely disposed to welcome this – especially after the conclusion of the wide-ranging Franco-Italian agreement of 30 June 1902.

The letters of several senior French Jesuits and Assumptionists display a particular concern, notably at the turn of the century, that the Vatican might sacrifice the religious orders in France to the maintenance of good relations with the French government. Few, if any, of them were aware of the degree of importance that the Vatican attached to the Roman Question; but they were strongly aware that the Vatican was very anxious to preserve formal relations with France and was deeply committed to maintaining Napoleon's Concordat, which governed relations between the Church and the French State. For the French secular clergy – the bishops and parish priests – state salaries were the prime advantage of the Concordat; but they were not its most important aspect for the Vatican. Indeed, as was later to be shown in the Vatican's handling of the disestablishment issue in 1905–6, it was quite prepared to abandon £16 millions' worth of property – ten times the annual value of the state salaries – in order to assert its principles on what it saw as the prime importance of the Concordat. The Concordat, like the maintenance of formal diplomatic links between Paris and the Vatican, was a symbol of French government respect for the Church and the Vatican's authority in the Church. These and other signs of formal deference meant a great deal to an organisation that felt desperately insecure; and the diplomatic links had the particular attraction of being attributes that were usually associated with temporal powers.

The Assumptionist Father Emmanuel Bailly wrote to his brother in February 1902, 'In everything that concerns France, the Vatican's guiding principle is this: every possible sacrifice is to be made rather than lose official diplomatic contact or the Concordat. Consequently, if one has to sacrifice monks, nuns, projects, newspapers and colleges . . . Rome will breathe heavy sighs, but will not make it a matter for breaking off diplomatic relations.'[7] A senior Jesuit, M.G. Labrosse, was shortly to complain about what he saw as a growing concordance of attitude between Rome and the government, concerning the orders.[8] The nuncio himself, somewhat unfairly, had accused both the Jesuits and the Assumptionists of seeking the wealth of rich anti-Republicans, and told Rampolla about Léon Harmel's recent outburst to Father Vincent Bailly, 'the cult of Mammon will be your ruin!'[9]

The Vatican unquestionably made many protests against the pro-scription of the orders, both publicly and through diplomatic channels. Whatever criticisms Lorenzelli made about various orders to other ecclesiastics, he loyally defended them in his interviews with Delcassé. Much of his time with the foreign minister was taken up with the issue, despite the fact that he knew that Delcassé was personally hostile to much of the cabinet's anticlerical programme. Yet these protests remained expressions of sorrow and dismay, without suggestion of sanction – although it could be argued that the Vatican had few significant sanctions at its command. De Mun's suggestion that the Vatican should threaten to break off the Concordat and diplomatic relations was unlikely to impress a government that was well aware of Leo's double attachment to the Concordat and to the formal diplomatic link.[10]

The fate of the orders depended on the Chamber elections of April–May 1902; and it was to be the strengthening of the anticlerical Left in the new parliament that gave Combes confidence to pursue to the full his ruthless programme against the orders, when he took over the premiership from Waldeck-Rousseau several weeks later (see pp. 43–4). Catholics had put great effort into limiting the extent of the anticlerical victory. The Ralliés had hitherto remained loyal to Leo XIII's favoured policy of attempting to form broad conservative alliances with other 'moderate' Republicans – rather than creating a distinctive Catholic party, with its obvious risks of falling into a ghetto situation. But the impending threat to the religious orders had decided them to form a party in June 1901 – Action Libérale – which, while eschewing a Catholic title, was openly recognised as an instrument of Church defence in the forthcoming elections. Its leader, Jacques Piou, exhorted the Vatican to persuade the Jesuits, Dominicans, Carthusians and Marist Brothers to set an example to the other religious orders by providing the party with several hundred thousand francs for the electoral campaign. Playing the card that was most likely to stir Rome into action, Piou pointed out that a victory for the Left might also imperil the Concordat.[11] Even so, the request was full of danger. If it became known that the orders were financing the electoral campaign, the worst accusations of the anticlericals would appear justified. On the other hand a Left-wing victory at the polls would make the truth of such accusations a matter of academic interest as far as the future of the orders was concerned. Rampolla's replies were broadly sympathetic on the principle, but were initially unspecific as to what action the Vatican was prepared to take.[12]

Much more daring was Rampolla's response to the suggestion of Bishop Touchet of Orléans, that 'those [French] bishops who were in favour of the proposal' should be verbally authorised by the nuncio to contribute 'twenty or thirty thousand francs from the diocesan treasury for Deputy Piou's operations' – an expedient which, if widely followed, could cover most of the campaign's expenses. Lorenzelli took the precaution of transmitting the idea in a coded letter, carried by a Franciscan friar to Rampolla's deputy, Mgr. Giacomo della Chiesa (later to become Pope Benedict XV). Lorenzelli invited Rampolla to reply by sending a telegram with the simple message, 'utique' ('everywhere'), or 'minime' (as little as possible').[13] Rampolla's immediate reply was 'utique'.[14] Unfortunately for the historian, later correspondence reveals nothing of the implementation and the harvest of the plan; but implemented everywhere it would theoretically have raised two to three million francs. Despite this uncertainty, the large amount of money spent by Action Libérale on the campaign does suggest that a number of bishops may have been successfully approached.

The actual electoral outcome, however, was disappointing. In a Chamber of 588 seats, Action Libérale obtained only seventy-nine – twenty-four of whom were disconcertingly also members of the Nationalist group – while their allies among the moderate Republicans, the Progressistes, numbered a modest ninety-one. This left them unhealthily reliant on the extreme Right – the fifty-eight Nationalists and the dozen or so monarchists, who would automatically oppose the government's anticlerical policies as part of their anti-Republican stance. But even with these uncongenial companions, plus a score of independent deputies, there was numerically no hope of countering the anticlerical majority.

Pius X

The death of Leo XIII in August 1903 and the advent of Pius X (1903–14) brought about a sea-change in Vatican policy. Matters might have been different, had not the Viennese government intervened against the candidature of Cardinal Rampolla, Leo's Secretary of State, who was within thirteen votes of the decisive score and would presumably have continued with the main thrust of his late master's policies. The new papal Secretary of State, Rafael Merry del Val, saw little or no hope of recovering Rome and even less of French aid in bringing such a miracle about. Both he and Pius X were convinced of the necessity of a general detente with the Italian government. Not only would this ease the Church's pastoral work in Italy, but it would emancipate Vatican diplomacy from the constraints of the Roman Question. The papacy would be free to speak its mind on issues affecting the Church, whereas Leo and Rampolla had been continually afraid of alienating governments who they vainly hoped might help them recover Rome – notably France. There was consequently something of a diplomatic revolution with the change of Pope, albeit a gradual one. Whereas Leo had hoped to use France as an instrument against Italy, the new masters in the Vatican wanted to be on better terms with Italy, so as to leave their hands free in dealing with France, and with any other country which adopted a belligerent attitude towards the Church. At the same time Merry del Val favoured a gradual and discreet replacement of the Roman issue with an alternative policy: papal independence should increasingly come to be based on a steady strengthening of the Vatican's role and reputation in matters of international co-operation. Leo had already initiated a policy of trying to obtain representation for the Pope on various international bodies – but for Leo this attempt to increase papal prestige had been a supplementary policy to the recovery of Rome, not a substitute for it as with Merry del Val.[15]

If the historian is inclined to admire the greater realism of Pius and Merry del Val on the Roman Question, there is less to admire in their assessment of French affairs and French churchmen. In these matters Leo and Rampolla had the greater knowledge and the sharper perceptions – for all their over-optimism and wishful thinking. Without renouncing the Ralliement, Pius X and Merry del Val progressively undermined its spirit and strategy. It had been Leo XIII's policy to encourage an alliance between Catholics and conservative Republicans on the basis of keeping a tactical silence on Catholic demands that might embarrass the conservatives. Divisive issues were to be kept for the while in a bottom drawer – like 'the maximum programme' of the Socialists.

In Merry del Val's view this policy had been disastrous, and he regarded the current predicament of the French Church as its direct result. In June 1909 he announced on the Pope's behalf that 'the most practical and opportune policy was to rally all men of goodwill on to *le terrain nettement catholique et religieux*, according to papal instructions'.[16] This in effect was a reversal of Leo's strategy, in that it threatened to throw Royalists and Ralliés together in an alliance against everyone else, thereby creating the kind of ghetto mentality that Leo had been so anxious to avoid.

Within a year of Pius X becoming Pope, the French government was to break off diplomatic relations with the Vatican; and within three years it would unilaterally abolish the Concordat and separate Church and State in France. Whether events would have evolved differently with Rampolla as Pope can only be a matter of conjecture. Combes's heavy-handed attempts to use the threat of Separation as a stick to bully Rome into accepting his own rigorous interpretation of the State's rights under the Concordat created a situation that he could no longer control, and resulted in a Separation that neither he nor his successor, Maurice Rouvier, actually wanted. It may well be that even Rampolla's good will and dexterity could not have averted this outcome. Yet the opening of the Vatican archives reveals a sharp divergence of view between Rampolla and Merry del Val on so many of the issues that led to the breakdown that the historian must concede at least the possibility of a much less damaging denouement.

The rupture of diplomatic relations in July 1904 is a case in point. While intended as part of Combes's programme of intimidating the

Vatican into compliance, his formal excuse was Rome's summoning of two scapegrace bishops to Rome under pain of canonical suspension – Combes claiming that the suspension of a bishop, like an episcopal appointment, was a bilateral Concordatory matter, needing the government's assent. The Vatican archives contain a lengthy report on one of the bishops, Le Nordez of Dijon, from a French parish priest, which the nuncio had sent to Rampolla in April 1902.[17] It accused him of various sexual misdemeanours, financial dishonesty, arrogant behaviour and theological unorthodoxy. It also accused him of drunkenness and a certain robustness of vocabulary in private conversation, as when he dismissed several devotional practices as 'good for nothing but listening to angels farting'. The nuncio's opinion was that only the sexual charges should be taken seriously – but he concluded that 'Mgr. Le Nordez brings no honour to the Church', and that when the following elections were over, the Church should get together with the government and jointly arrange for his resignation.[18] It is clear from his letter that he believed that the matter could be resolved only in conjunction with the government, and that resignation, not dismissal, was the proper procedure. The implications are that had Rampolla not been replaced by Merry del Val, the issue might have been concluded more tactfully – and the same is arguable in the case of the other bishop, Geay of Laval. Whether Combes would have been amenable to negotiated resignations is another matter.

Certainly the consequences of Separation for the Church in France would have been materially less crippling if Rampolla had been in charge of papal policy. In his encyclical, *Gravissimo officii* of 10 August 1906, Pius X not only condemned the Law of Separation but prohibited Catholics from forming the *associations cultuelles* that the law prescribed as the future legal embodiment of the Church in France. The papal prohibition stripped the French Church of the legal means of retaining the property that the Separation Law designated as belonging to the Church, and also deprived it of the means of rebuilding new material resources on a basis of legal security. It was only when the prohibition was lifted much later, in 1924, that the French Church was able to regularise its position vis-à-vis the law, and undertake new building programmes without risk of legal complication. The property lost in 1906, however, was beyond recovery. It was to take half a century of dreary appeals and collections to replace the resources that had been so spectacularly discarded.

This enormous sacrifice ran counter to the wishes of most French Catholics. Faced with the problem of maintaining 42,000 French clergy and buying or renting the appropriate accommodation, they were not in a mood to add to these difficulties by accepting self-imposed burdens that would weaken the Church still further. If, as the Vatican alleged, there was a danger of Church property getting into the wrong hands, the refusal of the Church to form *associations* would encourage rather than prevent this danger.

The opening of the archives of the papal Secretariat of State for this period reveals in detail the opposing views of Rampolla and Merry del Val on this costly act of legal suicide. For Merry del Val the least forgivable feature of the Separation was that the government was attempting to impose a new legal constitution on the Church in France, without having made the least effort to secure the Vatican's consent. Merry del Val feared above all that if it were to accept the Law and the proposed *associations cultuelles*, other nations might conclude that the Vatican no longer had the determination to defend Church interests, and they might be tempted to embark on similar anticlerical programmes themselves.

This is especially evident in the minutes of the meetings of the Congregation of Extraordinary Ecclesiastical Affairs. It was this body that in effect abandoned to Merry del Val and the Pope the decision whether to accept or reject the *associations cultuelles*, following its inconclusive discussions on 12 and 19 July 1906, in which four of its members were in favour of accepting the *associations*, and four were against – with a ninth member abstaining, despite personal predilections for acceptance. Opposing acceptance, Merry del Val pointed out that

other governments will immediately invoke the precedent of France. You have only to look at the drift of legislation in other countries under the rule of the international sect [i.e. Freemasonry] to be convinced of it . . . The bills that are being prepared in Hungary, Spain and Portugal, not to speak of the republics of the Americas, are already invoking the example of France as a model of progress. Only last Friday, the Portuguese Ambassador was expressing his fears to me. The Madrid nuncio and other people are telling me about the intended programme of the liberal parties in Spain, a combination of all the forces of the republican and liberal parties in the country; and this programme, invoking the need to attain the level of France, seeks the abolition of Article 2 of the constitution, it wants civil marriage, the secularising of schools, the gradual but systematic expulsion of the religious orders. And the same in other countries.

To accept the *associations cultuelles* 'would be a fatal mistake for religion in France and a terrible wound for the Universal Church'.[19]

Merry del Val saw the world in domino terms, much as John Foster Dulles did in the depths of the Cold War. The minutes of the other meetings of the Congregation of Extraordinary Ecclesiastical Affairs during 1906 show Ecuador, Bolivia and Venezuela as posing analogous if less serious problems for Rome – the common denominator being an inclination for new-broom governments to envisage changes in the legal status of the Church without prior consultation with the Vatican.[20]

Rampolla opposed Merry del Val's conclusions at the meetings of both 12 and 19 July.[21] He argued that a papal ban on the *associations cultuelles*, far from deterring other governments from anticlerical measures, might positively encourage them in this direction, if the French Church was severely weakened as a result of the prohibition. The only circumstances in which the ban might deter other governments was in the event of the French Church emerging patently strengthened by its ordeal. But Rampolla thought this most unlikely. Not only would the Church be weakened by the sacrifice of the material resources that the Separation Law allowed it to retain, but the public would perceive this as a self-imposed sacrifice, for which the Church had itself principally to blame; it would not result in the outburst of antigovernmental anger that many intransigent Catholics seemed to hope would follow.

Merry del Val remained unmoved by Rampolla's arguments and those of the other three cardinals who supported him. Rejecting claims that the system of *associations cultuelles* did not necessarily threaten the authority of the bishops over Church property, he replied that it was the aim of 'the sect' (i.e. the Freemasons) to chloroform public opinion with vague words and valueless assurances. 'This is the opinion of the better French bishops, the more virtuous clergy and the great mass of rural clergy who are in touch with the people . . . in sum those on whom we should rely in the future.' And, as on previous occasions, he took heart in the popular demonstrations witnessed at the time of the government's assessment of Church property in February and March 1906. He discounted Rampolla's view that the French Catholic population were incapable of prolonged resistance, arguing that the resistance over the government inventories of Church property might well have been even more spectacular, had not the bishops advised the parish clergy to come secretly to terms with the authorities, allowing the bailiffs to enter the churches surreptitiously to take the inventories, while outwardly sympathising with the demonstrators. At the same time he expressed 'the little faith that the Holy See can have in quite a lot of the archbishops and bishops of France'.[22] In conclusion he praised the example of Pius VI, who had refused to accept the Civil Constitution of the Clergy in 1791, despite pressure from many French Catholics to do so. The Pope's intransigence had ultimately been justified by the eventual capitulation of the French government after years of popular resistance against the Revolutionary tyranny; and the outcome had been the Concordat with Napoleon.

The encyclical, *Gravissimo officii* of 10 August 1906, rejecting the *associations cultuelles*, said little of Merry del Val's real fears. To have spoken of the dangers of the French example might have provoked the onslaught elsewhere that the encyclical was designed to prevent. Moreover, it would have been embarrassingly obvious that it was the Church in France not the Vatican that was paying the price of this salvage operation. The encyclical therefore chose to lay its emphasis on the potential dangers of the *associations cultuelles* to the unity and security of the French Church. The difficulty here, however, was that a general assembly of the French bishops, called by the Vatican specifically to debate the issue in Paris on 30–31 May 1906, had voted in favour of giving the *associations* a try by forty-eight to twenty-six. For Rome this was an inconvenient decision, which eclipsed the assembly's formal condemnation of the principle of the *associations* by a virtually unanimous vote. Rome's purpose in calling the assembly had been to obtain episcopal backing for its intended condemnation of the *associations*; and the Pope had issued a number of public and private statements designed to leave the bishops in no doubt as to what was expected of them. But, infiltrated by intellectuals and a Gallic respect for material considerations, the bishops proved unwilling to make chivalrous gestures of doubtful utility; and the Vatican's hopes backfired. The only consolation for Merry del Val was that the bishops were canonically pledged to public silence on how the votes had gone.

The encyclical therefore chose to say nothing about the bishops' affirmative vote on the real issue – and, having chosen reticence on this, it would have been wise to keep a consistent silence on the rest of the assembly's proceedings. But it could not resist making what capital it could from the bishops' formal condemnation of the principle of the *associations* – 'We see that we must fully confirm with our apostolic authority *la délibération presque unanime* of your assembly' – thereby giving the impression that the papal prohibition was a confirmation of the bishops' wishes. And even when Bishop Lacroix of Tarentaise supplied an anonymous report of the assembly's proceedings to *Le Temps*, revealing the disingenuous nature of the encyclical's claims, Merry del Val stuck to his guns. Instructing the papal *chargé d'affaires* in Paris to refute the accusation, he told him: 'The question put to the bishops was a *practical* one, to know whether one could set up *associations cultuelles, telles que les voulait la loi* without violating the essential rights of the Church. The reply was "No", with virtual unanimity. The minutes are clear. Naturally one cannot give all the details to the press.'[23]

Any charitable explanation of Merry del Val's duplicity must assume one of two possibilities: first, that available accounts of what happened at the assembly are erroneous; or, secondly, that the Vatican misunderstood or was misled by the official secret minutes that were sent to it. The opening of the archives of the papal Secretariat of State, however, confirms that neither hypothesis is sustainable; and it is significant that the Vatican carefully avoided making a specific denial of the clandestine accounts – only a denial of the significance of the votes taken. The Secretariat's archives contain not only the official minutes of the assembly, which corroborate Lacroix's leaked account, but also much revealing comment and supplementary detail from participating bishops, not only on the assembly itself but on the developments that brought it about.[24]

What clearly emerges is the important role of Bishop Chapon of Nice, who – rather like Francis de Pressensé on the side of the anticlerical architects of Separation – played a major but underrated part in securing the Church's eventual acceptance of the Separation Law.[25] Chapon's role in the ultimate settlement of 1924 is well known; but his activities in 1906, which have not been sufficiently recognised, can be seen in retrospect as laying the foundations of the eventual resolution of these problems. It was he who first suggested to Merry del Val that there should be a general assembly of the French bishops to discuss the issue; it was he who proposed that the vice-president and effective leader of the assembly should be Archbishop Fulbert-Petit of Besançon – who was later to emerge as a realistic architect of how a practical trial of the *associations cultuelles* might be reconciled with a formal condemnation of the Separation Law in principle.[26] It never occurred to a man of Chapon's integrity that the Vatican would abuse the confidentiality of the assembly to twist the bishops' recommendations into something suggesting the contrary of what they proposed; and he, for his part, had made clear to Merry del Val from the outset his belief that it would be disastrous to reject the *associations cultuelles*.

Chapon was particularly perceptive on French politics, and was a source of good advice to the Vatican on the forthcoming elections in May 1906, even if it was insufficiently heeded.[27] He warned the Vatican against the temptations of trying to form a specifically Catholic party, and suggested that the bishops should discreetly advise Catholics to campaign with the moderate parties of the Centre to keep out the Radicals and other anticlericals – without trying to extract from the Centre a commitment to repeal anticlerical legislation, as had been disastrously attempted at local level in the 1898 elections. When Chapon's views were discussed at the Congregation of Extraordinary Ecclesiastical Affairs, Rampolla spoke strongly in their favour – his own memories of the mistakes of 1898 convincing him of their wisdom.[28] The only dissentient note came from Merry del Val who said that the final strategy should depend on what happened to public opinion in the meantime. This was an ominous comment, in that it betrayed Merry del Val's perennial hope that the basic instinct of the Catholic common man would rescue France from the hesitations of the French bishops and intellectuals, whom Merry del Val profoundly distrusted.

But the disappointing election results of May 1906 did not dispose the assembly of French bishops to heroic decisions of self-sacrifice in the matter of the *associations cultuelles*; and Chapon's securing of Fulbert-Petit as effective leader of the assembly helped to ensure that this was so. Fulbert-Petit began impressively by defusing the bomb which the Pope had sent to awe the assembly into clear thinking. In a letter sent to Cardinal Richard, to be read to the bishops, the Pope reminded them that 'we are born for war: *non veni pacem mittere, sed gladium*', and asked them whether 'we would not be open to blame in trusting a government which resorts to trickery when it cannot use violence'.[29] Fulbert-Petit then cheered the spirits of the stunned bishops by pointing out that the letter had been written a couple of months previously (4 March) – since when circumstances had changed. He called upon Léon Amette, auxiliary bishop of Paris, to tell the assembly the current attitude of the Pope, Amette declaring:

The Pope told me positively that the bishops were quite free in the advice that they had to give him, that he was not seeking to weigh on their consciences, and that he did not wish to direct them one way or the other. Those then who interpret the [Pope's] letter to Cardinal Richard as an indication of the Pope's wishes are quite mistaken . . . The cardinals think so too, Cardinal Vanutelli, and especially Cardinal Rampolla.

That, according to Bishop Touchet of Orléans, produced a huge sigh of relief in the assembly.[30] This deft pulling of the rug from under the Pope's initial warning must undoubtedly have greatly angered Merry del Val when he learnt of it a few days later; and it may well have been a factor in the subsequent deep distrust that he displayed towards Amette when he eventually became Archbishop of Paris in 1908.

Bishop Touchet of Orléans was the Vatican's prime source of information on the atmosphere of the assembly, since his *ad hominem* comments went far beyond the formal account contained in the official report. Touchet was a strong-minded, intelligent man whose presence among the opponents of the *associations cultuelles* surprised a number of his contemporaries, who assumed that his realism would put him in the other camp. The private report on the assembly that he sent to the Pope was a bitter indictment of the pro-*associations* lobby, remarkable for the sardonic irony of his résumés of their arguments. Paraphrasing Archbishop Mignot of Albi, '"The *associations* are doubtless execrable. The Pope has expressed it admirably; we think the same and we have said so by our vote yesterday; but, at the end of the day, it's a choice of living or dying – and living is better than dying, wouldn't you say?" Much applauded.' Touchet laid emphasis on the important role played by Chapon and his carefully prepared report in favour of accepting the *associations*, which the bishops likewise greeted with much applause. In the ballot that followed – the crucial vote on whether to give the *associations* a try – Touchet reckoned that all the cardinals and archbishops voted in favour of acceptance, including those like Cardinal Richard of Paris who had been hostile to the *associations*. The bulk of the bishops did likewise. Touchet believed that the opposing minority of twenty-six – Rome's angels – almost certainly included the thirteen new bishops present, France's first non-Concordatory appointments, who in their purity owed nothing to government favour, and who had heard the Pope denounce the *associations* at their consecration two months earlier. In addition to these holy innocents, Touchet listed twelve battle-scarred stalwarts, and hazarded guesses as to the twenty-sixth.[31]

Apart from his steering of the discussions, Fulbert-Petit had also justified Chapon's confidence in him by the draft statutes that he had presented to the assembly, demonstrating how episcopal control could be guaranteed over the *associations cultuelles*. The Separation Law allowed the Church complete freedom to secure this control by imposing its own rules on Catholic *associations*; and the Church could make obedience to the hierarchy a formal condition of membership – as the framers of the Law were quick to point out, and as Fulbert-Petit's draft statutes impressively illustrated. The assembly gratefully voted its approval of these by fifty-nine votes to fifteen.

The reluctance of the French bishops to give a rousing cheer as the ship went down was a matter of bitter regret for Merry del Val. Speaking in a different context at the end of the year, he was to tell two Assumptionist visitors:

It would seem in effect that French Catholics are not interested in religious liberty, and that they wearily take up a defensive posture only when Rome demands it. It is, on the contrary, the duty of French Catholics to push intransigence to its ultimate limits, to reject utterly the laws that the government formulates against them, to go much further than Rome in resisting them, to be so militant that we need to restrain them . . . If our role was limited to being a moderating influence, you would have the situation that existed in Germany.

There, resistance was vigorous, with no quarter given; the Catholics were admirably intransigent; Rome had to moderate them, and it was by no means easy to hold them back . . . But what a splendid position for the Papacy which thereby became the arbiter of the situation. In France, unfortunately, it's just the other way round . . . Is it because le sens catholique no longer exists there?[32]

Always an admirer of self-solicited suffering, Merry del Val told several of his French Catholic visitors in the course of 1906 of the invigorating example of the General of the Jesuits who had refused anaesthetic during a recent operation on his arm, while firmly holding a crucifix in the other hand. 'To be a good Catholic, one must suffer.'[33] As for the Pope, his verdict on the plight of the clergy in post-Separation France was simple: 'The good ones will pull through; as for the bad, so much the worse for them.' On the educated French laity and their political leaders, his verdict was equally simple: 'French Catholics are cowardly, and they are as pig-headed as the Germans – which is saying a lot.'[34]

If Rampolla had not been deprived of the tiara by the intervention of Austria in 1903, the lot of the French Church in the years to come would undoubtedly have been much happier. The Combes era was short-lived; and, under the ministries that followed, the Church in France arguably suffered more at the hands of Rome than at the hands of the French government. Vatican attitudes during the Pius X era were an added impediment to the assimilation of committed Catholics into the Republican establishment, and thereby created further difficulties for those seeking to penetrate the more closely guarded branches of French state service. Their difficulties – both real and imaginary – are the subject of the next section of this book.

Part 2

As it was: Catholics and State employment, 1890–1914

All citizens . . . are equally eligible for all honours, places and public employment, according to their abilities, and without any distinction other than their virtues and talents.

> Article 6 of the Declaration of Rights of Man and of the Citizen,
> 27 August 1789

Sire, we teach respect for your dynasty because it rules by virtue of the country's constitution, just as we would teach respect for the Republic, if it were the current form of government. As long as you last, that is to your advantage.

> The Grand Master of the Université to Napoleon, 1811

While you owe justice to everyone . . . you keep your favours for those who have unmistakably proved their fidelity to Republican institutions.

> Circular of Emile Combes to prefects, 20 June 1902

4   Problems and principles

An acute and much-travelled English observer of French life, J. E. C. Bodley, wrote in 1898, 'a French citizen who is dependent on the State for his livelihood is not always at liberty to accompany his wife and children to Mass on Sunday morning, without risking his future prospects and their means of sustenance'.[1] Bodley's personal sympathies were admittedly with the Church rather than with its critics – and he viewed with a jaundiced eye what he saw as the profiteers in the contemporary political climate. His son recounts an occasion when he and his father had seen pass by an open carriage, bearing Edward VII and his current host, an eminent Jewish businessman. Bodley had thereupon raised his silk hat and in loyal ringing tones shouted 'Hail, King of the Jews!' Yet Bodley's remark on France reflected a belief that was widely held at the time, and was also shared by many later writers, who claim that it was extremely difficult for a practising Catholic to make a career for himself in the more politically sensitive branches of the public service – not only in the Ministry of the Interior, but in varying degrees elsewhere. Others reply that insofar as this was the case, it was a result of the anti-Republican record of the milieux from which the rejected applicants came; but that Catholics who kept a low profile and loyally supported the regime had no difficulty in obtaining entry or advancement. The matter has not been systematically studied by historians – partly because of the difficulty of obtaining access to the personal dossiers of civil servants.

Problems of approach

A law of 3 January 1979 extended official secrecy on public servants' personal files from a hundred years to a hundred and twenty years. It was claimed that advances in medical science made this necessary: not so much because some devoted old *rond-de-cuir*, coughing out his last days at the age of a hundred and nineteen, might object to his personal affairs becoming public, but rather that his immediate family, enjoying their extended life, might find their pleasure marred by unwelcome intrusion

71

into matters that were perhaps best forgotten. The practical result of this enlargement of official delicacy is that the historian is effectively denied access to alphabetical runs of dossiers for *fonctionnaires* whose in-service careers began significantly less than a century before the date of consultation – education and military service happily taking care of their first twenty-odd years of life. While archivists vary in the rigour with which they interpret the law – and a lunch-hour request to an inexperienced or inattentive stand-in may produce undreamt-of treasure – runs of dossiers that border on the forbidden period can normally be obtained only if an obliging archivist is prepared to take the time and trouble to remove from the run those individuals whose date of birth puts them out of bounds for the enquirer. Otherwise it is a matter of requesting by name the dossiers of specific individuals whom the researcher knows to be safely clear of the hundred-and-twenty-year limit – knowledge that he may not have, if his concern is with sample slices of the civil service, rather than particular men. The result is that no quantitative survey of the main theme of this book is yet possible for this period, and the following pages are therefore based on piecemeal archival findings and on other sources of information.

Even when access to personal dossiers is obtained, they are often disappointingly uninformative. In 1905, civil servants were given the right to inspect their own dossiers if they were the object of some sort of complaint; and this right of consultation was put on a routine basis by several ministries in the years to come (see pp. 117–18). One imagines that there may well have been a fair amount of document-burning by office-heads when this right was established; so it is conceivable that many of the more politically revealing documents may simply have gone up in smoke.

An alternative way of approaching the problem is to examine the records of Catholic private secondary schools and attempt to assess how many of their former pupils succeeded in entering the civil service. Such an exercise, of course, can be of only limited significance. Enrolment in a Catholic secondary school is much more indicative of the inclinations of the parents rather than the child. Presumably few children begged to be sent *chez les Jésuites* or *chez les bonnes sœurs* for the good of their souls and the supplementary graces of decorous manipulation of a knife and fork – even if emulation of an admired or envied neighbour's child might lead to such a request. And the fact remains that many parents who sent their children to such schools were not themselves practising Catholics – and did so for social reasons. At the same time a fair number of youths who were despatched there reacted violently against what they found and emerged hating everything the school supposedly stood for. It was –

and still remains – a staple theme in literature. Indeed the imprudence of equating a Catholic schooling with Catholic commitment is eloquently revealed by a perusal of the old-boys' lists and year books of any of these schools, where the names of future famous *mangeurs de curés* may be found in surprising company – and sometimes credited with surprising prizes. If Ste Geneviève boasted many generals and distinguished churchmen, it was also less inclined to celebrate Joseph Caillaux, partner (if circumspect partner) in Waldeck-Rousseau's anticlerical programme. Apart from these intrinsic pitfalls, reliance on the records of Catholic schools leaves out of account the many committed Catholic families who sent their children to the state *lycées* and colleges, especially if they were fortunate enough to win a *bourse* – which of its nature could be held only in the public sector. Nor should it be forgotten that even after the Separation of Church and State, the state secondary schools with boarding facilities continued to have chaplains, many of whom had a small but devoted following, whatever the ethos of the masters' common room.

Apart from the uncertain significance of a Catholic schooling, it is often difficult to identify the schools where civil servants originated. In a country with a unified national examination system, success in the *baccalauréat* counted more in a public servant's record than the particular school that had nurtured that success – with the result that many official dossiers contained no mention of the *fonctionnaire*'s secondary schooling. His higher education by contrast was of particular interest – especially if he was a product of the *grandes écoles*. And in a large number of ministries there was always the safety-filter of the ministry *concours* – which enabled them to test the particular qualities of mind and personality that they were seeking.

If ministry records display a seeming indifference to their employees' secondary schooling, the records of the secondary schools themselves present a patchy picture of their pupils' subsequent careers. The leading French Jesuit schools left the matter of links with old boys to the *associations amicales des anciens élèves*, which usually published sporadic information booklets on the recent doings of the school and its former pupils.[2] Inevitably the coverage was entirely dependent on the interest and zeal of individual boys, many of whom were only too glad to turn their backs on what had been a captivity, or whose subsequent careers and family life were more absorbing than curiosity as to what had become of their fellow captives. Such news was more appealing to those whose loyalty to friends or later drab futures lent a nostalgic aura of happiness to the past. Even in a hugely career-conscious school like Ste Geneviève, less than half of the old boys had kept the association up to date on their current addresses and occupations. Smaller schools, with fewer resources or ambitions, might leave the matter of contact with former pupils to some elderly, semi-retired teacher or ecclesiastic, whose age would guarantee some personal memory of the more mature alumni, but whose failing health often precluded the keeping of records in a systematic, business-like fashion. The shoals of glib-tongued, fund-raising sharks, with top-drawer-sounding names and honoraria to match, had not yet invaded the world of private education, transforming links of affection to matters of simple accountancy – but bringing, as compensation for the historian, ruthlessly efficient, computer-based address lists and career profiles, indicative of donor potential.[3]

A third field of enquiry for the investigator lies in the records of the *grandes écoles*, the golden gate between secondary school and the more prestigious sectors of public service. Yet these are unevenly informative on the past schooling of their entrants. As in the case of the civil service itself, they regarded success in the national examinations – and more especially in their own entrance examinations – as the prime guarantee of suitability. Yet the Polytechnique, for one, was assiduous in its records of secondary schooling, even if there appears to have been less provision in the system for the archetypal English headmaster's letter, testifying that the candidate 'is a useful tail-end bat and has done sterling work as a cold-dinner monitor'. Such matters appear to have cut less ice in France, even if there were those who later claimed that the French were to pay for it all in 1940, when a stronger presence of dedicated cold-dinner monitors might have kept back Guderian's panzers.

Given these limitations to the more obvious sources of information, the researcher is obliged to turn to other material – obituaries, retirement tributes, announcements of weddings and funerals, the wording of which (e.g. 'muni des sacrements de l'Eglise', etc.) might give some indication of at least the family's outward attitude to religion. And such time-consuming searches are applicable only to *fonctionnaires* of sufficient rank or distinction to have been accorded obituaries and tributes of this sort. When attempted, however, they can produce illuminating results – as exemplified by a recent study of a thousand 'elite' figures at the turn of the century.[4] Yet even with this relatively circumscribed sample, the author had difficulty in assessing the religious commitment of his subjects – and his study largely leaves the issue to one side. Even so, his survey showed that only a tenth of the senior civil servants among his subjects had received their secondary education at a private establishment – as against double that proportion among the businessmen. And the proportion among middle-ranking *fonctionnaires* was less than one in twenty.[5] As always, the factors that determined the choice of public or private education were only partly religious. The higher the parents' income, the greater the chance of their sending their children to private schools, where social contacts and character-building were a recognised asset of the system. In the case of boys destined for the business world, these factors counted as much as academic excellence. By contrast moneyed families, who envisaged careers for their sons that involved passing rigorous examinations, preferred the prestigious state *lycées* (especially those of Paris) that would prepare them for the *grandes écoles*, and thence the senior civil service and leading professions. Some parents sought to combine the virtues of both systems by supplementing daytime enrolment at a Paris *lycée* with parallel enrolment at a private boarding school.[6]

Barbarians behind the desk

If routine officialdom was surprisingly indifferent towards the academic provenance of its employees, this was not true of the Left-wing politicians – especially after the rumours of 'barbarians at the gate' in the later 'nineties. In the mid-'nineties, however, the more immediate concern of anticlericals was the presence of civil servants' children at Catholic schools – since this was a direct indictment of the *fonctionnaire* himself, rather than of his own parents who had sent him to a Catholic school, perhaps against his will. As indicated earlier (see pp. 39–42), the personal papers of Emile Combes, then Minister of Education, contain a lengthy digest of the reports that the sixteen Académies provided on this matter in 1895–6.[7]

The report of the Académie de Paris was relatively reassuring: the bulk of senior civil servants sent their daughters to the public sector, as well as their sons. But although judges and magistrates were less prejudiced against the state sector than the military, they tended, like the officers, to follow the lead of their superiors. Yet, like the Army, even the magistrates tended to transfer their boys to the *lycées*, if they had their eyes on the *grandes écoles*. Moving clockwise to the vintage lands of the Académie de Dijon, an area where religious observance was relatively weak, a number of senior magistrates were reported as hostile to the state sector, as were 'nearly all' of the senior officials of the *administration des forêts* – a technical department where politico-religious opinions were not a barrier to entry and promotion. The report listed the names of faithless *receveurs* and *percepteurs* who 'give their sons to clerical establishments'; and, with a cry of despair, it asked 'Just how many defections from the state schools can we expect among the officials of the Ponts et Chausées, when in Dijon even the chief engineer refuses to entrust his children to us!' Like forests, the pick-swinging, theodolite-orientated world of highways and bridges was a technical fraternity where politico-religious issues counted little in the recruitment and promotion of its staff – and where parental choice was less inhibited by fear of what superiors would think.

As Stendhal's Julien Sorel had known to his cost seventy years earlier, the greenswards and fir-clad hills of the Académie de Besançon were a region of comparatively high religious practice among the local population; and the rector's report gave a blacklist of *fonctionnaires* with children in Catholic schools. 'In the Haute-Saône, we cannot count upon the support of leading Republicans; and civil servants of all descriptions limp along behind them, not hesitating to entrust their children to establishments where the present form of government and liberal ideas are scarcely held in respect.' And when a captain of the gendarmerie was gently reproved for moving his son from the public to the private sector, he protested that the boy was 'picking up bad habits' in the state school, while another erring chief engineer of the Ponts et Chaussées, with a son *chez les Jésuites*, riposted 'that Monsieur Y—, a republican *conseiller général*, has two sons with the Eudistes, while Senator B— had his son reared by the Marists, which did not prevent the boy becoming a sub-prefect – and no doubt a prefect of the Republic one day.'

The Lyon Académie report covered an area which in part had a high level of religious observance – and this was reflected in the large number of Catholic private schools. In the department of the Rhône itself, over 60 per cent of the secondary-school population was in the private sector, mostly run by the religious orders. Most of the magistrates, senior civil servants and even the university teachers sent their children there – and, what the author found most shocking, five of the teachers in the Lycée Ampère sent their daughters to congregationist schools. Lyon also had a rogue chief engineer – in this instance, of mines – who, despite the fact that he was also *directeur* of the Ecole des mines, sent his boys to the private sector. By contrast, the Académie of Chambéry sent a fairly sanguine report, perhaps surprising for an area where religious observance was relatively high. Children of state employees (including army officers) made up 40 per cent of the enrolment of the Lycée Berthollet, while a quarter to a half of the pupils of the smaller state secondary schools were likewise from such families. On the other hand, the Académie of Clermont report presented a disturbing picture of the situation in Riom (Puy-de-Dôme), a borderland between high and average religious observance. Although several of the magistrates and the sub-prefect supported the state secondary school, 'nearly all the civil servants send their children to St Mary's'. Not surprisingly matters were scarcely more encouraging in the Haute-Loire with its high level of religious practice. The magistracy was divided in its allegiance between public and private schools; and although the heads of the various branches of the civil administration sent their children to the state sector, they were only partially followed by their subordinates, some of whom split their families between the two systems. In Moulins in the Allier, however, where religious observance was lower, most civil servants used the public sector.

The Académie of Aix-en-Provence was an area of relatively low religious commitment. Yet

Long is the list of *fonctionnaires* who in the Basses-Alpes, the Bouches-du-Rhône and the Var, put their children, both boys and girls, in religious establishments; and one does not need to emphasise the deplorable example that is given in small towns by this disregard of what is the strictest of duties. The school-roll of the Lycée de jeunes filles de Marseille contains not one daughter of a magistrate.

And the report notes with some bitterness that while public employees were happy enough to entrust to the state schools those of their children who obtained a *bourse*, they all too often turned to the Catholic schools when it was a matter of having to pay.

With the Académie of Bordeaux, this clockwise survey moves westwards into the stronghold of French Radicalism, where religious practice was low and anticlerical attitudes widespread. Loyalty to the state boys' secondary schools was relatively high, even if in the Dordogne 'each year retired army officers and retired magistrates come to live in Sarlat, so as to entrust their children to the Jesuits', rather like the moult migration of little-studied wildfowl. The main concern of the Académie was the reluctance of state employees to make use of the public girls' secondary schools. The same was true of the Lycée de jeunes filles d'Agen in the Lot-et-Garonne, where

we receive no one from the various departments of the Finance administration. And is it no wonder? Politicians of the Republican party, those who on the Conseil Général vote for grants for boarders at the lycée, are the first to send their own daughters to the convents. It is only natural that civil servants follow their example in the direction where their wives and fashion are already pushing them.

And when the former *procureur général* became the first magistrate to send his daughter to the state *lycée*, 'his example was scarcely contagious' – just two more magistrates followed suit, one of whom was a Protestant.

The area covered by the Académie of Poitiers was likewise a region of low religious observance – with the notable exception of the Vendée and the north-western part of the Deux-Sèvres. The situation appeared to be fairly satisfactory, apart from a judge and eight *fonctionnaires*, mainly finance officials, with children at Catholic schools. In sharp contrast, the Académie of Rennes was embedded in the heartland of traditional Catholicism. Yet the *lycées* of Nantes (Loire-Inférieure) and Laval (Mayenne) enjoyed the patronage of 'nearly all the civil servants' – unlike the state college in Saumur (Maine-et-Loire) which was regarded with hostility by the bulk of *fonctionnaires*, and where even the public primary-school teachers, who were supposed to feed it with recruits, forbore to speak well of it. Malicious gossip was likewise a problem in the neighbouring Académie of Caen, which was not a region noted for its religious enthusiasm – with the exception of parts of the Manche, the Orne and the Seine-Inférieure. In the Calvados, the calumnies came from the staff of the state secondary schools themselves, and helped to aggravate a situation where many magistrates and most of the law-court officials patronised the private sector, as did a number of finance officials. It was a common practice among government officials to make use of the junior classes of the public primary schools, but then transfer their children to Catholic schools when the approach of puberty and cross-class friendships became a matter for parental concern.

This then was the situation that Combes uncovered in the mid-'nineties. But already in 1893, the Masonic lodges of eastern France had called upon the government 'to halt the promotion of *fonctionnaires* guilty of hostility to the Republic – either through sending their children to be educated by the religious orders or by publicly criticising Republican laws'.[8] In the following year, the Grand Orient appointed a member of its secretariat to keep records of the political reliability of civil servants, as well as assessments of the utility of fellow Masons as sources of information.[9] Combes's enquiry may itself have served to augment disquiet among the fairly restricted milieux who were aware that it was being carried out – while the following years of government docility towards the Church, practised by the Méline ministry, increased claims that clerical schools were establishing bridgeheads in the civil service. Talk of this kind multiplied after Henry's suicide in 1898. November found members of parliament denouncing 'the invasion of the Ecoles nationales by pupils of the religious orders'; and the Conseil Général of the Seine department urged the *grandes écoles* to refuse anyone who had not spent at least four years in a state school.[10]

The result was a bill from the Socialists (24 November 1898) proposing that the state educational system be given a monopoly of entry into the civil and armed services, as well as into the *grandes écoles*. This, and a couple of analogous bills, were sent to the Education Committee of the Chamber – a body of thirty-three members, tantalisingly split between sixteen members who were broadly in favour of some such measure, and sixteen who were against, plus a potential floating vote.[11] If such a measure were to survive the misgivings of middle-class constituents who, for social reasons, had sent their boys into the private sector, a more tactful variant would be required. It was also highly questionable whether the nation's defence capabilities could withstand such a dramatic restriction of the catchment area of their officer corps.

In the meantime the events of 1899 had brought to power the Waldeck-Rousseau ministry, pledged to suppress subversion; and the cry of 'traitors in the camp' could not be lightly ignored by a government of Republican defence. Waldeck-Rousseau sought to appease it by instructing his Minister of Education, Georges Leygues, to put forward a bill on the government's behalf. Dated 14 November 1899, it was personally defended by Waldeck-Rousseau himself in a meeting with the Education Committee in the following month.[12] It restricted the impact of the bill to those echelons of the public services that required applicants to have at least a secondary schooling; and it limited the stipulation that they be state-educated to the final three years of their secondary schooling. To give intending applicants in private schools sufficient time to transfer to a state school for the necessary three years, the bill would not become operative until 1903. Similar provisions were made for prospective entrants into the *grandes écoles*. The bill further stipulated that private boarding schools that wanted to send pupils to state schools during the day – so as to fulfil the *stage scolaire* – must themselves be in conformity with the law; and this potentially excluded the many religious orders and establishments that were not officially authorised.

The preamble to the bill tersely summed up Republican thinking on what was expected of a state employee: 'There should be between the State and its collaborators a concordance of sentiments and views on the fundamental principles of society and on the political institutions that govern the relations between society and the State.' The government 'has an incontestable right to assure itself of a loyal and devoted co-operation on their part'. Speaking to the bill, Waldeck-Rousseau denied that the individual had 'some sort of personal right to be a civil servant; such a right is not to be found in the rights of the citizen. The state has the right to bestow or withhold public service.'

The leader of the Catholic opposition to the bill was the Lyon banker, Edouard Aynard, father of a dozen children and official *rapporteur* of the committee.[13] His response to this argument was to recite Article 6 of the Declaration of Rights: 'All citizens . . . are equally eligible for all honours, places and public employment, according to their abilities, and without any distinction other than their virtues and talents.' And he made a persuasive distinction between what he saw as two broad types of public servant: 'some are politically neutral by the very nature of their duties – or they may be merely executants of the public departments they work for; others may be first and foremost direct agents, and of necessity political agents, of the government'. In the first category he put the armed services – 'The officer must above all be silent' – and Aynard castigated the Restoration monarchy for having ostracised the senior officers of Napoleon. He similarly put the judiciary and the state education system in this category, claiming that impartiality was the essence of their role; and he added to them 'the many civil servants who merely run the non-political functions of the State: finance, registries, customs, forests, etc.'. In contrast to them, there was the second category, 'ministers and their immediate collaborators within the ministries, the administrative judges, sub-prefects, prefects and mayors, colonial officials up to governors-general, Councillors of State, ambassadors'. These, by their nature, should be attuned to the overall policy of the government – yet ironically it was candidates for these sections of the public service who would be less immediately affected by the *stage scolaire*, since their route to office did not specifically lie via the *grandes écoles*, unlike the more technical ministries. Even if their accession to public employment was ultimately barred at the actual point of entry into state service, they still had the benefit of whatever higher education they had received, whereas the aspirant to the more technical, politically neutral ministries would be denied access to the *grandes écoles* – which was the royal road not only to these ministries but to many private careers as well. Moreover the *stage scolaire*, restricted as it was to secondary schooling, would leave unaffected the primary-school teachers and *juges de paix* – who were commonly regarded as ambassadors of the militant Republic, but who did not require secondary education as part of their formal qualifications. In any case, Aynard added, the bill was punishing children for the decisions of their parents; and the government was in danger of creating 'a secular original sin'.

Aynard's report to the Chamber concluded with the observation,

Ministers come and go: civil servants remain. The ministers of a term or a year may have opposing views on the fundamental principles of society, and even on political institutions . . . The civil servant neither hates nor betrays: he merely changes with what the country wants, because he himself cannot change his profession . . . That is why it is said that France was formerly an absolute monarchy tempered by songs, while now it is a bureaucracy tempered by revolutions. It is the instability of regimes and governments which is responsible for the endless growth of the latent strength of the civil servant. The Grand Master of the University under the First Empire, M. de Fontanes, dared to say to Napoleon in 1811: 'Sire, we teach respect for your dynasty because it rules by virtue of the country's constitution, just as we would teach respect for the Republic, if it were the current form of government. As long as you last, that is to your advantage.' The whole of the political psychology of the French civil servant is contained in these words, 'As long as you last, that is to your advantage.'

That the bill was eventually rejected by the education committee (by fourteen to nine, with one abstention) was largely a result of the absence of seven supporters of the bill on the day of the vote – while only two of its opponents were away.[14] It is hard to know whether a favourable vote would have led to an ultimate adoption by parliament. As it was, Aynard's report skilfully exploited the misgivings of politicians of both the Left and the Centre; and, contrary to the expectations of many members, it proved to be the last word on the matter.

Catholics and the *grandes écoles*

Had the *stage-scolaire* bill become law, the two schools hardest hit would have been the Jesuit Ecole Ste Geneviève and the Marianist Collège Stanislas. The bill would have abolished their large entry into St Cyr and the Polytechnique (see pp. 37–9), and this would not only have reduced the Catholic presence in the Army, but it would also have curtailed their numbers in civilian occupations as well, since an increasing proportion of *polytechniciens* opted for non-military careers. In the case of the Ste Geneviève *polytechniciens*, the proportion entering the civilian sector rose from 32 per cent in 1875 to 87 per cent by 1906.[15] The Ecole Centrale des Arts et Manufactures was another *grande école* that would have been closed to Catholic-school products; it had taken no fewer than 392 candidates from Ste Geneviève alone in the 1881–1901 period, and even in the hard, anticlerical years of 1902–13, 8 per cent of its places were to go to *postards*.[16] The overwhelming majority of these went into the private sector of the economy – mines, railways and industry – and were thus no threat to the Republican purity of the public service. The same was true of the Institut National Agronomique, which took thirty-eight *postards* in the pre-war period, after special preparatory classes for it were inaugurated by Ste Geneviève in 1907 – while Stanislas was providing it with an annual contingent that rose from two or three in the 'nineties to half a dozen in the pre-war years.[17]

Anticlericals could take some reassurance from the fact that only one or two Stanislas boys found their way each year into the Ecole Normale Supérieure de Paris, while very few *postards* gained entry into this Athenaeum of Republican distinction until the inter-war years. Even so the Rue d'Ulm had its small but formidable 'Tala' elements ('vont à la messe'), including a number of subsequent famous names – while its librarian, Lucien Herr, the celebrated mentor of Left-wing intellectuals, was to have as his assistant an active Catholic Sillonist, Dominique Anziani. Indeed, by the 1930s, the list of former *normaliens* was to include a dozen Catholic priests and several teachers in Catholic private schools.[18]

If anticlericals were frustrated in their attempt to put the *grandes écoles* out of bounds to the progeny of private schools, equally frustrating was the fact that another ladder for future senior civil servants, the Ecole Libre des Sciences Politiques, was still in private hands and even less easy to protect against Catholic infiltration. Until the foundation of the Ecole Nationale d'Administration in 1945, there existed no state institution in France specifically dedicated to the training of fledgling high-flyers; and in the meantime, the Ecole Libre, first opened in 1872, increasingly attempted to fill this gap.[19] The faculties of law had made desultory attempts to provide a grounding for candidates for the more prestigious branches of the civil service, but their prime concerns lay elsewhere and it was left to the Ecole Libre to secure the participation of senior civil servants in the instruction of future entrants into their ranks. The result was that many aspiring candidates for the civil service simultaneously followed courses at the Ecole Libre and at a law faculty – an arrangement which the faculties tacitly recognised as mutually convenient. It was particularly the Cour des Comptes, the Inspection des Finances, the Conseil d'Etat and the Quai d'Orsay that looked to the Ecole Libre for suitable recruits. Two-thirds of their intake came from the school in the 1880–1900 period, and the proportion was to rise to 90 per cent in the next thirty years. An early architect of the secular Republic, Jules Ferry, had made a brief abortive attempt to nationalise the school in 1881; but the grooming of future mandarins of the regime continued relatively unmolested in private hands for the rest of the Third Republic.[20] The students of the Ecole Libre des Sciences Politiques were for the most part well heeled, since paying fees to both the school and a law faculty was an expensive business – to say nothing of renting a room in Paris, if the student came from the provinces. The comfortable, conservative milieu from which many of its students consequently came was one where the Church was regarded with more indulgence than in militantly Republican circles; and it was not surprising that the school acquired a fair number of practising Catholics. The Collège Stanislas was particularly well represented, supplying some 15 per cent of the school's total intake in 1895.[21] On the other hand Ste Geneviève's admittedly incomplete records reveal only one entrant in the pre-war years – law being one of the weaker sectors of *postard* ambition.[22]

La règle du jeu

A government's scope for political or religious preference in its public services largely depended on whether there were truly competitive entrance examinations, limiting its freedom of choice. The French bureaucracy was broadly divided into two categories, the *rédacteurs* who were administrative officers, implementing the instructions of their superiors and composing the directives and letters that embodied them, and the *commis expéditionnaires* who were clerks with little or no opportunity for exercising discretionary responsibility. Many ministries had started in the 1880s to use competitive examinations in appointing both *rédacteurs* and *expéditionnaires* in their central offices.[23] Yet it was a notorious fact that selection committees often sought to retain scope for political or personal preference by giving favoured candidates easy questions in the oral examinations. And indeed a more common complaint was the undemanding nature of many of the examinations, which by favouring everyone left the selectors free to fill posts as they pleased. In fact the low standards and old-fashioned format of these examinations was partly the product of an attempt to offer tried-and-true *expéditionnaires* the chance of becoming *rédacteurs*.[24]

The growing practice of promoting *expéditionnaires* to more senior posts after a token examination had an ambivalent effect on the composition of the civil service. Having initially entered it on the lowest rung, they would have escaped the more serious vetting process that *rédacteurs* underwent – especially if their appointments dated back to the less politically fraught periods of the nineteenth century. And since their superiors within the ministries were interested in their administrative competence rather than their politics, they might well escape political screening altogether. On the other hand it reduced the number of available places for outside candidates competing in the *concours* – which in turn could make entry more difficult for able candidates whose political reports contained some mild adverse comment which could be gratefully seized upon by the selectors to resolve an *embarras de choix*.

After the turn of the century, the *concours* were put increasingly under the control of the Conseil d'Etat, which went some way to creating comparability of standards and reducing favouritism.[25] Yet attempts to create a common *concours* for the central offices of the various ministries got nowhere – despite a straw vote in its favour in the Chamber of Deputies (26 November 1908).[26] As for the elite sections of the public service – the Cour des Comptes, the Inspection des Finances, the Conseil d'Etat, etc. – their autonomy of selection procedures was doubly protected. The undoubted quality of their applicants and the rigour of their *concours* protected them against accusations of arranging the hurdles to suit political or personal friends – while the private status of the Ecole Libre des Sciences Politiques (see p. 82), which trained many of these applicants, complicated the task of any government contemplating a common selection procedure.[27] In many of the ministries, by contrast, the *rédacteurs* in their central offices were likely to be simple law graduates, without the careful grooming of the Ecole Libre.[28] In these ministries, the individual and less demanding nature of their *concours* gave potential scope for favouritism – often to the government's political advantage. Yet the particular hurdles of the elite bodies tended to create bias of a different kind. As already noted (p. 82), the educational springboard to these *grands corps* was expensive and therefore favoured candidates with means, whose families were often conservatively inclined and more disposed than those from a lower social drawer to view the Church with favour, or at least an easy-going tolerance. In consequence a respect for Catholicism was more in evidence in their ranks than the militant devotees of a secular republic would ideally have liked. This was a latent factor that acted as a counterweight to attempts of Left-wing governments to create an administration that was sympathetic to their anticlerical policies.

Entry into the civil service was one problem, promotion another. A *leitmotif* of contemporary advice to ambitious young bureaucrats was to aim for posts that were not necessarily lucrative or bearing much responsibility, but which brought the tyro in touch with the minister or central office *directeur*, since catching the esteem of the influential could be worth years of devoted service in terms of leapfrogging the system.[29] On the other hand it meant living under constant pressure, meeting sudden deadlines and working late at night when the minister had to be accurately briefed on some unexpected issue thrown up by an opposition ambush in parliament. Such positions were obviously more likely to come the way of men whose political persuasions sat comfortably with those of their masters.

At the turn of the century promotion by genuine merit was threatened both from above and from below. On the one hand, superiors exercised a wide potential for favouritism in their recommendations, while *fonctionnaires* themselves were strongly urging automatic promotion by seniority. Every six months there was a general review of personnel, and a *table d'avancement* was drawn up. But the value of this was often vitiated in many offices by the blanket inclusion of everyone with a conceivable claim – or conversely by arbitrary intervention from above in favour of individuals whom the minister or some senior official wished to advance. In effect both practices came to the same thing, since a cross-the-board recommendation of everyone could only be resolved by the minister or his various deputies choosing whom they wanted from the plethora of supposedly deserving cases. At the same time, the *table d'avancement* was confidential to the recommending council and to the minister and his entourage – while the assessments of each candidate gave no indication of who had actually composed them.[30] The scope for ministerial favouritism was further widened by the increasing blandness of these assessments.[31] With no effective indication from below of the true worth of those eligible, a minister's preferences were no worse than using a pin – or so apologists would argue. Favouritism apart, however, the general drift was towards Buggins's turn; and this tended to keep bureaucrats on the narrow ladder of their particular office, rather than encouraging lateral and diagonal movement between departments.

For this and for other reasons, promotion by seniority was increasingly shaping a higher bureaucracy that was conservative and insular in professional outlook – and by extension was often disposed to be conservative in political outlook as well. This was particularly true of many of those who had embarked on their civil service careers during the Ordre Moral of the 1870s and who would not be reaching retirement age until the immediate pre-war period.[32] This was a factor that tended to offset the disposition of militant ministries of the Combes era to favour *fonctionnaires* whose political views corresponded to their own.

Oiling the *piston*

Patronage within the administration was strongly buttressed – and counterbuttressed – by pressures from outside, notably from deputies and senators. Letters of recommendation are a valuable source for the historian, not only in what they reveal about the writers, but in what they have to say about their protégés – even if the claims on their behalf require cautious reading. They put flesh on the stereotyped formulas of the official dossiers – albeit over-florid flesh – and when, as sometimes happens, they are filed separately from the protégé's personal dossier, they may be the only source that the researcher can legally lay hands on.

As in many countries, the *piston* had a particular place in public appointments and promotion. There was in France an unwritten assumption that the more testimonials a job-seeker had from MPs in the government alliance, the more likely he was to get the post he sought. Politicians' recommendations operated on a variety of levels. At the lowest level they might simply be an attempt to win votes in the con-stituency by supporting applications from constituents whom the deputy scarcely knew; and in these cases it might be enough for the deputy to send a letter of support to the minister and then be able to tell the constituent that he had done so. In these cases, it did not greatly matter whether the constituent actually got the appointment; the fact that the deputy was seen to support him was enough. Indeed cynics might conclude that it could sometimes be more convenient for the deputy if the constituent did not get the post, since he would stay in the constituency and continue voting and perhaps canvassing for the deputy as long as he needed his letters of recommendation; whereas if success took him to a promoted post elsewhere, the deputy lost his support. In reality, however, pride probably prevailed, since most deputies and senators would prefer the prestige of being regarded as a politician who could produce the goods – especially since news of this sort travelled fast in the provinces. Letters of recommendation in such cases were usually fairly basic, restricted to a few lukewarm phrases: 'I should be happy if the request that Mademoiselle Delarue has asked me to transmit to you were viewed with favour.'[33] And the Minister of Education would write back a sufficient answer for the deputy: there was either no suitable post available, or the field of applicants was particularly strong and Mademoiselle Delarue would be borne in mind for future vacancies. That was as much as the deputy would need to demonstrate to his constituent that he had tried hard on her behalf.

Some letters of recommendation were very basic indeed: 'Monsieur Camille, after forty years of service, requests to be transferred to [wherever it was]' – without the slightest word of explanation or support.[34] Many of the deputies and senators had straightforward printed pro-forma letters of recommendation, with blanks for the name and desired appointment, concluding: 'Je porte un vif intérêt à [Monsieur Labragère]' – but not 'vif' enough for the deputy to write a letter in his own fair hand.[35]

Above these routine vote-catching exercises came the next level of letter, where the deputy was genuinely seeking a post on behalf of his client. These the minister would treat with more respect, because the minister too might well need the support of the deputy – if not immediately, then on some future occasion. And there was much straightforward horse-trading here. Some deputies let it be known in oblique but familiar terms that their support on a forthcoming crucial issue in parliament might depend on a favourable outcome to the request. Such letters often ended 'J'exige satisfaction pour [Monsieur Dupois].' And many of these letters were either disarmingly or cynically open in the arguments put forward in favour of the candidate: 'je porte beaucoup d'intérêt à sa famille', or 'Monsieur Ovide Dupont est mon ami et mon compatriote.'[36] Indeed one candidate's dossier had successive recommendations of this type. In 1893, his deputy wrote 'Monsieur Lambert is the son-in-law of one of my cousins whom I dearly love' – without a word about his qualities – while six years later, another of his patrons was writing 'Monsieur Lambert is one of my friends. I attach a real importance to this request.'[37] Other letters attempted to be more subtle – although the ploys adopted must have been tediously familiar to ministers. In the case of clients wanting a transfer to the Paris region from some distant rural exile, it was common to put 'sa femme supporte mal le climat de [Valognes]'. And indeed, in this particular case, one of his patrons also claimed that his client's daughter needed to be near Paris, so as to be able to get proper medical attention.[38] All of which may have been true – but all too familiar to the recipient.

5 Patterns of preferment: sectors with teeth

It was recognised by politicians of most persuasions that a major distinction had to be made between those ministries that were the instruments of the overall thrust of a government's policies – such as the Ministry of the Interior – and the more technical ministries, such as Agriculture and Public Works, whose expertise was directed to specific material problems, requiring professional rather than political judgement. It was accepted with varying degrees of conviction that the government needed to assure itself of loyal and understanding executants of its policies in the first category of ministry; and many politicians believed that a major change of government justified a corresponding change in senior personnel in such ministries. Few, on the other hand, thought this necessary in the technical ministries. Violent disagreement arose, however, as to which ministries should be in which category, and on how far down the administrative ladder changes of faces were justified. There was notoriously bitter controversy as to whether the Ministry of Justice belonged to the first group or the second; and endless dispute as to whether the personal, political and religious beliefs of public servants could legitimately disqualify them for various sectors of the administration.

These arguments reflected the fact that the concept of civil-service neutrality was much slower to develop in France than in Britain; and although French politicians never admitted to having an American-style spoils system, they harboured a certain tacit envy of it. Unlike Britain, France in the nineteenth century had undergone a succession of regimes, with violence accompanying many of the changes. In these circumstances it was inevitable that an incoming government should feel apprehensive about the reliability and fidelity of the instruments at its disposal. There were also the indirect repercussions of the French tradition of ministers having their own *cabinet personnel*, a cluster of trusted friends and followers who came and went with them. While this existed in varying degrees in other countries, it was a more established feature of French political life; and the ethos it encouraged may have indirectly coloured attitudes to the relationship between politicians and those civil servants entrusted with general government policy.

For the historian of these issues, a useful barometer is provided by the prefects' reports on candidates for the more politically-sensitive ministries. This took the form of a printed questionnaire, filled in by the prefecture of the department where the candidate last resided. The questions varied from ministry to ministry and from decade to decade. For a prospective sub-prefect in the 1890s they would include 'opinions politiques apparentes', immediately followed by 'sentiments politiques réels'; 'Préférences ou antipathie pour une classe de la société'; and 'Religion à laquelle il appartient'. His wife, if any, was of equal concern: 'Caractère, esprit et valeur de sa femme', 'Relations comme femme du monde', and 'Religion à laquelle elle appartient'.[1] In the time of Napoleon, questionnaires on prospective prefects included 'Taste for hunting, women, etc.' – the equivalent perhaps of the deceptively casual enquiry at British interviews, 'Play any games?' But later generations, after the purging fires of the Restoration and the Ordre Moral, had settled for 'Relations sociales'. Candidates for the more technical ministries would be subject to less scrutiny in these matters. But even in the case of ministries where such information was wanted, prefectures were often hard put to it to obtain much that was concrete – especially in the case of young men whose personal opinions were scarcely known to the maturer adults around them. To questions on religion, the prefecture might simply write 'catholique' – which merely signified that he was registered as a baptised Catholic, as the bulk of French people were. But in the case of candidates for the Ministry of the Interior and other key sectors, these questions were often answered in considerable detail.

The pertinence of such questions to suitability for the Ministries of the Interior and Justice was clearly demonstrated during the anticlerical phases of government policy – notably in the 1880s and in the Combes era. Prefectures and magistrates found themselves having to implement policies that most committed Catholics regarded as uncongenial or straightforwardly unacceptable – expelling nuns, friars and monks, and closing down their schools. These were contentious measures, engendering political protest, where the government wished to be able to count absolutely on the loyalty of its executants. It was always open to an official to resign, if he did not feel in conscience able to implement a policy; but the governments of the Third Republic were not prepared to run the risk of the upheaval, inconvenience and damaging publicity which resignations involved – and so were reluctant to appoint such people in the first place. And this is what many Catholics objected to: the prior assumption by the government that, irrespective of their political commitment to the Republic, they could not be relied upon.

Even in the technical branches of the public services, where politics counted for less, all local officials were to some degree under the watchful eye of the prefect of the department and his sub-prefects. And this was a tradition that went back to Napoleon. Even under a relatively benign ministry like that of Charles Dupuy in 1894, when relations with the Church were good, Dupuy was writing to the prefects on 5 October, asking them for information on all officials, including those of the Ministries of Agriculture and Public Works, and asking whether they could be relied on individually to give wholehearted support to the government's policies.[2] Seven years later, the new-broom premier, Waldeck-Rousseau, was predictably much more insistent. On 11 January 1901 he urged prefects to hurry with the submission of their reports on the reliability of civil servants, in view of the imminence of promotion procedures.[3] Three months afterwards he was asking prefects to keep a particular eye on the political attitudes of the *percepteurs des contributions directes*, and commented ominously that the prefects' reports could have a very real influence on these tax officials' future.[4] Moreover Waldeck-Rousseau's own personal notes in the Institut Français – which are a series of pencil jottings on scraps of paper – stressed the importance of having politically sympathetic tax officers – and added equally ominously 'secondary-school teachers are also civil servants'.[5] On one level this was a straightforward statement of fact, but in the context of his current preoccupations likewise had an element of menace behind it. Even so, his jottings also contained the following cryptic cuff-reminders: 'guarantee the liberty of conscience'; 'respect for institutions'; 'neither dupes nor sectarians' – which for him were probably a vigorous dialectic of intent, but for the historian may appear as a sad reflection on the difficulty of achieving a balance between these ends.[6]

Matters became much tighter under Combes in 1902. Within a fortnight of coming to office he told prefects that they must instil a clear sense of political purpose in *all* civil servants of *all* departments; and in a phrase that might have served as a motto for the regime, reminded them that 'while you owe justice to everyone . . . you keep your favours for those who have unmistakably proved their fidelity to Republican institutions' (20 June 1902).[7] Six months later, he wrote to them complaining of their lack of vigilance, and drawing their attention to the many cases of civil servants with their children at private schools, which he castigated as setting a highly regrettable example for the general public.[8]

When in 1904 Combes came under strong criticism over the *Affaire des fiches* (see pp. 50–1), he became much more circumspect in his handling of civil service matters. Writing to the prefects on 18 November 1904, he announced that in future they should send their reports on the political attitudes of civil servants to the minister of the appropriate department, rather than to him, and that they should base their information on the reports of responsible people such as MPs and accredited officials.[9] In other words, they must not resort to the Masonic grape-vine or any other network of enthusiastic amateurs. Convenient habits die hard, however, and the lack of contrition shown by the Grand Orient and its sympathisers in parliament (see pp. 51–2) suggests that matters would not necessarily change overnight.

A ministry-by-ministry survey of recruitment and promotion policies during this chequered period would not only require a huge team of researchers but also the formal granting of archival dispensations on an unprecedented scale. The following archival samples are tiny and random, their pattern dependent on luck and the kindness of their keepers. One of the aims of the exercise was to try to measure the difference between the recruiting policies of the *esprit-nouveau* governments and those of Waldeck-Rousseau and Combes. But although the prefects' reports on candidates frequently provide a valuable guide to candidates' politico-religious opinions, they do not of themselves provide a trustworthy graph of changing government policies. Governments usually fell more rapidly than officials changed posts, and it was only when there was a major sea-change in the complexion of government, sustained in a succession of ministries, that the reader becomes conscious of officials adopting a different tack or terminology in describing candidates. It must also be remembered that most reports were based on information provided by lower echelons of the administration. These junior informants were generally less vulnerable to the political shifts that affected prefects and *procureurs généraux* – and indeed were usually far less aware that change had taken place – with the result that they tempered their tune less often than their superiors. Although the prefecture, with its ear closer to the ground, might word matters differently – since it was well aware that reports told governments as much about the signatory as about the candidate – most prefects' reports largely reproduced what had been handed to them from below. The researcher therefore needs to supplement the perusal of *fonctionnaires'* dossiers with other indicators of recruitment policies – ministerial and Masonic correspondence, old-boys' almanachs and the other sources outlined in previous pages. Indeed the most interesting archival files are those on rejected candidates – which to the historian's eternal loss are very few. Faced with pressure on cupboard space, most ministries destroyed unsuccessful applications, once sufficient time had elapsed to make a renewed application from a particular individual unlikely. Indeed the influx of women bureaucrats into ministerial offices in the inter-war years, with their brisk concepts of tidiness, saw a rapid erosion of the cautious, hoarding instinct of the middle-aged man that had characterised the dusty dens of the pre-war *ronds-de-cuir*.

The Conseil d'Etat

Revered by foreigners as a hallowed body of wise, impartial experts – awesome in the manner of Zarastro's council of priests – the Conseil d'Etat might seem too exalted a brotherhood to fall prey to the political preferences of transient politicians. The reality of the Conseil was somewhat less forbidding – perhaps more like Sachs's mastersingers, ranging from frisky young *auditeurs*, delegated to a range of one-off tasks to keep them from under their seniors' feet, including those of the furrow-browed *maîtres de requêtes* with families and mortgages to think of, to the *conseillers* themselves, a group of comfortable distinction, combining varying degrees of *gravitas* with a wide spectrum of experience and perceptions. The ambience of the place likewise varied from room to room and day to day – alternating the leather-bound somnolence of an exclusive club with the sudden excitements of the Bourse. Its mixture of functions – vetting legislation for consistency, checking draft decrees and administrative regulations, as well as acting as a higher court of judgement and appeal in matters of administrative law – this wide-ranging role endowed it with a potential for political influence that governments felt unable to ignore. And in a Republic fearing subversion from both Right and Left, governments wanted the nation's legal experts to be loyal as well as wise and learned – and not inclined to inconvenient or obstructive attitudes and judgements.

The change from the Ordre Moral to the 'République des Républicains' in the late 'seventies had seen a purge of the Conseil d'Etat, followed by indignant resignations, which cumulatively resulted in the replacement of all but four pre-purge *conseillers*. This transformation of the senior membership of the Conseil d'Etat had the effect of discouraging young men of Right-wing or well-known Catholic backgrounds from choosing it as a career – a consequence that was reinforced by the involvement of the Conseil d'Etat in the legal disputes arising from the anticlerical legislation of the 1880s. Paradoxically, however, the *conseillers d'état* in the late 'nineties included a somewhat larger number of Catholics than they had in the 'eighties. The young *auditeurs* and *maîtres de requêtes* of the 'seventies had largely survived the purge of 1877–80 that had seen the departure of so many of their senior colleagues; and they were now of an age and experience to be *conseillers* themselves. René Marguerie, a Stanislas old boy, and Henri Hebrard de Villeneuve, who had merely been *auditeurs* before the purge, had since become respected spokesmen of Catholic interests.[10]

Auditeurships of the Conseil d'Etat were often a springboard for other careers – the *corps préfectoral* or the magistracy – and they were also strong cards for future membership of a minister's personal *cabinet*. Ten old boys of the Collège Stanislas became *auditeurs* of the Conseil d'Etat in the 1880–1900 period; and the archives of the Conseil d'Etat indicate that a number of committed Catholics tried their luck and succeeded in entering its smooth-swinging, urbanely guarded portals, notably during the period of the Esprit Nouveau in the 'nineties.[11] André Dejean, an *avocat stagiaire* and Stanislas old boy, was first in the *concours* of December 1894. A report signed by the Préfet de la Seine, Eugène Poubelle, immortal founder of the Paris dustbin, described him as 'Catholic. Accompanies his mother to church each Sunday, but appears to be motivated both politically and religiously by very broad feelings of toleration and moderation . . . A Republican, like his father, who was always opposed to the [Second] Empire.'[12] It was a frequent feature of benevolent reports for the state services to mitigate the significance of Mass-going by the phrase 'accompanies his mother' – or more often 'his wife' – suggesting that his devotion was a matter of pair-bonding rather than personal conviction.

A less clear case is that of Marie-Joseph de Peyerimhoff, fourth in the *concours* of December 1894. Poubelle's report described him as 'Catholic. Studied in a religious institution.' Belonging to an Alsatian family, his grandfather distinguished himself as a defender of French interests in the Reichstag – a point heavily underlined by the recipient of the report.[13] There is no ambiguity, however, about the case of Louis Hannotin, an old boy of the Collège Stanislas and the leading candidate in the *concours* of December 1897. The prefecture reported: 'Religion, Catholic. The candidate appears to be following law courses at the Institut Catholique. . . He seems not to concern himself with politics.' A leading laureate of the Ecole Libre des Sciences Politiques, and holder of a state law degree, he elicited an overall verdict of 'très favorable' from the prefecture.[14] However, he later decided to stand in the legislative elections of 1902 and resigned from the Conseil d'Etat, informing the Minister of Justice 'I am standing essentially as a Republican candidate; nevertheless, since my electoral programme is at odds with the general policies followed by the government, I prefer to resign from my duties before the beginning of the electoral campaign.'[15] It should be noted, however, that he was a man of substantial private means who could afford to take risks of this kind. Unsuccessful in the election, he subsequently became an *avocat* at the Conseil d'Etat in 1906 and eventually president of the Order of *avocats* from 1926 to 1929. His legislative ambitions were realised in 1938, when he was elected as a conservative senator for his home department of the Ardennes where he had long been a spokesman of agricultural interests.

If these examples of Catholic appointments belonged to the era of the Esprit Nouveau, the Waldeck-Rousseau years contained one or two interesting if less clear-cut cases. Pierre Caillaux, a Paris *avocat*, came second in the *concours* of December 1901. In less understanding circles than the Conseil d'Etat, he might have been handicapped by his middle name, Xavier – as much a liability among secularists as 'Patrick Joseph' in Ulster – and by his education at the Jesuit college of Le Mans. Moreover a *procureur général*'s report commented on his family's mixing with Le Mans high society 'réputée peu favorable au gouvernement actuel'. He was, however, considered to be 'très libéral – and related to the Minister of Finance, Joseph Caillaux – while the Paris *commissariat de police* reported 'excellents renseignements sous tous les rapports'.[16]

These examples, however, are perhaps not that surprising for a body that retained considerable autonomy over its admissions procedures, and which drew most of its recruits from comfortable sections of society, given the expense of training for the *concours* (see p. 82). The Conseil was scarcely likely to respond like a weather-cock to every ministerial change of wind; and success in the *concours* remained the prime criterion of choice. Even so the counterpart to the question of whether it was difficult or not for a committed Catholic to obtain entry into politically sensitive areas of public service was whether it was easier for Protestants and Jews with similar qualifications. As indicated in the first chapter, it was certainly easier for Protestants and Jews to accommodate themselves with the secular Republicanism of these years than for Catholics; and the claims of Catholics that Protestants and Jews were proportionately over-represented in the government service has some statistical basis to it. The prefects' reports on successful entrants to the Conseil d'Etat reveal that in the years 1894 to 1907, half of them were baptised Catholics – most of whom in all probability had ceased to practise their faith once they reached adolescence – but 15 per cent were Protestants, despite the fact that Protestants constituted less than 2 per cent of the population. Ten per cent of successful candidates were Jews, in stark contrast to Jews' making up less than 0.2 per cent of the nation.[17] It is arguable, however, that family milieu had as much to do with the matter. An independent sample of twenty-two *conseillers* in 1901 showed all but one emanating from the middle and upper bourgeoisie – where Protestants and Jews were proportionately well represented.[18] This social rather than politico-religious interpretation is also supported by the pattern of religious affiliations among the unsuccessful candidates, which largely corresponds to that among the successful, thereby diminishing the plausibility of discrimination on the part of the selectors.[19]

Among the successful Jewish candidates in the 1890s was Léon Blum. Poubelle's report of November 1894 on this future leader of the Popular Front – France's first Socialist prime minister – remarked 'M. Blum ne fait pas de politique active, mais sa famille et lui ont la réputation d'être républicaine' – a fair enough assessment for the time. It also added 'While not endowed with a Herculean constitution, Monsieur Blum appears to be of sound health.' While these particular remarks appear to be in the hand of one of Poubelle's assistants, Poubelle himself cautiously added 'I think that this candidature can be accepted.'[20]

Impartial bearers of the scales of justice

The principle of the separation of powers is so deeply rooted in Western liberal rhetoric that it came as a surprise to British visitors that the political opinions of judges and magistrates were a major factor in their appointment and dismissal in Republican France. Throughout the nineteenth century it was assumed in France that a prime function of the judiciary was to encourage a state of affairs favourable to the current government. From the *juge de paix* to the president of the *cour d'appel* or the *procureur général*, no level of it was immune from government concern as to who held which post. Magistrates and would-be magistrates regarded their local MPs as their principal link with the Minister of Justice, the Garde des Sceaux; and a change of government found them besieging the Palais Bourbon, seeking the intercession of their deputies with the new Minister. One such minister, Jacques Trarieux, a later luminary in the Ligue des Droits de l'Homme, felt forced to comment in 1895 that 'merit and entitlement count less than patronage' in the recruitment and promotion of the judiciary; and the Cruppi report on the budget of the Ministry of Justice in 1901 likewise remarked that promotion was 'a matter of political pressures'.[21] The ardent Republican and Dreyfusard, Joseph Reinach, protested in 1906, 'Is it not humiliating and sad that in a democratic country, in a regime of equality and justice, magistrates should be the most avid, the most keen, at begging favours? Who among us has not received letters from magistrates similar to the one I received this morning, where I read these words: "If one does not continually beg, there is no promotion"?'[22] Indeed posts in the judiciary were often a means of compensating loyal politicians who had been beaten in recent elections – the only requirement being the usual minimum legal qualifications, which many already possessed, since a law degree and some brief legal experience were a common foundation for many aspiring politicians. And, as with the *corps préfectoral*, a spell in a minister's personal *cabinet* was also a strong card for any legally qualified aspirant to the magistracy.[23]

The Garde des Sceaux, like other government ministers, was a politician, and enjoyed virtual freedom in whom he appointed. In the early years of the Third Republic his choice had been confined to names put forward by the courts; but this disappeared in 1879, when the Republicans took over the Republic and endeavoured to wrest the judiciary from the local *notables* who had dominated it during the Second Empire and the Ordre Moral of the 1870s.[24] This was the point at which the politicisation of the Ministry of Justice sharply increased, with one quarter of the judges and magistrates losing their jobs altogether and many of the rest being shunted into less important posts.[25] Nor had this been the end of the matter. Hostility among judges to the government's anticlerical laws of the early 'eighties resulted in a major purge of the judiciary in 1883, in which 614 of its members lost their posts, including several senior judges who objected to what was happening to their junior colleagues.[26] Ironically the legislation of August 1883, which had enabled this drastic cleansing, also reaffirmed the principle of irremovability of judges – but with major exclusions, most notably the *juges de paix* who accounted for half the judiciary and who were politically vulnerable to local political pressures.[27]

Yet judges, like politicians and ecclesiastics, were not subject to the normal rules of retirement; and most of those who survived the political cleansing of the late 'seventies and early 'eighties continued as part of the system for decades to come. A sample of the judiciary (including *juges de paix*) at the turn of the century revealed that nearly two-thirds of them had been appointed before the purges.[28] While many of these had learned to trim with the wind, or had become genuine converts to Republican ideals, their numbers must also have contained a fair number of practising Catholics and quite a few men with little enthusiasm for the current thrust of government policy. Many were probably sustained in their uncomfortable role by a sense of dedication to the principle of social order and a belief that absence of firm government was worse than uncongenial government. Another factor that guaranteed a sizeable proportion of conservative and Catholic magistrates on the bench was the miserably low levels of salaries paid to judges. Despite improvements in 1883, it was difficult for men without personal means to undertake its duties; and until 1910 *juges suppléants* were not paid at all – a particularly grave matter, given the reliance of an undermanned judiciary on their services.[29] All of this gave an advantage to men of comfortable means, and was a factor that perpetuated a solid core which was *bien pensant, bien bourgeois*, to the distress of those Jacobins who would have preferred *la nation en toge*.

Certainly the Collège Stanislas was still very well represented in the Ministry of Justice at the turn of the century. It had twenty-three judges, a *procureur* and a couple of *greffiers*, while four more judges and a *greffier* were to be appointed from its ranks in the anticlerical years that immediately followed. There were additionally three old boys in the central administration of the ministry – and no fewer than eight *auditeurs* in the rarefied elegance of the Cour des Comptes.[30] As for the Jesuit schools, the traditionally high entry of the Immaculée Conception of the Rue de Vaugirard was shown in an overall total of thirty-five future judges and magistrats in the 1852–1908 period – even if some of them did not survive the decimation of the 1880s – plus three *procureurs* and two *sous-procureurs*. And in the same broad span, Ste Geneviève produced ten members of the judiciary.[31]

Catholic or conservative judges whose careers began in the 1870s and spanned several decades of the Third Republic inevitably found that the approbation of one government could be a liability under another. The historian is all too conscious of this when perusing their dossiers. It is not always clear whether the Ministry's underlinings in coloured pencil represent the approbatory response of a government favourable to the candidate's personal leanings, or whether they are a sharp reaction from a later government. These hazards are exemplified by the professional career of Louis de Lamy, self-confessed member of a family of seventeen, who at the age of thirty-one was made a *juge de paix* in September 1877 under the Duc de Broglie's *seize mai* cabinet, following warm praise from the district *procureur général* for his 'devotion to the conservative cause'.[32] Indeed a local mayor assured the Duc de Broglie that 'the appointment of Monsieur de Lamy is indispensable to the success of the conservative candidate in this constituency' – a frank enough expression of what was expected of the impartial bearers of the scales of justice.[33] He survived as a *juge de paix* under the Republican ascendancy but had to await the *esprit nouveau* of the Casimir-Périer ministry to become a salaried judge in April 1894. Although warily described in subsequent reports as 'républicain modéré' or more ominously as 'très modéré' and accorded the faint praise of observing 'une attitude politique correcte', he nevertheless succeeded in getting a letter of support from Chaumié, Minister of Education in Combes's cabinet.[34] By July 1904, however, he had descended a rung of the magisterial ladder, and was to remain there until his retirement thirteen years later. When the question then arose as to whether he be accorded the title of *juge honoraire*, the local prefect recommended rejection as he was 'a worthless magistrate', 'known as a reactionary, whose true beliefs are ill concealed by his obsequiousness'.[35] The district *procureur général*, however, interceded on the grounds that Lamy was 'correct' and harmless; and since the title cost the government nothing, the Ministry gave way.[36]

An interesting example of how even a sincere Republican's prospects could be threatened by his Catholic convictions and the milieux he frequented is provided by the case of the prophetically misnamed Legal La Salle. A supporter of the Republican victory of 1876, he was twice made sub-prefect – and suffered dismissal in the interim, during the Duc de Broglie's *seize mai* counter-attack. Yet when he subsequently sought to embark on a career in the judiciary, he was dogged by hostile *procureur général*'s reports, claiming that his marriage to a woman of anti-republican family would be 'badly received by the Republicans', and warning the Ministry that he was a 'catholique très pratiquant' – a comment heavily underlined by the Ministry.[37] Yet persistence and an irrefutable record of loyalty to the constitution ultimately brought its reward – a judge's appointment in the very Catholic Breton town of St Brieuc – where his religious convictions were at least congenial to the population, if not to the government. Like black faces under *képis* overseas, Catholics had their occasional uses for anticlerical governments – provided they knew on whose side they were fighting in the event of conflict.

At no time was this put more severely to the test than during Combes's expulsion of the religious orders. The parliamentary Left called for the suspension of magistrates who were lukewarm in their enforcement of these measures. And although Combes's Minister of Justice, Ernest Vallé, defended the irremovability of judges against this demand, he issued directives to the judges that they must do all that the government expected of them. Moreover he recommended that *magistrats instructeurs* should take personal charge of the actual eviction of monks, friars and nuns.[38] While magistrates continued to enjoy formal irremovability, a refusal on their part to implement the law was generally recognised as an occasion for resignation or dismissal – and there were numerous examples. Combes for his part warned the magistrates of the consequences of half-heartedness; and, exchanging the stick for the carrot, he asked to be informed of those magistrates who had shown particular zeal against the religious orders. Predictably the episode of the State inventories of Church property in 1906 (see p. 62) was the occasion of several dismissals and resignations.[39]

Dismissals and resignations created vacancies – and gave the government further opportunities for getting the sort of magistrates it wanted. But the *Affaire des fiches* had created a mood of vigilance towards the government's handling of the public services. Partly to counter allegations of ministerial packing of the lower echelons of the judiciary, a law of 12 July 1905 required *juges de paix* to hold a law diploma and to have served a probationary period in a legal or administrative office.[40] At the same time they were ostensibly given a greater measure of security in that any government sanction against them was subject to scrutiny by a commission composed of senior magistrates and officials. As before, however, support from political figures continued to be a major factor in their appointment – just as political considerations could be a major factor in their dismissal, despite the greater security that the new law theoretically gave them. Indeed the moderate Republican, Etienne Flandin, told parliament in November 1905 – with some exaggeration – that only the Ottoman Empire surpassed France in the subordination of the judiciary to the will of the government.[41] A brief attempt was made in August 1906 to limit the government's freedom of manoeuvre by instituting an annual *concours* for salaried magistrates. But this was replaced by an innocuous examination which in practice restored to the government its former liberty of choice.[42] And so matters rested until the inter-war period.

In the various courts and tribunals, even quite junior appointments were subject to the reports of prefects and *procureurs généraux* on the candidates' political attitudes; and the information was closely scrutinised by the Ministry, with an active coloured crayon at the ready. Many of these questionnaires were clearly designed for more senior posts, but this did not deter informants from giving dutifully thorough answers to them. A modest *clerc principal de l'huissier* contemplating a change of post might be the subject of lengthy questions on the 'situation, character, influence of his wife', 'state in which his house is kept' – even 'receptions', as though it were hoped that his appointment might transform the social life of the locality, and his dazzling soirées win over recalcitrants to the Republican regime.[43]

Notaries too were carefully vetted by the government for their political and religious views, despite the fact that they were simply empowered by the State to handle acts and contracts requiring official state recognition or sanction. They were appointed for life by the government, but could be dismissed for misconduct or incompetence. Apart from the intrinsic significance of their functions, the government's concern for their political rectitude may also have been semi-consciously influenced by an awareness that notaries, like cab-drivers, were an important source of local comment and gossip. A small-town notary, in his daily conversation with clients, could exercise a considerable influence in the locality – as was typically reflected in a senator's letter for an aspirant notary, in which he declared that the appointment of his protégé was 'an important political question'.[44] Whether an applicant was appointed or not depended a great deal on the attitude of the *procureur général* of the locality; and generally speaking the *procureur général* was much more interested in the candidate's professional and social skills than in his political and religious opinions. On the latter score, he was usually more inclined to be tolerant in his assessments than the local prefect. During the brief foretaste of militant anticlericalism under the Léon Bourgeois government of 1895–6, a report on a successful candidate for a notary-ship frankly remarked 'the candidate is not a republican, but there are no political objections to him'; and an equally successful candidate survived a report commenting on his 'hostile attitude to the government of the Republic', but tempered with the remark that he had agreed to steer clear of active politics.[45] Even during the high tide of anticlericalism under Combes, the reports of the *procureurs généraux* on candidates often confined themselves to a terse 'No objections on political grounds', while others urged that a clear distinction be made between the candidate's religious beliefs and his political acceptability. 'He is regarded as a clerical, but his attitude has always been correct' did not impede a successful candidature in October 1903; and favourable reports on applicants in the following year included: 'he is considered to be a clerical; but he observes a correct attitude and does not involve himself in politics, so it would be unjust to debar him'.[46] Or again, 'He is often regarded as a reactionary because of his religious convictions . . . but the *juge de paix* considers him a moderate republican.'[47] The differing perceptions of prefects and *procureurs généraux* were typically reflected in a clash in 1904, where the prefect was objecting to an honorary notary-ship being given to a lawyer, 'openly hostile to republicans', whose son wrote for *La Croix*. At the end of the day the prefect truculently gave way, 'on condition that this honour be seen purely as a reward for his professional services'.[48]

With this relatively tolerant attitude in the magistracy, it is not surprising that the turn of the century should find twenty-three old boys of the Collège Stanislas among the notaries and twenty-six among the notaries' clerks, with eight more becoming notaries and three notaries' clerks in the 1901–7 period.[49] There were additionally smaller numbers of notaries from the various Jesuit schools, notably Ste Geneviève and Caousou in Toulouse. Indeed one of the Caousou notaries was to play an important role in advising the religious orders on how to respond to the hostile legislation of 1901.[50]

The *corps préfectoral* and the Interior

There was – and is – universal agreement that the *corps préfectoral* was the most difficult sector for a committed Catholic to enter during the République des républicains. Several men from Catholic schools became sub-prefects during the Esprit Nouveau of the mid-'nineties (see pp. 6–8), but it would seem that none became prefects in the pre-war period. If, as is sometimes claimed, there existed two or three closet Catholic prefects in these years, their profile was so low as to be invisible to historians; and like the bears of the Pyrenees, they would have survived through a combination of remote location and shuffling around in comparative silence. It is conceivable that some of the more circumspect or little-known Catholic sub-prefects of the Ordre Moral in the 'seventies might have managed to escape the purges of the Republican victory, and by remaining circumspect might gradually have crept up the prefectoral ladder. But if they did, it would have been a triumph of camouflage, rather than a triumph of evident worth over government prejudice. They might have given praise to their Maker in the midnight privacy of their beds; but they could scarcely have afforded to be seen attending weekly Mass in their own localities. None of the old boys of the Collège Stanislas who were prefects under the Ordre Moral survived into the 'eighties – nor did any of the four prefects from Ste Geneviève or the three from the Rue de Vaugirard.[51] Indeed only one prefect in the whole of France managed to stay firmly in the saddle throughout the traumatic transition from the Republic of Dukes to the Republic of Whoever-next.[52]

This could scarcely have been otherwise, given that the prefect was traditionally the government's watchdog on the political loyalty of other public servants, as well as being its sheepdog in herding the local population along the *via dolorosa* of general government policy. If in an age of Republican virtue, the prefect was instructed to avoid any overt support for particular candidates in the elections he supervised, he was nevertheless expected to ensure that candidates favourable to the government profited to the full from the facilities, protection and opportunities that were legally open to them, while their opponents received no more than the minimum stipulated by law.[53] The prefects were likewise important channels of government economic aid to localities, which could often exercise a persuasive effect on voters whom parliamentary candidates were anxious to woo – thereby creating further links between the prefect and the government's supporters in the legislature. Added to this were the prefect's powers of patronage in local public employment, a continuing if contentious subject of correspondence between *parlementaires* and *préfecture*, in which the small change of clerkships and *bureaux de tabac* was endlessly disputed between rival claims of deserving constituents whose electoral support was eloquently portrayed as the only barrier against the triumph of reaction and the end of the Republic.

Such a role inevitably required close sympathy and trust between the prefect and the government in office. Not surprisingly the average span of a prefect's career was only seven or eight years in the pre-war Republic – most men being in their early forties when they obtained their first prefecture. And they would expect to remain in a particular post for only two or three years before being moved to another, depending on the government's electoral strategy or the prefect's success in securing promotion to a more prestigious prefecture with a higher salary.[54] Some, however, survived the course much longer. A famous example was Henri Paul whose administrative career began in the Second Empire and who first became a prefect in 1882, eventually finding himself Prefect of the Oise under Méline in 1896, where he remained until 1900 when, at his own request, he was transferred into the slippered ranks of *trésoriers-payeurs* at the age of sixty-two.[55] His impregnability against Left-wing accusations of clerical sympathies sprang from his embodiment of the conciliatory, realistic virtues that even stern-minded governments had to make use of in the minefield of local politics. His *chef de cabinet* in the Oise, J. A. Coulangheon, later made use of some of his master's traits in his humorous novel, *Les Jeux de la préfecture* (1902), which, after allowances are made for literary licence, catches the essence of an agile prefect's perpetual balancing act. Instructing his deputy, the prefect insists 'If anyone comes to you with requests and recommendations . . . give no promises, nothing concrete! Only hopes! Above all, hopes!' And, justifying his social contacts with a local, anti-Republican aristocrat, 'He plays a good hand at whist . . . Besides, he is a political adversary of undoubted integrity. I have got him to guarantee that the Catholic vote will go to [the moderate Republican candidate]. That's the real essence of the Ralliement!'[56]

When the *esprit nouveau* of the Méline ministry gave way to the harder-faced ethos of Republican concentration under Brisson in 1898, ten prefects were removed from the *corps* altogether and a third of the rest moved to other departments – some admittedly as part of the normal promotion procedure.[57] And what Brisson had begun, Combes continued. Within a few months of coming to office, he moved a fifth of the prefects. Eight prefects were made to leave the *corps* altogether in September 1904, and over a quarter of the rest were reshuffled.[58] However, even a sacked prefect could look forward to some sort of a state income. Successful prefects usually became *trésoriers-payeurs généraux* when they were put out to grass; but those who were seen as having failed the government might have to do with the management of a minor hospital or prison.[59] The Combes era, however, saw more generous terms offered to sacked prefects – partly on the promptings of his son, Edgar Combes, who was currently Secretary-General at the Ministry of the Interior – and succeeding governments maintained the tradition.[60]

Not only was there little likelihood of Republican governments appointing committed Catholics to posts of such pivotal importance to the survival and success of their overall policies; but, even given the chance, many Catholics would have experienced conflicts of conscience in taking responsibility for anticlerical policies in their localities. Many magistrates and army officers felt similar qualms when faced with implementing the laws against the religious orders; but they were at least the unwilling instruments of the decisions of a parliamentary democracy which they were powerless to alter. And these uncongenial tasks played a relatively small part in their overall careers of service to the nation. Prefects, however, were personally responsible for seeing that these tasks were carried out thoroughly and enthusiastically by their subordinates – and that the local population was persuaded to take an approving view of what was being done in their name. ·

The same was true, to a much lesser degree, of the sub-prefect. But the difference in degree was important. Not only was his personal responsibility and width of discretion only a fraction of that of his master; but his own attitudes and beliefs would be far less known to the Ministry than those of a serious candidate for a prefecture, despite the political reports on all applicants for the Ministry of the Interior (see pp. 89–91). Moreover the government had to find three times more sub-prefects than prefects, and therefore could not afford to be overfastidious at this junior level. It would therefore be easier for a closet Catholic to infiltrate their ranks – even if his chances of ascending the subsequent rungs of the *corps* ladder were remote. For what it is worth, four Stanislas old boys became sub-prefects during the Esprit Nouveau of the mid-1890s, all of whom continued in the *corps* despite the distasteful tasks subsequently imposed upon it by the Combes government.[61] Their fortunes will be looked at in a moment.

That said, entry was still extremely difficult for such men. Not only were sub-prefects the pool from which most prefects were subsequently fished, but like that of the subaltern in the trenches their role was a crucial one in the government's electoral battles. In periods when *scrutin d'arrondissement* was the prevailing electoral system – based on single-member constituencies – the sub-prefect was directly in the line of fire, as he was in local elections. And since it was representatives of local councils who largely elected the Senate, the sub-prefect was likewise an important if indirect influence on the composition of the upper house. No government would knowingly entrust this role to men with mental reservations about which side should win.

Unlike the situation in an increasing number of ministries, there were no formal qualifications required of an aspirant to be a sub-prefect or a prefecture secretary-general – or even a prefect. Until 1928, the only legal requirement for membership of the *corps préfectoral* was to have reached the age of twenty-one. This in principle gave the government much greater freedom to hire and fire the men it wanted than was the case in ministries where choice was limited to applicants who had been tempered by the fire and water of the *grandes écoles* or the demands of a *concours*. Yet in practice, a sizeable majority of sub-prefects had a law degree; and of those who eventually became prefects in this period over 80 per cent were law graduates.[62] Since many aspiring politicians were similarly qualified, the close relationship and interchange between ministers' personal *cabinets* and sub-prefectures made service in one role an aid to advancement in the other – thereby intensifying the political character of the *corps préfectoral*. Those who aspired to the *plumes blanches* of a prefect, however, were aware that as the leading representatives of the Republic in the provinces prefects were expected to impress and seduce local opinion with a certain *train de vie* and generous hospitality, not all of which could easily be met from current salary levels – even less from a sub-prefect's salary, if a would-be prefect was anxious to show his superiors that he and his wife knew how to entertain. Not only did this have an inhibiting effect on the democratisation of the *corps préfectoral* desired by the Left, but it encouraged ambitious sub-prefects to seek wealth in a future wife – and with wealth on the distaff side there often came a missal and a rosary. It would be difficult, however, to claim that many *bien pensant* women in *préfectures* exercised a softening effect on the executive zeal of their husbands in carrying out the government's anti-clerical policies. The pious wife of a Socialist politician like Jaurès did not prevent him leading to victory the campaign for the disestablishment of the Church; and even the violent blow across the face which an outraged Madame Chaumié dealt her husband – Combes's Minister of Education – did not cause him to reconsider his current measures against Catholic schools.[63] Prefects were no more likely to melt than politicians – and arguably had more to lose if compassion was condemned as insubordination, as their wives fully realised.

The Stanislas old boys who became sub-prefects during the Esprit Nouveau are illustrative of a frequent early career pattern in the *corps préfectoral*, even if they demonstrate little or nothing about the permeability of the *corps* to Catholic infiltration. Louis Piette – whose loyalty to his roots was reflected in his life-membership of the Stanislas old boys' association – took a law degree while attending the Ecole Libre des Sciences Politiques. He became a *rédacteur* in the Ministry of the Interior in 1893; and then obtained the very felicitous advantage of membership of the minister's *cabinet* in 1894, when Charles Dupuy was minister and premier. 1896 inaugurated a succession of brief appointments as sub-prefect in various towns, while 1902 found him Secretary-General of the prefecture of the Meurthe-et-Moselle. The *sales besognes* of the following years, however, may have given him second thoughts, for he left the *corps* during the *campagne laïque*.[64] Interesting in its similarities and differences is the career of Jacques Régnier – likewise a Stanislas life-member – who duplicated Piette's fortunes in becoming a member of Dupuy's *cabinet* at the Interior in 1894, after taking a law degree while at the Ecole Libre des Sciences Politiques. There likewise followed a string of sub prefectoral appointments – which in his case took him right through the chequered political era of Méline, Waldeck-Rousseau and Combes, to the happier times of Briand and beyond.[65] A comparable capacity to take the rough with the smooth was exemplified by another Stanislas life-member and law graduate, Henri Borromée, who became a sub-prefect during the Méline ministry and remained so during the dark days of Combisme before eventually emerging as Secretary-General of the Sommes prefecture.[66] The historian has no means of knowing how these men viewed the tasks consigned to them – or indeed what their beliefs were, or had become. If nothing else, they show that it was not impossible for private-school products to penetrate and climb the lower echelons of the *corps préfectoral*, the Republic's *Sturmabteilung* at this time – though at what cost, if any, to self-esteem can only be guessed at. Much more obscure is the case of the only other Stanislas sub-prefect of this period, Bernard Millon, who withdrew into private life at the early age of thirty in 1896 – though at whose behest, and for what reasons, is not clear.[67]

Among the relatively rare surviving dossiers of rejected candidates, an intriguing case is that of Lucien Burlet, who was seeking a sub-prefecture in the summer of 1894, during the early months of the Esprit Nouveau when Charles Dupuy was premier and Minister of the Interior. Burlet had been Jacques Piou's secretary and currently edited the Rallié newspaper *Le Libéral du Valois*. The customary confidential report on him from the Prefect of the Oise referred to his lack of administrative experience, or university degree, while admitting the breadth of his general culture. It also commented on his wife's lack of social experience, and the couple's slender private resources. These factors were perhaps enough on their own to kill his attractiveness as a candidate, but the attentive pencil of the Ministry also underlined his connections with Piou and the editorship of *Le Libéral du Valois*, 'founded by the reactionaries of Crépy-en-Valois, calling themselves *ralliés*. *Le Libéral* does not openly attack the government, and describes itself as liberal republican.' The report admitted that Burlet had not been in the locality long enough for an accurate assessment of his personal political opinions to be made – but the application got no further.[68] The fact, however, that Burlet thought it worthwhile applying at all indicates perhaps something of the hopes invested in the *esprit nouveau* by those Catholics who were seeking a rapprochement with the Republic.

Even before the Ralliement, there was the occasional prefect who was prepared to appoint a committed Catholic as his *chef de cabinet*, or recommend him as a *conseiller de préfecture* – both relatively modest posts as compared with the *corps préfectoral* itself. In November 1890, the prefect of the Manche described his former *chef de cabinet* as 'Catholic, religious by conviction . . . very independent of any influence of the clergy . . . a moderate Republican', and warmly proposed him as a *conseiller de préfecture*, preferably in the east or the north 'which would be more suited to his character' – perhaps because these were regions where Catholicism was fairly strong in some departments, without the 'reactionary' over-tones of Brittany and the Massif Central.[69] Whatever the outcome of this particular recommendation, the Stanislas old-boys list of 1901 was to include a *chef de cabinet du préfet* and a couple of *conseillers de préfecture*. It could likewise claim a *sous-chef de service*, a *rédacteur* and three *attachés* in the central administration of the Ministry of the Interior – all appointed in the 1890s, despite the Ministry's reputation as the powerhouse of Republican proselytism.[70] Unlike the *corps préfectoral*, the central office had established a *concours* in 1886, which helped to ensure that political acceptability and a manipulative mind were not the only criteria of entry, thereby giving strong candidates of less immediately pleasing backgrounds something of a chance.

6 *Ronds-de-cuir, genoux-de-chameau*: other sectors

And those who prayed were called 'camel-knees' by their companions.

Oratorian sermon

Pulling the purse strings

The financial sectors of state employment occupied a curiously intermediate position between the technical ministries and the more politicised branches of the French administration. Professional expertise was essential – as was acknowledged in the high hurdles set for intending *inspecteurs des finances* (see pp. 108–9), and in the rather more modest *concours* established for central-office staff in 1885.[1] Yet political factors could not be entirely ignored in recruitment and promotion. To some extent this was an inevitable result of the growing interventionism of modern European governments – and of the increasing expenditure and revenue-raising that it entailed. The activities of all other ministries were bound by what the Ministry of Finance was prepared to allow; and it would have been only too easy for a financial staff, hostile to government policy, to raise endless pecuniary objections to what the government intended. Conversely a sympathetic staff knew which ministerial back-pockets could be raided to realise a cherished government project – or at least they knew how to massage the accounts to minimise criticism.

As in all ministries in this period, there was a tendency for ministers of finance to bring in as *directeurs* men with whom they had worked before, often in other ministries or contexts – political cronies, whose views and judgement they considered reliable, but with sufficient financial ability to be able to challenge and override the traditional obstructive habits of an arthritic administration, set in its ways and unable to muster enthusiasm for short cuts to short-term political objectives. Civil servants, counting on a life-time in the ministry, never ceased to be shocked by the insouciance with which in-and-out politicians created dangerous precedents, the eventual nemesis of which would never concern them. They were even more disgruntled by the frustration of their promotion

prospects by this succession of alien *directeurs* parachuted in from outside
– blockage on the top rung stalling promotion all the way down. Of the
thirty-five *directeurs* appointed to the central offices of the Ministry of
Finance between 1885 and 1912, twenty-eight had been outsiders.[2]

Some observers regarded this intrusion of political friends of the
ministers as a salutary counterpart to the conservatism of many of the
rédacteurs, intensified by some of the *bien pensant* appointments of
the Esprit Nouveau years. The anticlerical historian, Antonin Debidour,
claimed that the *enregistrement* in particular was riddled with them in the
1890s, and accused them of turning a blind eye to the fiscal irregularities
of the religious orders.[3] Whatever the truth of the matter – and Debidour
was not one to underplay his hand – the products of Catholic schools
were well represented in the finance ministry. At the turn of the century,
the Collège Stanislas had three *rédacteurs* and three *attachés* in the central
administration – and even had a *directeur des finances* during the Méline
thaw, albeit in the safe seclusion of Madagascar. There were additionally
three *receveurs*, a *percepteur*, three *receveurs-rédacteurs* and three other
members of the Enregistrement et Domaines, together with a number of
more peripheral appointments. The *trésorier-payeur général*, whom
Stanislas had on its list, was a former *trésorier d'Afrique*, seconded to the
French army of occupation in Tunis during the Esprit Nouveau –
thereby, cynics would say, conforming on three counts to the archetype
of Catholic bureaucrat (if Catholic he still was).[4] Caousou of Toulouse
had at least a couple of tax men among its alumni.[5]

It must also be recognised that political animosities were not allowed
to interfere too much with the normal routine and courtesies of the Palais
Bourbon and the Pavillon de Rohan, separated by a short digestive-
settling stroll across the Seine. While Déroulède was more or less openly
plotting against the Republic, his recommendations for various government appointments were affably received by the relevant ministers and
prefects, and in several cases met with success. Thus his former
Boulangist friend, Francis de Susini, one-time deputy for Corsica, was
appointed to a *recette buraliste* in Tulle (Corrèze) by Henri Brisson's
Minister of Finance, Paul Peytral, who had stood against Boulangist
candidates in previous elections.[6]

A branch of public finance with courtesies of its own was the
Inspection des Finances – although it was only in 1895 that it became
entirely separated from the Ministry. Candidates for its *concours* were
expected to be law graduates – although after 1892 graduates in other
relevant subjects became eligible. From 1906, however, they were also
expected to have a diploma from the Ecole Libre des Sciences
Politiques.[7] This, of its nature, favoured men with family resources (see

p. 82); but even before then a sample of sixty-six *inspecteurs des finances* in 1901 showed all but one as coming from the middle and upper bourgeoisie, and, as noted elsewhere, this milieu favoured a tolerant if not necessarily indulgent attitude towards the Church.[8] Catholic schools were undoubtedly well represented in the ranks of the Inspection. The Collège Stanislas alone provided at least nine *inspecteurs* between 1880 and 1900, and a couple more by 1907, while among more chequered career patterns a couple of *postards* who graduated from the Ecole Polytechnique in the early 'eighties eventually became *inspecteurs des finances*.[9] Perhaps the most famous *postard* to become an *inspecteur des finances* was Joseph Caillaux (1881–3), a man with bitter memories of Ste Geneviève, who when he eventually became Minister of Finance in Waldeck-Rousseau's government gradually brought in as *directeurs* old acquaintances from the Inspection des Finances, after easing out the existing incumbents.[10] He was not, however, a *postard* of whom the school was particularly proud; and its publications simply list him as 'inspecteur des finances', without mention of his subsequent political career, which one must assume was insufficiently *Ad maiorem gloriam Dei* for the school record.[11]

The lists of *inspecteurs des finances* at the turn of the century included a number of illustrious family names strongly identified with Catholic interests; and in the period 1890 to 1914, nearly 10 per cent of *inspecteurs généraux* carried a *particule* to their names.[12] The career of Charles Georges Picot exemplifies not only the well-heeled, incense-flavoured world from which a number of *inspecteurs* came, but also the Inspection's pioneer role in the art of *pantouflage*, which was later to become such a marked feature of certain sections of the French civil service.[13] A close relative of the Church defender, Georges Picot, Charles became an *inspecteur* in 1893, before eventually leaving in 1900 to take up a series of prestigious appointments in the private sector – a move that appears to have been dictated by personal advantage rather than unease with the increasingly anticlerical policies of the government. The financial expertise of *inspecteurs* and their intimate knowledge of the legal limits to which money-making could be stretched made them invaluable adjuncts to banks and commercial enterprises; and, between 1850 and 1914, about a third of *inspecteurs* finished their careers in the private sector.[14]

The knowledge that such opportunities were open to them encouraged a certain independence of mind which contrasted with the more circumspect attitude of *fonctionnaires* whose prospects were dependent on outward conformity to the broad policies of government. It also, in theory at least, allowed them the luxury of resigning in protest against current government policies. But few appear to have availed themselves of this luxury – which like death or retirement can be exercised only once. In any case, governments came and went; and the financial sectors were too peripheral to the government's campaign against the religious orders for a resignation to be publicly perceived as a relevant protest. Indeed many members of the *grands corps* regarded themselves as a continuing guarantee of the traditional decencies in government, which would outlive the transient terms of office of their brief-lived overlords. Even so, a large number of *inspecteurs* were attached to various ministerial *cabinets* – the Minister of Finance alone having perhaps half a dozen, as was the case in the Waldeck-Rousseau government.[15] Given the heavily political concerns of the *cabinets du ministre*, influence and advancement were inevitably easier for *inspecteurs* whose general political attitudes were not sharply out of step with the minister's. Similarly, the itinerant 'en mission' work which increasingly took up the time of *inspecteurs* inevitably made the *inspecteur* something of a representative of central authority in the provinces – which meant that governments could not entirely ignore the political outlook of their *inspecteurs*. Encouragements to prudence or parsimony would come less convincingly from a man who was unsympathetic to the government's overall policies. Targets of the roving eye of an *inspecteur* included the local *trésoriers-payeurs généraux*; these were often former prefects who had been moved into their new role because their views were insufficiently in harmony with those of the incoming government.[16] It would not do to have their new roles overseen by someone who was even less in tune with government than they themselves were. Conversely, pro-government former prefects, retired merely for reasons of age, would not relish being inspected by critics of the regime.

Bread-and-butter ministries

The Ministry of Commerce did not play a political role like those already examined – not even in the indirect fashion of the Ministry of Finance. Yet it had rewards at its disposal – services, concessions and jobs – which were highly sought after in the country at large, and whose distribution was often influenced by political considerations. If this did not necessarily require the recruitment of a bureaucracy that shared the government's enthusiasms, it at least required a bureaucracy that was discreet in channelling the government's generosity. It was not an attractive ministry for a young man of spirit who relished a swift climb; 'complete stagnation among the staff and virtually no promotion', as one guide put it, unless one obtained a post in proximity to the minister.[17] In earlier decades the ministry had undergone rapid development to cope with the growing complexity of the modern economy and the government's increasing involvement in its regulation. It had been a time of rapid promotion for young ambition, with the result that the higher echelons were filled by individuals with long years of service in front of them, thereby blocking the promotion prospects of those beneath.

Recruitment of *rédacteurs* for the central administration was by *concours*; and candidates were the subject of a letter from the police or the prefecture to the Minister, rather than of an answered questionnaire. Many of these letters made no specific mention of the candidate's politics or religious commitment; candidates for this relatively mundane ministry would not necessarily be vociferous in their opinions, and the Ministry seems to have been content to accept the frequent formula that available information was 'favourable from all points of view'.[18]

Some letters, however, particularly from the late 'nineties, were more explicit – although not always with the thoroughness that the government would have wished. An interesting case was that of Marcel Lecoq, a successful applicant for a *rédacteur*ship in the central office of the Ministry.[19] A committed Catholic, he was to be closely if briefly linked with Marc Sangnier's Sillon. Reporting on him favourably in October 1899, the prefect of police added, in the conditional tense of caution, 'il ne s'occuperait pas de politique'. Following his appointment, his first two years in the Ministry were the subject of a good report (4 December 1901), which had nothing to say on his politics or religion. He was then given permission to take open-ended leave to make a study on social policy, relevant to his ministerial work. It was then, however, that he fell foul of the Radical-Socialist deputy for the Nord, Ferdinand Lepez, a dedicated anticlerical – the issue being the archetypal bone of contention in Clochemerle-style politics, a *bureau de tabac*. Lecoq's mother, who herself lived in the south of France, was *titulaire* of a *bureau de tabac* in Bruay-sur-Escaut in the Nord. When the tenancy came up for renewal in September 1903, Madame Lecoq proposed to the Prefect of the Nord a tenant who the Prefect admitted 'was perhaps making a more attractive offer than his competitors, but which I refused to authorise since, from a political point of view, it did not provide sufficient guarantees'; according to the hostile deputy, Lepez, the proposed tenant was 'secretary of the Cercle Catholique'. The situation engendered a prolonged four-sided correspondence, in which Lepez not only accused Lecoq of intriguing with 'le parti réactionnaire' to secure his protégé's case, but threatened to petition the Ministry to rescind Madame Lecoq's proprietary rights. He likewise presented Lecoq's recent discussions of social policy with the Catholic Action Libérale deputy, Paul Lerolle, as dealings with the Nationalists. His accusations led the Ministry of Commerce to ask the prefect whether Lecoq was taking 'a hostile attitude to republican institutions' – to which the prefect replied that Lecoq's behaviour in the department appeared to be perfectly proper and directed simply to ensuring that his mother got a fair return on the *bureau de tabac*.

While the Lecoq case indicates the need for caution among employees of even the 'non-political' ministries, it strikingly illustrates the importance of political factors in appointments to *bureaux de tabac*. Tobacco being a government monopoly, these *bureaux* were theoretically the gift of the Ministry of Finance, which in practice it delegated to the local prefect. They were much sought after; and it was government policy to bestow them on deserving individuals who needed the steady income that they supplied. Since the deserving always outnumbered the *bureaux*, this gave the government an added means of rewarding Republican loyalty, or at least a satisfying occasion for saying 'no' to political dissidents or to the lukewarm.

Although the Ministry of Public Works was an important channel of largesse to localities that the government wished to favour, it showed relatively little curiosity about the political and religious attitudes of aspiring entrants into its ranks. The staff of its central offices had been admitted by *concours* since 1885; but a sampling of their dossiers revealed nothing of their politico-religious sympathies, while considerations of this kind appear to have weighed even less in the appointment of ministry engineers.[20] However it was alleged during the parliamentary debates on the *Affaire des fiches* that prefects had been interfering on political grounds in staff promotions. Whether this had gone beyond the limits enjoined on prefects by recent ministerial circulars is not clear. But, whatever the truth of the matter, the Collège Stanislas provided at least twenty-two engineers for the Ponts et Chaussées between 1880 and 1900, and five more during the *campagne laïque* that followed – which was scarcely surprising, given the school's large entry into the Polytechnique (see p. 39).[21] And similar considerations ensured a strong entry from the Jesuit schools. Of the two hundred *postards* who graduated from the Polytechnique between 1880 and 1891, at least six became engineers with the Ponts et Chaussées; and by the time of the Ste Geneviève diamond jubilee on the eve of the First World War, the school had provided no fewer than fifty-three engineers for the Ponts et Chaussées, to say nothing of 149 for other branches of the public service – all of which reflected Ste Geneviève's strong technical curricula.[22] Vaugirard, for its part, had a more modest record of state engineers for this overall period: a couple with the Ponts et Chaussées, and a further thirteen elsewhere in the state sector – while at least two Caousou alumni of the late nineteenth century became engineers with the Ministry of Public Works.[23]

The relative political innocence of the Ministry of Public Works was also to be found in the Ministry of Agriculture – even if, like Public Works, Agriculture was a spring of generous benefaction for the provinces. A sample of *rédacteurs'* dossiers in the central administration revealed no prefects' reports on them – although the possibility of subsequent removal cannot be entirely ruled out. Some contained the entrance-examination papers written by the candidates – the main skills tested being literacy, numeracy, geography and administrative law.[24] Away from the central offices, political insouciance was even more marked; and whereas by the end of the century the Collège Stanislas had merely a couple of old boys in the central administration, it had no fewer than thirty-one *inspecteurs des eaux et forêts* – an occupation more arduous than its idyllic, nymph-like title might suggest, as was that of the Oberonesque *chef du bureau des alignements et des promenades et plantations* at the Préfecture de la Seine.[25] At least two *postards* who emerged from the Polytechnique in the early 1880s went into state forestry, while the state stud-farms contained at least four former *postards* and a Vaugirard product in the period 1852–1913 – arguably an unremarkable figure when ability to handle horses was often in inverse ratio to sympathy for the Republic.[26] Descending to the humbler levels of *gardes forestiers, chasseurs*, and *brigadiers domaniaux*, the official questionnaires on applicants had no specific questions on their political and religious views; and the only questions which were of a personal nature concerned their financial means, character, appearance, private behaviour, and convictions for offences.[27]

Within the Ministry of Public Works, life in the Postes et Télégraphes was not a career for anyone seeking the fast lane to the top: in one vademecum's words, 'an easy examination; work requiring a lot of assiduity but simple, hard and monotonous; slow promotion; struggling beginnings and a modest conclusion to one's career'.[28] A sample of dossiers of its junior officials included nothing on their politics or religion – which is perhaps mildly surprising when one considers the splendid opportunities for intercepting information or sowing misinformation that would be open to any would-be subversive employed in the transmission of letters and telegrams. At a more elevated level, the Collège Stanislas had a couple of old boys in the central administration at the turn of the century, and another in the Paris telegraph office – while in the sixty years before the First World War eight Ste Geneviève products made their way into the service.[29] (Whether confusion over the term 'postard' gave their applications an unaccustomed tactical advantage can only be a matter for the idlest speculation.)

At the sharp end, and bends, of the service, the dossiers of postmen in the Dordogne *fin de siècle* contained no comments on their politico-religious attitudes – the capacity to negotiate a bicycle, Jacques-Tati fashion, around the precipitous hairpin turns of the district being perhaps the prime requisite for this hazardous occupation.[30] But the service's choice of postmen was not dictated purely by professional skills of literacy, numeracy and dexterity. When Paul Déroulède recommended a fellow bard for a postman's job in the neighbouring department of the Charente in January 1899, the prefect regretfully but affably replied that a recent circular of the Sous-Secrétaire d'Etat des Postes et Télégraphes instructed prefects to reserve positions as postmen to former NCOs, and that only in the absence of suitable military applicants with stripes should other categories be considered.[31]

France abroad

Like the Army, the Quai d'Orsay struck casual observers as a ministry where the ideological exiles of the Republic were positively welcome. Although the advent of the République des Républicains in 1879 had seen three-quarters of the ambassadors replaced, the government still liked to have in the senior ranks of its embassies and consulates benign-voiced patricians with private incomes and social graces.[32] Such men could demonstrate to a largely monarchical Europe that a republic could still equal or outshine the embassies of other countries in its *savoir-faire* and hospitality, despite the humiliating inheritance of a massive military defeat. The families from which these national ornaments were drawn were largely Catholic in sympathy and patronised the private sector of secondary education.

But breeding and wealth had to be complemented by genuine ability. Debutants for junior responsible posts, such as *attaché d'ambassade* or *consul suppléant*, were selected by *le grand concours* which had been instituted in the late 1870s, while a *petit concours* controlled entry into the lower echelons of the consular service. As in other ministries there were competitive examinations for *rédacteurs*.[33] Informed observers such as Victor Turquan claimed that the foreign ministry was difficult to enter – but, once in, promotion came 'à son tour de bête'. Even so, private income and a title were great advantages for anyone aspiring to foreign postings; and Turquan warned that 'Jews are regarded with great disfavour. A diplomatic career is in practice forbidden to them.'[34] Conversely the Collège Stanislas in 1900 could list nineteen members of the diplomatic and consular staff abroad, including four consuls, and seven members of the central administration.[35] The Jesuits too were very well represented. Since the 1850s, Vaugirard had supplied twenty-nine members, although the few who became consuls and chargés d'affaires were largely posted to the Catholic obscurity of Latin America, to wrestle with the legacy of their seventeenth-century Jesuit predecessors. There were also sixteen *postards* in the same period.[36]

If the situation in the foreign ministry seemed to reflect Gambetta's famous dictum that 'anticlericalism is not for export', this maxim was less clearly evident in the colonial office. It is a commonplace of popular history that anticlerical governments worked hand in glove with French missionaries. This assertion had some truth to it in the periods preceding annexation; and it could still be true when the French were dealing with suspicious natives or rival colonial powers. Once French rule was established, however, relations became more ambivalent. There were French officials at home and in the colonies who believed that France's *mission civilisatrice* was a secular one and who questioned their colleagues' tendency to view French missionaries as all part of the *mission sacrée* of French interests. All this requires critical investigation. The old boys' lists of Catholic schools contain fewer names of colonial officials than one might expect. Three Stanislas products for 1880–1900, plus five *postards* and a Vaugirardian in the years 1852 to 1913 is not a large haul for such a long and politically varied period.[37]

Religion and regional origins

A reader following this tour of ministries on foot would increasingly become aware that those bodies which were curious as to their staff's political and religious beliefs were all situated on the Right Bank, while those which were largely unconcerned were on the Left. There was a complex mix of political, social and architectural reasons why this was so, but no simple causal connection. Historians are similarly reluctant to make simple causal links between the geographical origins of ministerial staff and the politico-religious complexion of each ministry.

Yet the differing levels of Catholic representation in the various ministries were matched by differing patterns of regional recruitment among their staff; and it is tempting to see this congruency as in some way causally connected. Historians who have made separate studies of the more politicised branches of the public service have independently commented on the southern provenance of many of their members. In the case of the *corps préfectoral* over 27 per cent of prefects under the Third Republic originated in Aquitaine and the Mediterranean provinces – areas which held less than 14 per cent of the French population in 1900. By contrast fewer than 8 per cent of the prefects came from the western peninsula and the northern provinces bordering on Belgium – areas which collectively held over 17 per cent of the population in 1900.[38] Indeed an independent study of a sample of prefects at the turn of the century showed no fewer than 35 per cent coming from Aquitaine and what the author terms 'the south' – an inconveniently broad area, stretching from the Bay of Biscay to the Italian border – and just over 18 per cent from 'the west' (i.e. west of the line Calvados–Vendée) and 'the north' (i.e. north of the line Seine-Inférieure–Ardennes).[39] A comparable sample of magistrates of the Cour de Cassation reveals 32 per cent originating in Aquitaine and 'the south', and only 14 per cent in 'the west' and 'the north'.[40] The author also looks at the regional roots of a sample of *directeurs*, drawn from a wide spectrum of the civil service – *directeurs* often being the most 'politicised' members of a ministry, apart from the *cabinet personnel* of the Minister. They too show a similar if less strong pattern – 22 per cent from Aquitaine and 'the south', as against just over 10 per cent from 'the west' and 'the north'.[41]

While both authors are too experienced to hazard easy explanations, the first of them speaks of the southerner's penchant for *la fonction publique*, arising from the lack of alternative attractive careers, from their 'taste for legal studies, display and speech-making, social relations, and exercise of authority', to say nothing of 'the practice of patronage'.[42] These may indeed be factors; but other possibilities would also be worth investigating, including the negative factor of elimination on politico-religious grounds. The broad geographical terms employed, particularly in the second survey, make it difficult to compare their coverage with maps of religious observance. Nevertheless it would be largely true to say that levels of Sunday Mass-going and Easter communion were much lower in Aquitaine and the Mediterranean provinces than in the western peninsula and several of the 'northern' departments – with important exceptions. The obvious dangers of attempting a correlation of this kind lie principally in the uncertainty of knowing what proportion of the *fonctionnaires* from 'the south' came from the predominant areas of low religious observance and what proportion from the less typical areas of high religious observance. Even so the patterns of regional origin in the politicised services may partially reflect the difficulties that Catholics encountered – or assumed they would encounter – in gaining entry into these sectors. The Catholic regions would consequently be under-represented, leaving room for more entrants from the areas of low religious observance.

The plausibility of this suggestion is borne out by other interesting findings in these investigations, notably in the study which compares its figures for the turn of the century with similar samples for the Second Empire. These comparisons show that the regional contrasts became much more marked between the Second Empire and 1900, which would coincide with the increase in anticlerical attitudes in the recruitment of the politicised branches of state employment, without necessarily demonstrating a causal link. The proportion of prefects originating in 'the south' nearly doubled in this period (from 12 per cent to 21 per cent), as did that of magistrates from the Cour de Cassation (14 per cent to 23 per cent). Conversely the percentage of magistrates from 'the north' dropped from over 12 per cent to 7 per cent, and those from 'the west' by a similar amount. The figures for *directeurs* reveal a similar if less dramatic rise from to 9 per cent to over 12 per cent in 'the south' and 6 per cent to nearly 10 per cent in Aquitaine – with a corresponding drop in 'the north' from 9 per cent to 5 per cent, but with a barely perceptible decline in 'the west' (from an already low 5.8 per cent to 5.4 per cent).[43]

Further grist for the politico-religious hypothesis is the gradual reversal of these regional trends in the later decades of the twentieth century (see pp. 200–1), when Catholic areas made relative gains in membership of the political services, coinciding with the evaporation of anticlerical vigilance in these sectors. Equally interesting, if no more conclusive, are the figures for the non-political services in 1901, where Aquitaine and 'the south' account for a much smaller proportion of senior membership, but 'the north' correspondingly more – over 20 per cent in the case of Ponts et Chaussées and 13 per cent for the Inspection des Finances.[44] This obviously owes much to the growing industrial and commercial wealth of 'the north'; but one might also have expected some reflection of this 'northern' wealth in the entry-patterns of the politicised sectors, even if on a much more limited scale. The fact that their entry-patterns show the very reverse of this expectation suggests that the politico-religious factor is worth investigating.

Bids to restore trust

Although most ministries appear to have been relatively free from politico-religious prejudice, there was inevitable unease following the *Affaire des fiches* and the resignation of Combes. It was widely asked if the Masonic surveillance of army officers had its counterpart in the civil service; and the issue gave rise to bitter parliamentary debate.

In the short term the most important outcome was that *fonctionnaires* acquired the right to inspect their own personal dossiers if a charge was brought against them or if their promotion was blocked (22 April 1905).[45] The new War Minister, Maurice Berteaux, had given a lead in his circular of January 1905, which ordered the destruction of any unofficial secret reports on army officers that might feature in their personal files, while a companion circular gave every officer the right to peruse his file and any report written by a superior. In the hierarchical plain-speaking world of the armed services, where junior officers were used to being sworn at by their superiors, this did not pose any particular embarrassment and was to become an established feature of many European armies in the twentieth century, when it became customary for officers to queue up to sign the reports of their commanding officers, with the unquestioning submissiveness of boys entering the headmaster's study. But the issue was more delicate in the notionally liberated world of civilian life, where the need to earn a living was the principal servitude, and where family and friends were curious to know one's standing with the boss.

That the measure had become a reality in the civil service was largely the result of a stormy debate in the Chamber on 9 December 1904. Critics of Combes had not been mollified by his circular of 18 November, forbidding the political surveillance of *fonctionnaires*, except by accredited public officials. Even this, opponents claimed, was odious delation. To save the principle of political surveillance, Combes's successor, Maurice Rouvier, conceded the right of *fonctionnaires* to see what had been written about them 'when they are the subject of a disciplinary measure or of a delay in promotion by seniority' (22 April 1905).

In practice, however, the right was largely confined to cases where civil servants were specifically accused of misconduct or inadequacy and wished to see the incriminating evidence. It was rare for it to be invoked by them to gain access to the routine reports on their competence, political reliability or suitability for promotion. Even so, the recently created Ministry of Labour and Social Security gave its staff this option (30 July 1907), limiting consultation to the months of November and December, so as to discourage neurotics from making daily requests to harassed secretaries for their files to be brought up from records. Other ministries followed suit in the next few years, thus bringing to the pre-Christmas period something of the old penitential spirit of Advent.

If the government sought to create a civil service that was loyal to the Republic, there was no shortage of outside bodies ready to advise it. Prominent among these were the Freemasons, particularly the Grand Orient.

Freemasonry in France is often portrayed as a surrogate secular church of the French Radical tradition – an image that was strengthened by its vocabulary. It described non-Masons as 'les profanes'; and it explained the decline of Masonic influence on government during the Esprit Nouveau as symptomatic of 'the spread of scepticism' – a curious semantic reversal of roles, turning the Enlightenment on its head.[1] Masonry in fact was a form of solidarity for men who shared a number of broad democratic and secular assumptions. Its ideology was accepted, because its basic content corresponded with what most Radical free-thinkers already believed. And not only Radicals, for by 1905 a third of the Grand Orient's *ateliers* were Socialist.[2] Its ritual and language were not taken very seriously. In practice Masons were active members of their lodges for only about five years on average – generally at the point of their career when they were most in need of professional or political advancement. Masonry in France was nevertheless on the increase. Its total membership grew from some 24,000 in 1903 to 32,000 five years later. It was believed, moreover, that well over a third of the new Chamber of Deputies of 1902 were Masons – as were a third to a half of the Senate. Emile Combes's cabinet of 1902 consisted almost entirely of Masons, with the paradoxical exception of General André (see pp. 46–7) and the arguable exception of Delcassé, who had been nominally a Mason, but who had long since ceased to show up at Masonic meetings. Yet to condemn the Combes cabinet for its Masonry was to mistake a symptom for a cause. Masonry was a function rather than a factor of the secular movement in French politics. Masonic membership was generally a means to an end. The real power of Masonry lay at the local level.[3] It was there that its favours or animosity could make or break. The provincial lodges generally knew more about local affairs than the prefects or the ministries in Paris, whose life span was generally too short to acquire comparable information on who was who at grass roots level. It was therefore understandable that civil servants and Radical politicians should use the lodges as additional sources of information. In a country where the *piston* was a central ingredient of the selection system, it was inevitable that Masonic protection should be a major force. But in this, as in so much else, it largely duplicated and extended existing methods and channels of influence.

Some of these interventions were of a relatively straightforward kind, of the type that a British MP might make to a minister on behalf of a constituent. Typical of these was a letter from one of the Grand Orient's leading luminaries, Frédéric Desmons, to Méline's War Minister, requesting three months' compassionate leave for a military bandsman whose father had recently died.[4] But the Masonic archives contain large numbers of letters sent by provincial lodges to the Rue Cadet, requesting support for lodge members seeking particular government posts. The Secretary-General of the Grand Orient would then transmit what he regarded as deserving or plausible requests to a Masonic deputy or senator in the region where the petitioner was seeking a post. The MP would then usually write to the relevant office responsible for the appointment, arguing his client's case on merit and political acceptability, without specific reference to his Masonic connections. Even if the recipient of the letter was himself a Mason, it would not do that overtly Masonic recommendations should be passed around among appointing committees or remain in files for less sympathetic eyes to see. However, the anticlerical high-tide of 1899–1905 found the Grand Orient less inhibited in its utterances and much readier to mention the candidate's Masonic affiliation, if it was likely to strengthen his appeal.

The Grand Orient was insistent that individual Masons should submit their petitions to the Rue Cadet via their local lodges – which were then expected to vet the worthiness of each application and the degree of priority to be given to it.[5] It was also emphatic that local lodges and their members should not make direct requests for favours to Masons in positions of influence: 'it is preferable that the lodge of the petitioner should apply to the Grand Orient, which, being better informed on the worth and opinions of the Masons who might be approached, can effectively set the matter in motion'.[6] Thus when a local lodge asked the Grand Orient to approach on its behalf four particular deputies to push a request in February 1897, the secretary was quick to reply that only two of the four were active Masons and that nothing was to be gained by approaching the others.[7]

Masonic membership was a card to play or conceal, depending on circumstance; and many Masons did not wish their membership to be generally known. For this reason the Grand Orient vigorously rejected a well-meant but imprudent proposal in 1897–8 that Masons be given a list of fellow Masons in their electoral constituencies.[8] Caution was particularly advisable during the Esprit Nouveau; and there were many signs of Masonry's awareness of the unpropitious climate under the Méline ministry for seeking favours from the government. The situation was not without irony in that two of the Esprit Nouveau premiers, Charles Dupuy and Jules Méline, were Masons – which did not prevent Méline being reviled by the Grand Orient for ignoring Masonic warnings on the infiltration of the civil service by Catholics.[9] As the secretary said, in reply to a local lodge's entreaty on behalf of one of its members, 'One has clearly to recognise that the moment is scarcely favourable for an effective intervention, since the current government does not often give its protection to true republicans.'[10] His records are full of letters to many disappointed provincial lodges, whose requests had not yet borne fruit. All that he could wearily repeat was that he was prepared to 'intervenir de nouveau' 'au Ministère des Travaux Publics', 'au Ministère des Colonies', 'au Sous-secrétaire d'Etat des Postes et Télégraphes', etc, etc.[11] And when in desperation the Grand Orient decided that the time had come for the supplicant himself to write to the minister concerned, jogging his memory on some unsatisfied plea, the secretary, Bergère, usually added the caveat 'while avoiding, of course, any appeal to your being a Mason'.[12] But after two years of the Méline ministry, Bergère felt obliged to tell the latest job-seeking lodge, 'I have to tell you that it is difficult. Everything is tied up everywhere.'[13] Indeed it was only in distant colonies, remote from the shifts in government policy, that the Grand Orient could count on its accustomed clout; and even this depended on the colony – and, above all, its governor.

The Rue Cadet kept careful records not only of its members but also of rejected applications for membership, many longstanding – much in the spirit of present-day credit companies' lists of unreliable clients. Indeed its Livre des Refusés was often more informative on provincial rejects than the local lodge's own records. Thus when a lodge in Valence tentatively proposed a new member in January 1898, the secretary swiftly riposted that the Valence lodge itself had unanimously rejected the man a number of years earlier on the strength of three unfavourable reports.[14] In the same way lapsed members, though very numerous, were not quickly forgiven by their former brethren. Thus the bulletin of the Grand Orient in the mid-'nineties made several barbed references to ex-Brother

Alfred Rambaud, eminent historian and currently Minister of Education, whom it accused of favouring royalists and imperialists and cold-shouldering Masons.

The reign of the profane proved short-lived, however, and great was the rejoicing in Masonry's *heiligen Hallen* when the worsening Church–State relations at the turn of the century restored the influence of the brotherhood. At the same time the increasingly dominant role of Narcisse-Amédée Vadecard in the secretariat of the Grand Orient ushered in a more direct-style of Masonic intervention, appropriate to the new reign of virtue. It was an era of confidence, in which the cautious circumspection of the Méline years gave way to a brisk assumption that Masonry now had the ear of those who hired and fired. The Grand Orient's correspondence files display a much greater quantity of petitioning letters sent direct to the ministries, rather than through inter-mediaries or by word of mouth. And the emphasis of each request is on the candidate's Republican credentials, rather than on his professional skills. Given the provenance of the letter, there was no need to mention his Masonic connections – though Vadecard usually did this, if he felt confident of the recipient's Masonic sympathies.

The rank and file of Masonry were quick to realise that happy days were here again; and Vadecard was flooded with demands. By the end of 1900 he himself was forwarding an average of five a day, after rejecting the non-starters and weak applicants. The secretariat received 4,000 more letters in 1900 than in 1899, most of which concerned appoint-ments and favours; and in desperation Vadecard begged that each request be made the subject of a separate letter, accompanied by a summary that could be sent to the appropriate minister.[15] The point was being reached where the ministries were no longer capable of giving serious consideration to the applications, let alone gratify them.[16] Faced with the volume of Masonic requests in the later part of 1900, 'all the ministers reply to you that they are busy with the discussion of the budget' – though Vadecard characteristically took out extra personal insurance by adding 'unfortunately [the council of the Grand Orient] has no means of forcing the hands of reactionary administrative bodies'.[17]

His expressions of virtuous exasperation with the tardiness of ministries in granting favours to Masons were largely attempts to reassure disappointed petitioners that he was doing all he could for them. 'Is one forced to conclude that governmental preferment – which in many cases is merely the fulfilment of the claimant's entitlement – is kept only for opponents of the Republic? Whatever the truth of the matter, not one of our good friends whom we are supporting has yet been included in the appointments recently listed in the *Journal Officiel*. It is truly extraordinary!!'[18] It was true, of course, that Waldeck-Rousseau was not himself a Mason – neither was Joseph Caillaux of Finance nor Georges Leygues of Education – which did not deter Vadecard from bombarding all three with requests. The day after he blew the warning whistle to the over-insistent lodges, he was himself enlisting the Masonic deputy of the Loiret in an unsuccessful bid to obtain from Waldeck-Rousseau the transfer of a Mason from the secretary-generalship of the Gers prefecture to that of the Loiret.[19] Similarly, although Vadecard warned petitioners that the Minister of Education 'is far from being one of us', education continued to be a field where the Grand Orient was particularly active in seeking favours for its members.[20] And the same was true of the Ministry of Finance, despite the fact that candidates were many and success usually went to those from comfortably bourgeois backgrounds. 'Besides, the minister [Joseph Caillaux] is not one of us.'[21] On the other hand the Minister of Public Works, Pierre Baudin, was a good Mason, and Vadecard had no hesitation in writing discreetly to him for even quite junior appointments. January 1900 found him requesting the post of lock-keeper on a minor canal for a Mason who was 'sincèrement dévoué à nos institutions'. Moreover, in the termination of his letter, he addressed the Minister as 'Monsieur le Ministre et Très Cher Frère'.[22]

Vadecard was equally active in pursuing overseas posts and advantages. His concern for Masons in Algeria extended to the Muslim population – albeit with guarded enthusiasm. Supporting a Muslim Mason's quest for the rosette of Officier of the Légion d'Honneur, he sought to reassure his intermediary that his client was 'devoid of any fanaticism (which is rare with Muslims)'.[23] Vadecard's letters to the Governor-General of Indo-China, personally addressed to 'Brother Paul Doumer', covered a wide spectrum of patronage, ranging from education via civil administration to engineering; and a fair proportion of these requests bore fruit.[24]

Many Masonic recommendations placed their emphasis on political factors rather than professional merit. This was particularly true in the educational field.[25] And just as MPs, urging the case for a more congenial posting for their protégés, often pleaded the state of health of their client's wife, so a common argument put forward by the Masons was that they or their protégés were being harassed by their superiors, in the hope that they would resign. Thus a couple of persistent petitioners from Annecy claimed in December 1900 that, as *juges de paix*, they were being badgered by the Parquet of Chambéry, which was dominated by clerical and anti-Masonic elements.[26] A recurring theme in Vadecard's

letters is the fear that Masonic membership was depriving worthy
fonctionnaires of their just reward – typified by his concern that a
fonctionnaire with thirty-eight years' service might be denied a decoration
because his personal dossier contained a note describing him as
'personnage important de la Franc-Maçonnerie'.[27] It is hard to know
how genuinely felt were these fears – or whether they were merely a lever
or form of blackmail to obtain support from politicians who either had
Masonic sympathies or recognised that it would be embarrassing if
claims of anti-Masonic discrimination were to be made. The political
card was played no less energetically in overseas France. Even in the
West Indies – relatively remote from the political wrangles of metro-
politan France – Vadecard's candidate for *receveur municipal officiel*
at Saint Pierre was put forward first and foremost as 'a militant
republican'.[28]

Yet despite these heady days of Masonic ascendancy in government
circles, the Grand Orient was prudent in the phraseology of its requests
for posts. While Vadecard had no hesitation in addressing a minister who
was a Mason as 'Brother', and would draw specific attention to the
Masonic credentials of the candidate, more caution was shown in
approaching civil servants. This is particularly evident in the letters of
Masonic MPs.[29] Nor were these intermediaries prepared to risk their
credit supporting feeble or unsavoury applicants. As one of them replied
to Vadecard – when asked to solicit the decoration of Officier du Mérite
agricole for a fellow Mason – 'The support of the Grand Orient counts
for a great deal with me, but I cannot invoke it with the *profanes* who hold
the key to the matter.'[30] Vadecard increasingly shared this concern, and
was well aware that there were limits to the credibility of the Grand
Orient. Not only did he complain about the lack of professional
information that politicians sent to him, but he was especially angry
when lodges put forward for support candidates who turned out to be
unsuitable or unworthy. He commented bitterly on one such proposal:
'He is, it appears, a good *fonctionnaire* from an administrative point of
view, that is to say that he conscientiously harasses his subordinates.
Always ready to sacrifice an unfortunate primary-school teacher, if this
cowardice can get him out of the least difficulty . . . That is the man
whom *our friends* have been happy to unload on us!'[31]

Masonic influence was wielded to obtain dispensations as well as
honours and advancement. Vadecard wrote to ex-premier and fellow-
Mason, Léon Bourgeois, to intervene with the Minister of Education on
behalf of a Masonic *instituteur* in Rouen, who wished to study for the
licence ès lettres but who had been refused a dispensation from the
baccalauréat.

And our friends from Rouen, heartbroken by this outcome, are saying to us, 'Can't you appeal to the excellent Masonic sentiments of Brother Bourgeois, a former minister, and get him to be so kind as to make a personal appeal to the Minister of Education himself. ' . . . You would thereby be helping *un brave père de famille*, entirely devoted to the Republic, who simply asks to work yet harder and make himself more and more useful to humanity.[32]

The counterpart to obtaining jobs for friends was evicting enemies. But getting rid of uncongenial officials was often a more difficult matter than provincial lodges imagined – as Vadecard was at pains to tell them. Responding to disgruntled Masons in St Amand in December 1900, he pointed out that many magistrates were irremovable by the nature of their appointment. 'To have any chance of success, you must always work in conjunction with the republican representatives of the constituencies in which the people concerned are based. It is more or less obligatory!' The Grand Orient would do what was possible, 'but, alas, it is far from able to do what it would like to do!'[33] A fortnight later he was explaining to another provincial lodge his failure to get rid of a 'reactionary magistrate' – the result of the 'ill will of certain clerical administrative bodies, still plentiful, alas!!!'[34] A tantalising example is the case of the Prefect of the Basses-Alpes, Alexandre Offroy-Durieu, who had been appointed in March 1895, during the moderate ministry of Alexandre Ribot. The Fraternité-Provençale lodge of St Auban wrote to the Grand Orient's Conseil de l'Ordre on 15 May 1901 asking for his removal in the forthcoming *mouvement*, since he was 'openly reactionary'. A week later, the Conseil de l'Ordre referred the matter to brother Mason and militant anticlerical, Gustave Hubbard, the newly elected independent Radical-Socialist deputy for the Basses-Alpes, victor of a recent bye-election.[35] Whatever the influence of a deputy whose electoral success was still news and whose formal adhesion to the Radical-Socialists was being eagerly solicited, the Prefect lost his job two months later and disappeared from the *corps préfectoral*. He was admittedly fifty-nine – well above the normal prefectoral age. Having successfully got rid of its prefect in 1901, the Fraternité-Provençale lodge of St Auban then proposed to do battle in the educational field in the following year. It insisted that the prime minister, Combes, should be warned that training colleges were being put into the hands of clericals and turned into 'véritables jésuitières'. Combes should be asked to see that his Minister of Education, Joseph Chaumié, be made aware of the danger of leaving at their posts the current *directeur de l'enseignement primaire* and the *chef du personnel*, 'who bar the way to any *fonctionnaire* once they know that he belongs to Freemasonry' – significantly amended to 'that he is a republican'.[36]

It would require teams of researchers to chart the success-rate of these Masonic interventions for appointments and dismissals – even supposing that the enquirers were granted access to the relevant personal dossiers. Since job-seekers vastly outnumbered places, only a small number of recommendations could be successful; and what counted most with the ministries was the political clout of the deputies and senators transmitting these requests, rather than their Masonic connections – even if the deputies and senators themselves were responsive to Masonic pressures, especially when local and press support at election time could be affected by their readiness to respond.

Dealing with governments, however, was only part of the activity of the Masonic network. It was also concerned with the world of private business and family life. March 1898 found the secretary making discreet enquiries among the Masons of Perpignan about the financial and family situation of a young man whom a girl from a Masonic family in Paris was thinking of marrying.[37] And job-finding in the world of private enterprise was also part of their function. Indeed the secretary was deeply lamenting in January 1898 that the Grand Orient did not possess some sort of Masonic Yellow Pages, in which Masons were listed by profession, thereby facilitating contact with the men who mattered. Surprisingly all they had was an unclassified alphabetical list of Masons – and nothing so sophisticated as the Collège Stanislas's lists which grouped old boys by region and profession as well as by seniority. The Grand Orient was therefore unable to help, for example, a Mason from Algiers, who was seeking a place as a *contre-maître mécanicien*, since it had no classified list of potential employers.[38]

The pervasiveness of Masonry in the domain of job-seeking led both its enemies and its friends to assume that it would be equally unstinting in the support of Masonic candidates in national and local elections. While this was true in terms of exercising whatever persuasive influence it could, it seems usually to have stopped short of directly supplying funds. For an organisation so deeply involved in politics, it might seem disingenuous for the Rue Cadet to inform local lodges that it was against its principles to provide money to help Masonic candidates – something on a par in duplicity with the government's formal instructions to prefects to remain politically neutral. Yet this appears to have been its policy in practice as well as in principle. Besides, as Vadecard somewhat disarmingly remarked in January 1900, the Grand Orient was rather short of money anyway.[39] As an organisation, the Masons were not particularly wealthy, even though a fair number of their individual members were; and politically and electorally matters in France were going sufficiently their way for it not to be necessary to give them a further push with financial help. Their current situation was very different from that of the Church, which felt that it was fighting for its life, and so was prepared to take risks (see pp. 57–8) and spend money that it would otherwise have sooner kept for more straightforward religious and charitable projects.

8   Marianne at school

For both Church and Republic, educating the young was the prime task; it determined what sort of society France would be. Given these high stakes, the Republic might predictably have insisted that its teachers at all levels should be committed to the vision of society that the Republic represented – even if that vision could be expressed only in terms of benign disenthralment: freedom of thought, freedom from obscurantism, freedom of the individual to make his or her own choices in life, etc. (Anything more prescriptive would immediately have run the risk of splitting the Republicans between those who believed in social equality and those who preferred to settle for equality of opportunity – to say nothing of creating war between the intermediate staging posts, all stoutly defended by their particular enthusiasts.) The creation of a sternly Republicanised teaching body might have seemed all the more likely and justified, given the sacrifice of effort and goodwill that had been given to ridding the country of such a sizeable sector of the rival Catholic school system. There would seem little point in wrecking the enemy's installations, while allowing its troops to infiltrate the home citadel. Yet recruitment of the State's educational forces involved much less political scrutiny than is commonly supposed.

As far as secondary teachers and university lecturers were concerned, archival records indicate an ambivalence of attitudes in the relevant sections of the Ministry of Education. It recognised the impossibility of ignoring political issues, yet there was more than a hint of fastidious distaste for having to take such matters into consideration. Reports on candidates for university teaching posts were usually accompanied by reports on their political and religious attitudes, but it is hard to tell how seriously these considerations were taken. Some of the reports were quite detailed and strongly worded; yet, somewhat like the technical ministries, higher and secondary education were areas where expertise and academic competence tended to be the prime concern in recruitment and advancement. This is exemplified in the dossiers of a professor of Greek literature in the Faculté des Lettres of Montpellier. When he emerged from the Ecole Normale Supérieure in August 1868 – long before the advent of the anticlerical Republic – his report described him as 'narrow-minded and somewhat false. A very sincere Catholic, he is nevertheless conscientious in his duties as a student of the school.'[1] Twenty-two years later – when the Radical Léon Bourgeois was Minister for Education – the ministry's Directeur de l'Enseignement Supérieur was writing of the professor, with equivocal delicacy, 'Deservedly respected, particularly in the aristocratic circles which he has always favoured.' The report was nevertheless a favourable one, recommending his being made a Chevalier de la Légion d'Honneur as soon as possible.[2] And, for what it may signify, nine university professors were appointed from among the ranks of the old boys of the Collège Stanislas during the years 1880–1900, with another thirteen in the following decade, while the Jesuit Caousou school of Toulouse provided the town university with a professor of law in the same period.[3]

Yet a sample of university teachers at the end of the nineteenth century showed under 8 per cent of them as products of private education.[4] To some extent, this reflected the academic excellence of the leading state *lycées*, especially those with preparatory classes for the Ecole Normale Supérieure. It may also have reflected the somewhat wider social catchment area of the universities, as compared with the *grands corps*. Although higher education involved financial outlay for families, the university ladder was less expensive than that of the *grandes écoles*; and the senior ranks of the academic world contained a larger minority of people from the lower-middle classes where *bien pensant* attitudes and private education were less widespread.[5] If Catholics were nevertheless a real if modest presence among university staff, they could become targets of punitive action if they raised their heads too high above the parapet – especially if their activities or utterances were open to political connotation. Several of these victims were well-known members of Action Française, and probably were singled out for retribution as much for their political polemics as for their defence of Catholic interests.[6]

It is perhaps surprising that a sample of secondary-school teachers' dossiers revealed virtually no official comment on their political or religious sympathies – far less than in the case of university teachers. It has to be remembered that, unlike primary-school teachers, they were dealing with a tiny, privileged percentage of the youth of France (see pp. 29–30); and once again academic ability was the main consideration, especially since the French system gave opportunities for the best of them to move into university teaching. Indeed the Catholic Collège Stanislas had twenty of its old boys appointed to the teaching staff of state *lycées* between 1880 and 1900 – and a further six by 1909 – though, as one would expect, there were nearly five times as many in the private sector.[7] And the Jesuit Caousou school of Toulouse produced at least one state *lycée* teacher in these years.[8] The size of the Catholic presence was indicated by the fact that when a teacher at the *lycée* of Coutances, Joseph Lotte, established an association of Catholic secondary-school teachers in 1910, it acquired 545 members within a few years.[9]

A very informative study of women secondary-school teachers in the 1880–1914 period – conducted before the imposition of the 1979 law – concludes, 'Jews apart, it would be difficult to cite any dossier of a state teacher who was genuinely harmed in her career as a result of her religious convictions.'[10] The author consulted over 2,500 dossiers, mainly concerning teachers who embarked on state employment before 1900; and 86.7 per cent of them make no mention of the teacher's religion.[11] The survey, of course, was confined to those who succeeded in entering the profession; and those dossiers consulted suggest that well-disposed reports and letters of recommendation made mention of religion only if it was in the teacher's interest to do so. Thus although Protestants made up only 6 to 10 per cent of women secondary-school teachers, the bulk of dossiers that mentioned religion concerned Protestants. The phrase, 'fervent Protestant', was intended and seen as a recommendation, whereas 'fervent Catholic' was avoided as a potential liability to the success of the candidate. Protestants seem to have been disproportionately successful in becoming headmistresses, perhaps because they were widely seen as combining high moral commitment with an absence of clerical associations – but also perhaps as a result of the strong Protestant presence in the administration and among the theorists of the state secondary-school department.[12] Jews, on the other hand, were regarded with some misgiving, especially for headships, where fear of parental reaction was given as a reason for preferring other candidates.[13]

But if political and religious issues were remarkable for their relative absence in the official reports on secondary-school teachers of both sexes, this was not the case in the various letters that were written on their behalf by deputies and senators who were supporting their requests for transfers or promotion to teacher-training colleges, especially to college headships. It might be argued that politicians did not know any better, and that was the way their minds worked. But in the light of Waldeck-Rousseau's remark, cited earlier (see p. 90), that the secondary-school teacher was also a civil servant who required surveillance, they may have been closer to government thinking than their high-minded critics realised. Characteristically when a Radical deputy of the Jura wrote to the Minister of Education in September 1898, supporting the candidature of a protégé for the directorship of a training college, he prefaced his encomium with the information, 'Monsieur Dunac is the son-in-law of the Mayor of Montbourg, one of the strongest supporters of Monsieur Bourgeois in his constituency' – Bourgeois being the writer's fellow deputy in the Jura.[14] Politicians' letters were as necessary to deflect thunderbolts as to secure appointments – though ministers knew how to respond to these, if the defendant's case was weak. Thus when a senator of the Ardennes complained to the Minister of Education about the transfer of a secondary-school teacher to another school, the Minister drily replied 'His classes were veritable fairgrounds, where the pupils took to unbuttoning the waistcoat of their teacher and unknotting his tie, without his daring to demur; and in some cases they set about playing cards, forcing Monsieur Dhaleine to join in their game.'[15]

Overt sympathy for subversive political groups could bring retribution. August 1889 had seen the dismissal of a number of secondary teachers who had sent letters or tokens of sympathy to General Boulanger; and more recently Louis Dimier of Action Française was sacked from the teaching staff of the Collège de Valenciennes in 1904, for having defended the schools of the religious orders.[16] In his case there could be no doubt as to his anti-Republican commitment – which was equally true of two other Action Française luminaries, Henri Vaugeois and Pierre Lasserre, likewise removed from their *lycée* appointments. Nor should it be forgotten that these punishments of Right-wing teachers had their counterpart on the Left, where notable critics of compulsory military service lost their posts.

Despite the anticlerical vigilance of the pre-war period, there ran parallel with it a fair measure of tolerance within the secondary schools themselves. This reflected on the one hand the liberal intellectual tradition of the Université, and the tendency for friendships and mutual respect for professional competence to transcend political differences among colleagues. But it also arose from a realistic awareness that the private sector of secondary education remained a powerful and attractive alternative in the eyes of many middle-class families, despite the campaigns of Combism. Indeed the growing role of laymen in post-Combes Catholic schools tended to lessen the gulf between their style and ambience and those of the public sector.

Grass roots

The village primary-school teacher was commonly regarded as the missionary of the secular Republic in hazardous country. In very small communities where the school consisted of a single classroom, in which the *instituteur* taught all the village children single-handed, the teacher tended on balance to be a man – women usually finding themselves in schools where there were two or more staff, or in charge of the girls' classes when the size of the community permitted separation of the sexes. As the accredited *instruit* of the village, he was also commonly called upon to be the mayor's secretary – a role which required on his part at least a reticent neutrality towards the politics and policies of the mayor and, in the eyes of some mayors, a degree of enthusiastic commitment as well. The political sympathies of the *instituteur* were therefore a matter of interest to the village, whatever its attitude and that of its mayor towards the current government in Paris.

His mandate – and that of the *institutrice* – was not only to dispel ignorance and instil socially useful attitudes, but also to emancipate young minds from the constricting influence of clericalism – at least insofar as it damaged open attitudes and dictated political choices. In the early 1880s religious instruction had been replaced in state primary schools by moral and civic education, based on what Jules Ferry liked to call 'the good old morality of our fathers', without seeking to dissect what its historical and conceptual foundations might be. Initially it had included 'duties towards God', but these were increasingly dropped – in some regions more slowly than in others – and the principle grew that there was to be neither talk of God nor denial of the existence of God, teachers being theoretically expected to observe neutrality in such matters. Even so, in many schools in Brittany and the Massif Central, where Catholicism was strong, moral and civic education continued to be broadly Catholic in character – and often made specific use of the Catholic catechism, depending on the teacher. Prefectures and *académies* tolerated this situation, since they were all too conscious that in these regions the state was competing with the strongly entrenched Catholic private schools; if they insisted too rigidly on the letter of government policy, the public sector would fail to win over the Catholic clientele of the private schools, despite the fact that public primary education had been declared free in 1881.

Moreover just as there existed geographical disparities in secular rigour, so there were important age-group differences in teachers' commitment to neutrality. Any teacher who entered the profession before the *campagne laïque* of the early 'eighties would have escaped the new-style secular training that was introduced into the departmental teachers' training colleges. It was unrealistic to assume that older teachers would, or could, change their methods and attitudes overnight as a result of new directives – especially in one-teacher schools where the only witnesses of what went on were the children, who were even less responsive to state directives than the teachers themselves. Some anti-clerical parents might complain at what they heard their children relate at home. But since the bulk of French children, even in areas of low observance, made their *communion solennelle* at the age of twelve or there-abouts, few parents would go to great lengths to ensure that a secure boundary-fence was maintained between what their children heard from the *instituteur* in school hours and what they heard in the *curé*'s pre-communion catechism classes. Only the annual visit of the *inspecteur* acted as a check on the *instituteur*'s freedom of speech – and the many *inspecteurs* who were themselves of a similar vintage well understood the problems of teaching old dogs new tricks, especially in localities where the old tricks were preferred by parents. Departmental studies suggest that in many regions secularisation did not fundamentally change the teaching profession until the turn of the century – the point at which the products of the Republicanised training colleges were just beginning to outnumber the older generation.[17] The transformation came even later in the case of women teachers. Given the tardy development in France of public education for girls, it was not until the 1890s that there was a significant body of *institutrices* trained by the Republican *écoles normales*. Until then the bulk of those women primary teachers in the public sector who had received any formal teacher training had done so at the hands of the Dames du Bon Sauveur – and many of these still had decades of service before them.[18]

The cat-and-dog relationship between parish priest and *instituteur* became an established feature of village life only in the early years of the twentieth century – and in a very uneven fashion, depending on the locality and the personalities of the individuals themselves. This hostility became a cliché of popular fiction – and it was further fanned by the polemical journalism of the time. The Catholic *Courrier de Vitré* in 1904 offered this amiable description:

a man whom we ought to brand and nail to the pillory, this man is the damned soul, the evil spirit of the countryside. Look at his low, receding forehead; one would think him laden with all the curses of the world. Pathetic man, bad citizen, sweating hate and deep envy from every pore, skilled at destroying but not at creating. This man is the *instituteur* . . . Good people, shun him like the plague.[19]

In many small communities, however, there was often a secret and some-times open sympathy between the teacher and the priest – the only two educated men in a rather desolate world. This was sadly exemplified by the remarks made by a *curé* to an incoming *instituteur* in the Tarn-et-Garonne, who had paid him a visit.

Castelmayran has two ferociously hostile clans, the republicans and the clericals: they keep their distance and are committed to an eternal mutual hatred. The one frequents the Café Bayrou, the other the Café Bouché: the youth of the Left meets in a dance-hall which only they use; the young Right also has its own. In the same way each clan has its own grocer and butcher . . . Everyone here is classified, labelled . . .

We, the *instituteur* and the *curé*, are seen as implacable enemies. You certainly have all my sympathy, but in our own interests we cannot meet again. If you were seen entering the presbytery, I should lose the respect of my parishioners; they would try to get the bishop to move me elsewhere. As for you, the republicans would hate you and create difficulties for you until you too had to leave, whether you wanted to or not.[20]

Matters worsened after the Separation of Church and State in that, freed from the sanctions of the Concordat, bishops and parish priests became more forthright in their denunciation of the public sector of education. A number of text-books used in municipal schools were condemned by the Church, notably history books; and the so-called *guerre des manuels* in 1909–10 found priests in many localities encouraging children and parents to refuse to use them. More seriously, a number of priests were warning parents that by sending their children to the public sector they were endangering their souls. In areas where there was a large and militant practising Catholic population, teachers who were regarded as enthusiastic executants of the government's secularising policies could find themselves the victims of violence – windows broken, washing stolen or trampled in the mud, and their lives made a misery.

Even so, the stereotype presented by fiction and polemical literature needs softening. A questionnaire distributed in the 1960s among primary-school teachers who had entered the profession before the First World War revealed some interesting if incomplete indications of their political and religious sympathies.[21] Inevitably their accuracy was coloured to some extent by hindsight; and, in the case of women who did not have the vote before 1945, their memories of their pre-war political beliefs tended sometimes to be coloured by the political views they subsequently held when they were eventually enfranchised. Among the men, a fifth of their fathers were peasants, a fifth were shopkeepers, while a further fifth were teachers. As compared with the men, a slightly larger proportion of women teachers came from lower-middle class as distinct from peasant or artisanal backgrounds. Of the men questioned, 37 per cent claimed to have had Socialist sympathies before the First World War, and 20 per cent Radical – with 27 per cent not replying to the

question. Only 35 per cent of the women questioned regarded themselves as having had strong political views in that period, although a
surprising two-thirds of these described their views at the time as
Socialist.

The replies to the questions on religion were predictably the most
ambiguous. Thirty-five per cent of men and 56 per cent of women
classified themselves as Catholic (in many cases merely by baptism or
early upbringing), 4 per cent of both sexes were nominally Protestant,
while 41 per cent of men and 24 per cent of women claimed to be free-
thinkers. But when it came to religious practice, only about 10 per cent
of the two sexes combined claimed to have been practising in the
pre-1914 period, with 32 per cent not practising, and a tantalising 57 per
cent not replying to the question. Presumably the percentage of men who
were practising would have been even lower than the 10 per cent of the
sexes combined. Apart from the patchiness of the information, it
inevitably raises many questions. One wonders to what degree the low
level of religious practice reflected personal inclination, and to what
extent it reflected fear, justified or unjustified, that church-going might
prejudice professional advancement.

Given the role of village teachers, as perceived by the Republic and its
enemies, one might have expected a strong degree of political vetting in
their selection. The means lay easily to hand in that until November
1944, primary-school teachers were technically appointed by the prefect
of the department, rather than the *recteur* of the Académie – even if the
opinion of the *inspecteurs d'académie* was the prime factor in prefectoral
choices. But routine comment on candidates' political and religious
sympathies was limited by the fact that the whole structure of primary
education was departmentally based, with *instituteurs* and *institutrices*
largely recruited and trained within the confines of the department where
most of them were destined to spend the rest of their careers. In these
conditions prefects' political reports would largely have been for auto-
consumption, destined to impress no one other than subordinates and
later prefects. It would serve little purpose to devote time and energy to
their completion, especially since the political sympathies of young
training-college products were unlikely to have made much impact on
the milieu where the prefectures took soundings in compiling their
reports.

But the departmental *écoles primaires supérieures, écoles pratiques* and
écoles normales were another matter. Although appointments to these
more prestigious institutions were still made at departmental rather than
national level, they did give rise to prefects' reports, especially if they
involved giving opportunities for the felicitous phrases and psychological

insights of one prefect to be known and admired by his peers and senior colleagues. More seriously, these were appointments requiring experience and proven ability, and candidates were of an age for their political inclinations, if any, to be known in the locality. Thus, when a teacher in the department of Finistère sought a transfer to the Ecole Pratique de Narbonne (Aude), the prefect of Finistère was asked by pro-forma letter for 'confidential information on [his] conduct, past record, personal financial means, family and political attitudes and opinions' – but with no specific question on his religious opinions.[22] These questions were usually answered with a fair degree of attentiveness – not with the one-line blanket formulas that became the norm after the First World War.

In the case of ordinary primary-school teachers, however, political vetting started to become serious only when they were seeking promotion or transfer to more congenial localities – or when their behaviour or reputation in their current post made a rapid transfer desirable. Teachers by that time had some sort of track-record which could be evaluated by the local *académie* and prefecture. With first-time appointments, however, the pro-forma 'Renseignements sur l'Elève-Maître' which training colleges issued on their products was largely restricted to matters of academic ability and health, their ranking in the year and the future posts they preferred. Only under 'Avis du Directeur de l'Ecole Normale' was there any scope for political comment – and none was given in the samples of dossiers examined.[23] Similarly the pro-forma reports on primary teachers completing their probationary periods contained nothing specific on political matters;[24] nor did the regular inspectors' reports on tenured teachers. These were confined to academic issues – and, in any case, they had to be countersigned by the teachers themselves, thereby discouraging any comment that an inspector was not prepared to sustain in face of appeal.[25]

In the case of teachers with overall responsibility for a school, the pro-forma for the inspector's annual report often contained the question, 'Relations with families and the authorities', which could acquire a political connotation in the case of actively militant individuals; but it otherwise merely sought an assurance that the teacher could be on reasonably good terms with parents and outside bodies.[26] Teacher–parent relationships were certainly a matter of particular concern to a regime which saw itself as having a civilising mission in the country at large; and the authorities felt disappointment and distress when learning of setbacks in this domain. Such a case was the confrontation between an *instituteur* and a mother, following his eviction of her son from class with the comment 'Get out, you stink!' The teacher, whose name was

Adreani, terminated the interview by shouting at the mother, 'Get out, you stink as much as your son!' – to which she replied with mounting degrees of insult, 'Filthy Corsican! Filthy Italian!!!'[27] This was not what Jules Ferry had envisaged in designing the fabric of the new Jerusalem.

While politico-religious issues scarcely featured at all in the routine reports of the great majority of teachers, this was not the case with supporting letters from politicians, which, as with other sectors of public employment, displayed no compunction in appealing to personal as well as political factors: 'I am an old friend of her family and am always interested in her future', etc.[28] In the same way teachers in trouble would seek support by stressing their Republican credentials. An *instituteur* put on indefinite unpaid leave for alleged sexual abuse of his charges wrote to Ferdinand Buisson, archangel of Republican *laïcité* and President of the Ligue Française de l'Enseignement, recounting his activities in local elections on behalf of the Comité de Concentration Républicaine and emphasising his commitment to *l'enseignement laïque*.[29] He claimed that he was the victim of political factions, punishing him for his recent entry 'dans la Grande Famille Maçonnique'; but Buisson merely passed on the letter to the local prefecture and Direction de l'Enseignement, commenting, 'I do not know the petitioner.'

While pro-government sentiments were an advantage to an upwardly aspirant *instituteur*, the authorities were aware that if they were too loudly displayed they could narrow the esteem in which he was held by the local population and reduce his effectiveness as a representative of the Republic. For similar reasons, some senior officials were uneasy about *instituteurs* standing as candidates in local or national elections, and pointed out that by allowing pro-government candidatures, it became logically difficult to refuse others.[30] Governments remained in several minds on this issue; and the teaching profession, at all levels, continued to be well represented at the hustings – albeit on the side of Republican concentration.

What officialdom tolerated in a teacher varied from region to region. In areas of high religious observance, with an attractive counterforce of private Catholic schools, prefectures and *académies* would close their eyes to what would have entailed disciplinary action elsewhere. An interesting mixture of terrain was provided by the department of the Tarn in the diocese of Albi. In the western, arable half, religious observance was confined to about a third of the adult male population in 1900, with a majority of the electorate voting for Radical and other Left-wing candidates. In the more pastoral east of the department, half to three-quarters of men went to Easter Communion, and only a minority supported the Left. In the department as a whole, teachers were out-numbered by parish priests; and religious observance continued to be widespread among *instituteurs* until the opening years of the twentieth century.[31] In the early 1890s there were still *instituteurs* who were teaching the Catholic catechism in class and taking their charges to Mass on Sundays and feastdays – for which they earned a small public indemnity for the incursion into their free time.[32] The authorities tolerated the situation as preferable to a rise in the enrolment at the local Catholic school. Indeed in some cases the appearance of a new private school would result in the resumption of catechism teaching in its public counterpart – as happened in Lesgraisses in 1895. But little of this survived the Combes era. By 1914 scarcely any of the training-college male students from the Tarn were Mass-goers – and this was also true of several neighbouring departments. On the other hand religious practice remained high among *institutrices* in the Tarn. As one of them said: 'training college does not destroy your faith; those who go there as believers, stay that way'. In any case even non-practising villages tended to regard a church-going *institutrice* as a good influence.[33]

Political and religious friction involving primary-school teachers was largely a grass-roots matter that came to the notice of the prefecture or the *académie* only in the event of a formal complaint or appeal. In the Tarn as elsewhere, the dominant concern of most senior administrative staff was to minimise fuss and discontent, and to ensure a quiet life. While this encouraged on the one hand a lenient and understanding attitude towards the teacher and a reluctance to resort to disciplinary sanctions, it nevertheless sometimes resulted in pacifying tactics that could be more damaging to the teacher in the long run. Patently unjust accusations against a teacher might still lead to his transfer to another school if local tranquillity was at stake – or prevent his appointment to a post that he coveted. A typical case was that of Georges Becq, an *instituteur* who wished to be appointed as *adjoint* in Gaillac, where his parents lived. The *inspecteur primaire*, reporting the matter to the Inspecteur d'Académie d'Albi, described him as apparently 'intelligent', 'hard-working and dedicated', and his parents as 'very honourable people' – 'but – for there is a serious "but" – his father is a sacristan at the church of St Michel in Gaillac. For this reason alone the mayor has told me that Monsieur Becq's appointment to Gaillac would be very badly received, and he gave me to understand, though not officially, that he would oppose the appointment with all his strength.' And the inspector sadly concluded that 'it would not be wise to propose Monsieur Becq for the post at Gaillac . . . Unfortunately his position there would be a very delicate one on account of his family, which, rightly or wrongly, is regarded as reactionary.'[34] In many ways the situation was on a par with the policy adopted in cases of domestic scandal where the *instituteur* was the innocent party. The *instituteur* of Loupiac had found his wife – 'une véritable Messaline' – in bed with a young man, and the matter had become common knowledge in the village. Although the intruder was currently away on military service, the inspector advised the *instituteur* to apply for a transfer before the youth returned to the locality. In fact the *instituteur* decided to stand his ground, which he did until his eventual retirement twenty-one years later. He was widely regarded as an able teacher; and although a personal enemy accused him of absenting himself from class and playing cards with the *curé*, the inspector reported that the sessions took place only outside school hours on Thursdays and Sundays.[35]

It was inevitably difficult to disentangle genuine politico-religious friction from personal animosities and clashes of individual interests – especially when the school and the teacher's living accommodation were part of the same ensemble as the *mairie*. In these cases the activities of the *instituteur*'s wife (who, after the turn of the century, was often herself an *institutrice*) could be an additional source of trouble. The drama of Marsal exemplifies the point. The municipal elections of 1892 had resulted in Marsal acquiring a more conservative administration, which refused to keep on as mayor's secretary the same *instituteur* whose political sympathies reflected those of his illustrious namesake, Louis Blanc. Mounting tension was brought to the prefect's notice when the mayor angrily reported to him that as he was leaving the *mairie* one evening, 'the contents of *un grand vase d'eaux sales et d'ordures* was forcefully thrown in my direction and spread out at my feet'. As proof of the malevolent intent behind this summary disposal of domestic effluent, 'the spot where the contents fell is a distance of approximately five metres from the perpendicular line of the window'. And the mayor, with enviable presence of mind and legal percipience, immediately summoned two passing villagers to testify to the mathematical accuracy of his survey – each duly designated as 'sieur' and 'dame' in the separately signed testimony that he sent to the prefect.[36] The *instituteur*, defending his wife's action, claimed that the contents of the pot were less offensive than the mayor implied; but the *inspecteur primaire* eventually felt obliged to recommend to the Inspecteur d'Académie that Louis Blanc be moved to a post where he had fewer political enemies. In another commune of the region, the mayor accused the *instituteur* of refusing to unlock the school paddock on the eve of market-day to allow the overnight pasturage of pigs prior to sale. Later complaints from the mayor claimed that the *instituteur* had shown no such inhibition about affording parallel hospitality to a young woman who had clearly spent the night in his apartment.[37]

Given the assumptions of the democratic process, mayors were commonly supposed by higher authority to represent the prevailing political opinion of the locality – with the result that their word was often preferred to that of the *instituteur*. Not that this was always so. Like the *procureur général* in cases involving accusations against magistrates, the *inspecteur primaire* often found himself in the role of defending counsel when the prefect reported alleged misdemeanours by *instituteurs*. When in 1901 the prefect reported that the *instituteur* of Camalières was said to have favoured the conservative candidate in a recent election, the *inspecteur primaire* personally interviewed his accusers and ascertained that he had apparently done no more than vote for the conservative – which, as the *inspecteur* told his superiors, was not a sufficient reason for transferring him.[38] Likewise, during the high tide of Combisme, the *inspecteur primaire* dismissed claims that the *instituteur* of Lacaze had supported the clericals in the last election, and insisted that it was in the public interest to keep him in his post. In such cases the *inspecteur* was anxious to keep a clear distinction between breach of government regulations, on the one hand, and lack of personal enthusiasm for the government parties on the other.[39] A typical example occurred in St Salvi de la Balme, where the *instituteur* was accused of 'a deplorable and clearly hostile attitude to the republican candidate' during the 1902 election and of having distributed copies of the *Conservateur*, 'journal réactionnaire de Mazanet'. The *inspecteur primaire* discounted the claims, when the accusers failed to turn up at the appointed time for questioning; and it also transpired that it was the teacher's son, not the teacher himself, who was hawking the paper. On the other hand the *inspecteur* was inclined to take much more seriously the teacher's own admission that he had continued to conduct formal prayers in school, despite recent legislation forbidding this in state secular schools. Indeed his accusers had discerned a sly political manoeuvre in his choosing the week immediately before the elections to terminate the practice, saying: 'My poor children, I have the profound sorrow of no longer being able to ask you to pray . . . by order of my superiors.' Even so, the *inspecteur* was disposed to limit retribution to a reprimand; but he nevertheless thought the teacher should be offered a transfer to another comparable post when one became vacant – a compromise which the teacher was prepared to accept.[40]

Despite the apparent desire of many *inspecteurs primaires* to ensure that justice was not sacrificed to the cause of peace in these village feuds, this concern was perhaps more evident in quarrels between pro-government *instituteur*s and local 'reactionary' forces, than in reverse. Thus in 1904 an investigating *inspecteur primaire* described as 'unlikely' accusations that the *instituteur* of Villelongue 'is living with a concubine, and has made his classroom a place of debauchery'. The *instituteur* dismissed his accusers as political friends of Baron Reille, a prominent spokesman of Catholic interests (see p. 19); but he admitted that at a noisy dinner at his home a friend of his 'between the dessert and the cheese . . . had the unhappy idea of singing "Down with the clericals!"' while another guest sang 'the Song of Progress, which lays bare the moral and intellectual turpitude of the clergy'. Passers-by reported the matter to the *curé*, who proceeded to organise a petition against him. The *instituteur* also had a long history of unpaid tradesmen's bills, many of them wine merchants'. But he was a good teacher, and the *inspecteur* wrote with sympathy of his attempts to deal with his debts.[41] At the end of the day, the *inspecteur* merely suggested that in view of his health he should perhaps be offered a post in a less bleak locality – but in fact ill-health caused him to resign before such an opportunity occurred.

The department of the Charente Inférieure presented a more compli-cated politico-religious pattern than the Tarn. An area of relatively low religious observance in the population at large, it nevertheless contained significant pockets of Protestantism. More recently the fact that Emile Combes was a loyal and grateful son of the department inclined the local authorities to show themselves equally loyal to their illustrious benefactor during his ministry. Yet, in fairness, their attempts to resolve the conflicts of mayor, priest and teacher were genuinely marked by equity and common sense. Public primary teachers who displayed their Catholicism too militantly might be moved to other villages where it might cause fewer problems. Thus the *institutrice* of Chailevette whose 'somewhat intemperate religious zeal' was offending Protestant parents and causing tension with the municipality was required in 1892 to move to St Léger where she was less likely to provoke animosities.[42] Conversely the Mayor of La Rochelle expressed misgivings to the prefect in August 1899 about appointing a forthright Republican as *directrice* to the Valin primary school, for fear that *bien pensant* parents might seek to set up a private Catholic school in the locality.[43] Officialdom's desire for a quiet life involved curbs on Protestants, as well as on Catholics and anti-clericals. A Protestant *institutrice* at Doeuil was attacked in 1892 in two municipal petitions, complaining in unspecific fashion about her teaching. She retaliated by complaining to the prefect, claiming that the petitioners included Bonapartists and people of dubious morality. As for herself, 'I recognise myself as being guilty of nothing, except of not going to Mass.' A month later she was threatening to take legal action against her accusers, guilty of 'village gossip deformed by clerical malevolence'.[44] But already the Inspecteur d'Académie was proposing to move her to another school where most of the children would be Protestant.

Petitions against teachers often masked politico-religious motives with complaints about their teaching, morals or social shortcomings. Some, however, were specifically political in their accusations. In Lozay thirty villagers wrote to the prefect in 1900 that the newly appointed *instituteur* had a reputation for trying to build electoral coalitions around Rallié candidates; such a strategy, imported into Lozay politics, would break the Republican front and let in the enemy. The *inspecteur primaire* thereupon paid the *instituteur* a personal visit, urging on him 'the greatest tact' and 'an impeccably correct republican attitude'. In answer to the *inspecteur*'s questions, he admitted that in his previous post 'he sometimes went to Mass, and that he had sung with the rest of the congregation'. But he strongly denied that his daughter had regularly played the harmonium at the church – it had happened only once and, in any case, her inability to sing would guarantee that there would be no further prejudice to her father's academic career.[45] Petitions, however, cut in various directions, and the Church occasionally found support in unexpected quarters for purely secular reasons. In 1892, 208 inhabitants of Portes on the Ile de Ré petitioned the prefect in favour of appointing a nun with medical skills to the local public primary school, since the nearest doctor was eight kilometres away. But, despite the support of the local republican council, the Inspecteur d'Académie replied that the law of 30 October 1886 left him no alternative but to appoint a laywoman.[46]

Most village-school conflicts were settled by *inspecteurs* and prefectures. Those where the teacher was accused of professional misconduct, rather than imprudence or political partiality, were a matter for the Ministry of Education. Hitting children, idleness, drunkenness, insubordination or running up debts were the commonest offences treated in this fashion. But politico-religious issues also featured widely. March 1902 found three *instituteurs* in the Ardennes alone reprimanded for allowing school premises to be used for political meetings, while a week later an *institutrice* in the Ardèche lost her job for participating in 'a political demonstration against the republican candidate' – although there were also admittedly additional charges of a professional nature.[47] The highly charged atmosphere of the hustings led to an *instituteur* in the Indre being censured for 'making a pupil sing in class a song that was hurtful to certain personages of the locality – and immoral in some of its words'.[48]

More seriously an *instituteur adjoint* in Algiers was censured, 'with specific mention in the bulletin', for 'encouraging his pupils to shout "Down with the Jews!" during a conducted walk. He then compounded his misdeed by thumping a boy who had shouted "Long live the Jews!"'[49]

Whatever else these grass-roots episodes exemplify, they bear witness to a thriving popular culture of political and anticlerical songs – some locally composed at the expense of regional worthies, and others addressing a wider clientele, distributed by Paris publishers. Combes's papers contain a selection of those sent to him by their proud authors.[50] Bouchard's and Nicolay's *Le Bloc: hommage à Monsieur Emile Combes* is perhaps more remarkable for the publisher's list of 'monologues et chansonnettes grivoises' printed on the back; these included 'Un drôle de couvent', 'Madame Putiphar', 'Les Pilules Groscolard (grand succès)' [shades of Félix Faure?], 'La Préfecture d'amour'. Indeed some of the national classics of later decades had their roots in these more modest pre-radio days – 'Madame la Marquise' owing more than a little to the same publisher's 'A part ça, ça s'est bien passé.'

If, for the youth of France, teachers were the face of education, so were the cleaners and caretakers. For each school cleaner there was a personal file at the departmental Direction de l'Enseignement Primaire, listing his or her 'Exactitude et régularité dans le service', 'Zèle et activité', 'Tenue', and 'Observations particulières et propositions', but with no specific sections on their political or religious opinions.[51] The same was true of school caretakers, with additional concern for their 'Instruction', 'Moralité' and 'Constitution physique'.[52] Consciously or otherwise, the Republic perhaps recognised that the school caretaker could be as formative an influence on children in the lunch-break as any teacher in class. When not clearing smokers out of the coke-hold or recovering balls from the roof, he was often an informative raconteur, regaling children with stories of his war-service or gossip about local dignitaries – 'Oh, celui-là! Ce que je pourrais vous dire à son sujet!' An elderly man in the 1920s could still recount what the school caretaker had told him sixty years earlier under the Second Empire. The caretaker had served as a youth in Napoleon's Grande Armée, and he would electrify his young audience with memories of his one brief encounter with the Emperor – 'He was small; he was dark; and when he looked you in the eye, it made you shit your breeches!'[53]

Part 3

As it became, 1914–1994

9   *La grande illusion?* 1914–1939

With the inter-war years, the concerns of this book enter a world of closed sources that limit investigation to the well-worn path of printed material. The availability of the Vatican archives ceases with the death of Benedict XV in 1922, while the 120-year rule governing the personal dossiers of French civil servants is even more difficult to circumvent for this period than it is for the pre-war years. Such material that has slipped the net is largely the fortuitous outcome of broad-band cataloguing – usually in sectors where the modest number of personal dossiers has resulted in a wide age-group being stored in the same boxes – or occasional misplacement. In both cases it is too sparse to be usefully illustrative, let alone a reliable reflection of how things were. Nor is there a compensating improvement in other sources. Old boys' records in private schools had yet to acquire the systematic thoroughness of the fund-raising revolution of recent times; and those retired *fonctionnaires* who still survive to relate their experiences were mostly entering their careers in the mid-1930s or later.

Such evidence as there is, however, suggests that matters had not greatly changed since the pre-war decades of the Third Republic. There was admittedly no recrudescence of Combism; and even the Herriot government's brief anticlerical offensive in the mid-1920s was largely a counterattack against what it perceived as the creeping subversion of the Republic's achievements in secularising France. Yet there was still a wariness about entrusting ministerial portfolios to committed Catholics or appointing them to the *corps préfectoral*. The few that achieved ministerial office were largely restricted to the more technical portfolios or to the open ground of national defence, where the trust of the armed services in the professional competence of their political masters was as necessary to a war or navy minister as the trust of his cabinet colleagues. It needed the ambivalent developments of the 1940s to challenge this situation – and even then the changes were uneven. The transformation of the Vichy years – more apparent than real in some sectors – was followed by the recriminations of the Liberation, with mixed but limited impact on the composition of the civil service. Even so the enfranchise-ment of women in 1944, the inclusion of Catholic ministers in most ministries of the Fourth Republic, and the nationalisation of significant parts of the economy, all in variously direct and indirect ways lowered or removed the surviving hurdles that had affected Catholic penetration of the politicised sections of state employment in the past. De Gaulle's decade in power furthered the process – as did the fall in religious observance in the late 'sixties and the dispersal of Catholic political activity in different directions. All of this was to leave anticlericals bewildered as to whether there was any quarry worth hunting, and, if so, where it was to be found. Indeed in the 1960s and 'seventies, the historian enters a politico-religious landscape that has close affinity with the home ground of the present.

The Great War

Yet the First World War undoubtedly affected perceptions of the Church, just as it affected perceptions of class and national differences. This reappraisal of what united and what divided humanity found varied expression in the years that followed, not least in Jean Renoir's celebrated film, *La Grande Illusion* (1937). Even so, the film's ambiguity about where 'la grande illusion' really lay – in national or class differences, or in any notional distinctions between human beings – reflected deep uncertainty in society itself. And the same uncertainty coloured attitudes towards the reformulated relations between Church and Republic that followed the war.

The German challenge demanded a unified French response in which internal differences should be temporarily shelved. On the outbreak of war, the militantly anticlerical Minister of the Interior, Louis Malvy, suspended the programme of closing Catholic schools that were in breach of the Combist legislation against the religious orders. With Catholic priests serving in the trenches, anticlericalism seemed increas-ingly to be an irrelevance. Clergy, whose professional lives had largely consisted of ministering to Sunday gatherings of women, children and old men, suddenly found themselves in continual contact with men of their own age, sharing their mingled fear and boredom and mutually dependent on each other's loyalty and endurance. Well over a third of the clergy of France were mobilised; and in the first eighteen months of the war only 150 of these were serving as chaplains.[1] A further 395 voluntary chaplains were added to their number, as a result of an agree-ment which Albert de Mun arranged with the Viviani government in August 1914, while a number of the conscript clergy, serving with fighting or hospital units, supplemented their secular duties with pastoral functions. The other 25,000, however, were divided into two broad groups. The 13,000 who had been part of the established Church before the Separation of 1905 were allowed to serve as hospital staff, ambulance drivers, stretcher-bearers and the like. But priests and seminarists of a post-1905 vintage were treated no differently from other French citizens – even if individual commanding officers chose to temper the impartiality of the law by allocating some of them to functions where they were not directly called upon to take life. Admittedly the papal Holy Penitentiary had foreseen the moral dilemmas that conscripted clergy might face; and two years before the war it had temporarily lifted the prohibition on clergy taking up arms, if governments forced them to. Their numbers were supplemented by members of the regular orders of friars, brothers and monks who had never been covered by the provisions of Napoleon's Concordat; and they in turn were joined by considerable numbers of exiled regular clergy who came back to France to defend the nation in whatever way they could. Well over 15 per cent of the mobilised clergy were killed – a third of whom belonged to regular orders. At the same time some 12,000 nuns gave their services to military hospitals – with 300 killed in the battle areas. While the distinction between 'Mort pour la France' and 'Mort pour la République' was a difficult one to draw, many Frenchmen of all persuasions increasingly thought it pointless to try.

Running parallel to this camaraderie of the trenches was the Union Sacrée at governmental level.[2] Aristide Briand's ministry of October 1915 included the Catholic royalist, Denys Cochin, whose personal political preferences had always been subordinated to lessening tension between Church and government (see p. 39). His fellow ministers-without-portfolio included the arch-anticlerical Emile Combes, and the old war-horse of French Marxism, Jules Guesde, who happened to have as his chauffeur a conscripted priest from Bordeaux. Briand's reshuffle in December 1916 gave Cochin ministerial responsibility for the economic blockade, while his fellow Catholic at the Navy Ministry, Rear-Admiral Lucien Lacaze, was joined at the War Office by General Louis Lyautey, Catholic architect of French paternalism in Morocco (see p. 37). While Lyautey's appointment represented a triumph for Ste Geneviève, Lacaze was a product of the state system, despite having relatives at Ste Geneviève. This Catholic triumvirate did not last, however. Lyautey found it hard to temper his proconsular methods to suit the democratic ethos of government in Paris, and he departed after three months. Lacaze survived longer, until differences over naval strategy, compounded by the sniping of Left-wing deputies, precipitated his resignation from Ribot's cabinet in August 1917 – the month which also saw Cochin's departure after nearly two years in government.

Cochin's departure was more symptomatic of the problems that faced Catholics in government. He had not found Combes the most congenial of colleagues, *le petit père* muttering that facing death in the trenches did not entitle the religious orders to a better deal after the war. But after Combes departed in the course of Briand's reshuffle of December 1916, Cochin became increasingly aware of the evaporation of the good will that had characterised the initial months of the Union Sacrée – a union which in any case was a concentration of national effort against Germany, rather than an expression of mutual reconciliation. Central government was under pressure from the parliamentary Left to be far less indulgent towards what were seen as enthusiastic departures from official state neutrality in religious matters. Prefects were warned not to participate in religious ceremonies; and in February 1917 the formal distinction was abolished between Concordatory priests who had hitherto been allowed to restrict their war service to non-belligerent roles, and the rest of the enlisted clergy who served as fighting troops. In practice, the outcome was less drastic than was initially feared in that the clergy who now found themselves exchanging stretchers for rifles probably numbered 4,000 at most. Cochin nevertheless accused the Left of destroying the Union Sacrée.

Co-operation often worked better at a lower level, especially when it was directly geared to emergency welfare, where the encounter with appalling suffering shamed leaders into sinking their differences, if only temporarily. Symbolically the Comité de Secours National was under the joint patronage of the Archbishop of Paris, the Grand Rabbi, a Protestant pastor and the secretary of the CGT – with the Archbishop appropriately represented by Canon (now Mgr.) Odelin, who had helped unmask the *Affaire des fiches* ten years earlier (see pp. 45–52).

As frequently happens in times of personal crisis or national emergency, there was at first a sharp rise in religious observance. In some dioceses more people came to communion in August 1914 than had come in a whole year. The Battle of the Marne was presented by the Catholic press as a miracle; and in the German prisoner-of-war camps religious services provided French troops with a focus of solidarity that brought together men who had scarcely set foot in a church since they were children. Yet even fear becomes dulled with time; and by 1917 religious observance in France was no higher than it had been before the war.

If unaccustomed contact with the clergy in the combat of war softened many preconceptions among the rank and file, there was little affection engendered for the Vatican. Many French people, in and outside the Church, were glad enough to see the last of Pius X and Merry del Val, whose disastrous impact on French affairs was widely seen as a logical if indirect consequence of the Austrian intervention in the papal conclave of 1903 (see p. 58). But Benedict XV (1914–22) failed to fulfil the rather naïve expectations that his election had aroused among some of those who knew him as the Mgr. della Chiesa who had been a moderating voice of common sense in the Secretariat of State during the crisis years of Franco-Papal relations in 1904–6. It had seemed particularly propitious that Benedict replaced Merry del Val with the francophile Domenico Ferrata – and then with Pietro Gasparri, a kindred spirit in the Secretariat who shared with della Chiesa something of the benign pragmatism of Rampolla. Unfortunately the role of impartial, loving father of all Catholics in a time of war afforded Benedict little opportunity for compensating French Catholics for the rough deal that they had received from his saintly predecessor. Like most belligerents in the Great War, the French assumed that the iniquity of the other side was self-evident to all, except to the ignorant or prejudiced; and it came as a shock when the Pope in 1917 embarked on a campaign for a negotiated end to the war, with the postponement of contentious issues such as Alsace-Lorraine until peace enabled a calm and considered debate. Catholic liberal journals joined with the rest of the French press in declaring this unacceptable; and Catholic deputies, such as Denys Cochin, had an ungrateful task trying to defend the Vatican against charges of partiality – a doubly embarrassing role for Cochin since he had been engaged in prolonged unofficial negotiations with the Vatican in the vain hope of some mark of papal recognition of the justness of the Allied cause. But this was an impossible aspiration at a time when the Vatican was seeking wider recognition in the world as an independent source of wisdom and experience on moral issues. Many on the Allied side argued that Rome's ambitions would have been better served by publicly expressed papal sympathy for the side that to them seemed so clearly in the right. But Rome was not prepared to assume that this perception was widely shared elsewhere, and opted for a prudent silence on the rights and wrongs of the matter. As vicar of the Prince of Peace, the Pope's position had an undeniable logic, whatever disappointment it created among those who saw aggression being treated on an equal footing with legitimate self-defence. It was a perennial debate that was to re-emerge time and time again, notably in the Second World War, but also in more recent times in the Gulf War of the 1990s.

The Franco-papal rapprochement

Peace, however, was followed by the re-establishment in 1920 of formal diplomatic links between France and the Vatican.[3] This was not the result of the generous euphoria of victory or a warm-hearted impulse to let bygones be bygones. It sprang from the practical problems posed by the French regaining of Alsace-Lorraine. These provinces had been in German hands at the time of the French abolition of Napoleon's Concordat in 1905, with the result that the sees of Strasbourg and Metz were still subject to the old Concordatory methods of episcopal appointment, which required official contact between government and Pope. The clergy in the lost provinces had continued to enjoy their Concordatory state salaries, while the religious orders had been protected by the German frontier against the impact of the anticlerical laws of the 1880s and the Combes era. If anticlericals demanded that these scandalous anomalies be rectified, French governments, faced with the task of reintegrating into a secular France a heavily-practising Christian population, were inclined to move more cautiously. Prudence prevailed, and the state privileges of both Catholic and Lutheran communities were left intact. That this was so was substantially aided by the November elections of 1919, in which the voters favoured candidates associated with the national *élan* of the war years. Conversely those Socialists and anticlericals of other parties, who were popularly associated with the calls for a negotiated settlement with Germany in 1917–18, were accused of lack of patriotism and suffered accordingly at the polls. This brought into office a succession of ministers under moderates such as Millerand, Leygues and Briand, who were aware not only of the need to conciliate the *bien pensant* populations of the lost and found provinces, but also of the practical advantages of being on official speaking terms with the Vatican. Indeed a bonus came in that the continuation of Concordatory procedures for filling the sees of Strasbourg and Metz led the Vatican to make concessions in the method of appointing to the other French sees. Although Rome was still in principle free to appoint whom it liked, Cardinal Gasparri conceded in an *aide-mémoire* of May 1921 'that in the case of every episcopal nomination, the Holy See will consult with the French representative to discover whether the government has anything to say against the chosen candidate from a political point of view'.

Indeed Gasparri had as much reason as the French government to regret the absence of such an arrangement in the 1906–21 period. The post-Concordatory appointments and promotions of Pius X had created a much more intransigent body of bishops. An uncomfortable number of them were sympathetic to Action Française, for which a papal condemnation was pending; and given the general *esprit exalté* which pervaded them, it was not going to be easy convincing them of the need for compromise. For Gasparri, the well-being of the French Church depended on a *modus vivendi* with a modern capitalist Republic, not an idealised monarchy, based on a back-to-the-land ideology and a nostalgia for *le grand siècle*. It was true, of course, that many of the bishops who admired Maurras did so mainly for his anathemas against the government, rather than for his ideology, much of which was irreconcilable with Catholic teaching. But this did not lighten the load of the would-be architect of a lasting peace with France.

Yet in fairness to Pius X and Merry del Val, several of the bishops who were most warmly disposed towards Action Française were first appointed under the Concordat in the time of Leo XIII, when the government had the initiative in choosing candidates – even if their subsequent promotion was the work of Pius X's entourage and its advisers in the French seminary in Rome. Indeed the archives of the Secretariat of State reveal that Pius X's initial appointments in the post-Concordatory period made a serious effort to take account of French episcopal opinion in each of the archdioceses concerned.[4] It was essentially when differences arose between the Vatican and the French episcopate over the *associations cultuelles* (see pp. 60–7) that Merry del Val became convinced of the unreliability of many of the bishops and decided to abandon the current system of episcopal consultation in favour of a method that was little more than a token. Nor should it be forgotten that it was under Benedict XV and Gasparri himself that some of the most intransigent bishops were appointed or given archbishoprics – even if the extent of their predilection for Action Française was insufficiently appreciated at the time of their appointment. Not only did the inclinations of a number of these bishops make the papal condemnation of Action Française (1926–7) a protracted and embarrassing business, but it delayed the achievement of a practical accommodation with the Separation Law of 1905. Whereas a majority of the French bishops had been in favour of accepting the *associations cultuelles* in 1906 (see pp. 60–6), the balance had altered as a result of the colour of Pius X's appointments. Even so, the *soumissionistes* of 1906 still had intelligent and influential spokesmen. Bishop Henri Chapon of Nice, aided by the Abbé Ferdinand Renaud, had provided Rome with a compelling brief in favour of accepting the *associations cultuelles* on a diocesan basis.[5] To make sure of the ground, they had notably consulted with Briand on whether the government was likely to accept the principle of a single association for each diocese. This diocesan body would take the place of the various parochial associations envisaged by the Separation Law; it would be chaired by the bishop and consist entirely of diocesan clergy. Mercifully for France, the new pope, Pius XI (1922–39), decided to retain Gasparri as his Secretary of State. With Gasparri's encouragement, Pius was prepared to override the misgivings of the intransigent wing of post-Concordatory bishops and accept the terms of the Separation Law as embodied in the Chapon–Renaud proposals (18 January 1924). With the *associations diocésaines* the French Church could now corporately own property instead of being reliant on private individuals; and with a legal roof over its head, it could at long last terminate its eighteen years of mentally living with bags packed, ready to go no one knew where. But most of the Church property, initially recognised as belonging to the *associations cultuelles* by the Separation Law of 1905, had been sold off by the State as a result of the refusal of Rome in 1906 to allow Catholics to form these associations. There was no way of recovering this.

Nor was the matter a mere issue of worldly goods, as some of the intransigent votaries of Pius X claimed. The legal uncertainty surrounding the Church's material resources had led to a drop in seminary entrants in the first quarter of the twentieth century, and second thoughts among the more lukewarm candidates for ordination. It was no mere coincidence that the regularisation of the Church's legal position in 1924 saw recruitment to the seminaries picking up once more in the late 'twenties, resulting in a 38 per cent increase in fully fledged ordinands between 1933 and 1938, as these recruits emerged from their six years' training.

That all this came about owed much to the patience and common sense of Gasparri. Even so the good fortune that his persuasive skills fell on receptive ears in Rome was helped by the fact that papal independence had survived the test of war. Residence on Entente soil had not deprived the Pope of the respect of the Central Powers. If anything, it was the Entente countries who had felt short-changed and were heard to mutter unseemly comments about '*le pape boche*'. Like Leo XIII, however, Gasparri was Concordat-minded, and similarly considered the Roman Question a matter of importance for the Church, directly affecting its ability to pursue vigorous independent policies. Unlike Leo, however, he had very modest ideas of what was territorially necessary to secure this independence. The Lateran Treaty of 1929, which made the Vatican a sovereign state, was largely Gasparri's brain-child – and the product of many years' thinking. He had long been optimistic that his scheme would one day find acceptance; and these hopes may or may not have encouraged him to be indulgent with other countries, including France. A more obvious factor was his Concordat-mindedness, which made a settlement with France an attractive proposition. Even a mutually accepted Separation was paradoxically better than a situation where one side recognised the status quo and the other did not.

The French Church and the Republic

The regular clergy too benefited from the more relaxed atmosphere of the 1920s. The wartime moratorium on enforcing the Combes legislation against them was tacitly continued into the following decades, even if the statute book remained unchanged until the Vichy years. Not that this indulgence had gone unchallenged. The failure of Raymond Poincaré's Ruhr operation of 1923 had seen many Right-wing Radicals withdraw their support from the Bloc National and rejoin their former brethren in the Cartel des Gauches, which emerged as the chief beneficiary of the 1924 elections. The resultant Radical government of Edouard Herriot tried to breathe new life into the old cause of anticlericalism, the traditional cement of a Left that was deeply divided on socio-economic issues. Its agenda accordingly included the removal of the special status of the churches in Alsace-Lorraine, the discontinuance of diplomatic links with the Vatican, and a stricter observance of Combes's legislation against the religious orders. It also revived the routines of pre-war Combism in sending a circular to prefects in September 1924, instructing them to warn *fonctionnaires* not to send their children to private schools. But the anticlerical campaign met with little enthusiasm outside Left-wing circles; and the Cartel eventually broke up on the old familiar issue of social expenditure, with the Radicals refusing Socialist demands for higher taxation. This demonstration that the anticlerical drum could no longer rally the Left with the same resonance as in the past created growing confidence among committed Catholics that the Republic was a home in which they could feel relatively secure. It likewise discouraged the Left from raising the old tattered banners of militant *laïcisme* in subsequent elections. Even the Popular Front victory of 1936 saw very little attempt to regain the ground that die-hard *mangeurs de curés* claimed had been lost to creeping clericalism.

This situation had its counterpart on the Right, where the anti-Republican leagues of the 1930s found much less support among committed Catholics than had their forerunners of the pre-war years. For one thing, their ideology was closer to the modern secular nationalism of similar movements elsewhere between the wars, rather than to the nostalgic nostra of the militants of the Dreyfus era. The Pope's condemnation of Action Française in 1926 had damaged Royalism's appeal in Catholic circles, despite the attempts of the Duc de Guise and the Comte de Paris to distance themselves from Maurras and his followers in the years that followed. There were several prominent Catholics in the marching movements of the 'thirties; and it was a matter of some embarrassment that the leader of the Croix de Feu, François de La Rocque, was an old boy of Ste Geneviève. And to those who knew it, it was a matter of even greater embarrassment that Ste Geneviève's most distinguished retired soldier, Marshal Franchet d'Espérey, was supposedly connected with the Cagoule. While the Cagoule's scattered adherents in the Army claimed to be exclusively concerned with rooting out Communist cells in the armed services, anti-Communism was a familiar cover for anti-Republican subversion. Even so, the armed services remained on reasonably good terms with the Republican governments of the 1930s, including those of the Popular Front whose increased expenditure on rearmament was a matter of reassurance to officers who disliked its politics and the pacifist sympathies of a section of its supporters. There was an effective working relationship between Edouard Daladier at the Ministry of War and the new Chief of the General Staff, General Maurice Gamelin (1935–40), while the growing menace of Nazi Germany served to concentrate minds on the enemy without rather than on domestic differences. Gamelin was himself a Collège Stanislas product; and whatever the nature of his religious beliefs during his period of command, his subsequent imprisonment during the Occupation found him with a crucifix by his bedside.[6]

Despite a Catholic presence in the Right-wing leagues of the 'thirties, the bulk of Catholics preferred to look to the orthodox parliamentary conservatives of respectable politics to provide the best guarantee against the return of anticlerical government. The fact that many of them also favoured the socio-economic policies of the conservatives rather than those of the revolutionary Right was a further inducement to follow this preference.

French Catholics and inter-war politics

Since the time of Leo XIII, it had been widely recognised that the Church would lose rather than gain by the creation of a specifically Catholic party in parliament. The anticlerical onslaughts of pre-war years, however, had brought many Catholic deputies together in Action

Libérale Populaire (see pp. 57–65) – a loose parliamentary group which, despite its secular title, was unquestionably an instrument of Catholic defence. Its membership, however, had rarely exceeded eighty; and it had been able neither to prevent nor reverse the legislation of 1901–5. Indeed those slender ameliorations that were achieved came largely from the manoeuvres of the moderate Republicans in other parties. The lessons of these years and the relative absence of militantly anticlerical government after the war made a successor to Action Libérale Populaire seem both unnecessary and unwise. The Herriot attack of the mid-'twenties merely seemed – by its failure – to confirm these conclusions. It is true that Masonic groups all over France had campaigned vigorously in favour of the Cartel des Gauches in the May 1924 elections, and had greeted Herriot's anticlerical programme with enormous enthusiasm. This in turn had encouraged a distinguished old boy of Ste Geneviève, General Edouard de Castelnau, to denounce 'la dictature de la maçonnerie en France' and form a Fédération Nationale Catholique in February 1925 to campaign against Herriot's proposals. With over a million members and the *Echo de Paris* as a sympathetic mouthpiece, the federation made itself heard loudly and effectively, so much so that in the 1928 elections 277 deputies were to subscribe to its declaration on freedom of education and association. Indeed the foundation of the federation encouraged the French cardinals and arch-bishops to issue a joint declaration in March 1925, condemning not only the Herriot proposals but attacking the whole gamut of pre-war anti-clerical legislation, which Catholic advocates of compromise had thought best dealt with by stealth rather than denunciation. Yet the federation itself was essentially an extra-parliamentary organisation, using the press and public meetings as its principal weapons. Castelnau himself had lost his parliamentary seat in 1924, and the movement's representatives in parliament were a mixed bunch, ranging from loyal if drab defenders of Church interests to the saturnine Royalist, Xavier Vallat, who, having lost an eye and a leg in the First World War, was to lose his soul in the Second as one of Vichy's Commissioners for Jewish Affairs (see p. 180). The federation was of short-lived significance. The fact that the Herriot campaign was not renewed removed the movement's principal raison d'être, and by 1930 it was subsiding into relative obscurity.

It would be tempting to classify the Union Populaire Républicaine as a parliamentary party of Catholic defence, which in many ways it was. It essentially represented the Catholic interests of Alsace-Lorraine in the somewhat changed homeland of a secular republic – and the particular legal rights of the Catholic Church in Alsace-Lorraine were prominent among them. But its adherents numbered only nine in the Chamber of Deputies and five in the Senate. They were nevertheless a useful adjunct to the scattered forces of Catholicism in parliament; and at times of crisis they were an identifiable group that could be quickly mobilised.[7]

But crises for Catholicism were relatively few after the collapse of the Herriot campaign. Thereafter Catholic energies were increasingly invested in the various youth movements of the 1930s, which were rightly seen as sowing the seeds of widespread Catholic influence at the grass-roots level of industry, agriculture and the professions. It was these – Jeunesse Ouvrière Chrétienne, Jeunesse Agricole Chrétienne, etc. – that sought to rechristianise their particular socio-occupational milieux by displaying a persuasive combination of professional progressivism and social conscience; they would challenge the secular world on its own terms and transform it. It was these organisations that were also to provide a generation of articulate spokesmen who made their way into the parliamentary politics of post-Liberation France. The late 'forties were not only to find them of an age and experience to be able to enter the political arena with effective impact, but the enfranchisement of women in 1944 was to give them the electoral support that enabled them to do so in significant numbers. It was these products of the 1930s youth organisations who were to provide the progressive wing of the post-war Mouvement Républicain Populaire.

If this parliamentary harvest lay in the future, its programme was modestly foreshadowed in the inter-war years by the Parti Démocrate Populaire. Never fielding more than nineteen deputies in the years 1924 to 1940, it was not a Catholic defence group, but rather a Christian democrat party with a modest Sillon-style programme of social reform which Catholics of a more conservative stamp did not find particularly attractive.[8] In fact it came into being partly as a reaction to the attacks of Action Française rather than as a response to the threats of the Herriot programme. Even so, the PDP formed part of the opposition to both the Cartel of 1932 and the Popular Front of 1936. Although it was circumspect in its utterances concerning Blum's government, the pattern of its votes in parliament left no doubt as to where it stood in the political spectrum, despite occasional lukewarm tributes to the good intentions if not the good sense of the Popular Front. The only Catholic group to express enthusiasm for the Popular Front was Maurice Landrain's Chrétiens Révolutionnaires – which also included a number of Protestants – and their journal, *Terre Nouvelle*. But they did not attempt to enter parliament; and their posters depicting the crucifix surrounded by the hammer and sickle were hardly calculated to win

Rome's sympathy. To the surprise of few, papal condemnation came fairly swiftly.[9]

Catholics in government

The most influential committed Catholics of the inter-war parliaments were largely to be found in the secular parties that represented socioeconomic interests. Of the four Catholics who became ministers in the 1920s only Auguste Champetier de Ribes belonged to the PDP – and was to become its President in 1929.[10] An old boy of the Collège Stanislas, destined for a legal career, he was initially elected to the Chambre des Députés in 1924 on the Union Nationale ticket. Despite this, Edouard Herriot offered him a place in a broad-bottomed government that he was unsuccessfully attempting to form in 1926 to pull France through the financial crisis, but Champetier recognised a lost cause when he saw it and refused. Appointed by Tardieu as a junior finance minister in 1929, he was promoted to be Minister of Pensions in Tardieu's second cabinet in the following year, a post he regained under Laval in 1931 and was to retain until a chastened Herriot returned to power in June 1932. The equally chastened Edouard Daladier reappointed him to Pensions in April 1938, before moving him as his own junior colleague to the Quai d'Orsay at the outbreak of war – presenting the piquant example of the leader of the Radical party in close harness with a well-known spokesman of Catholic interests – one moreover who had refused to rescue Daladier's mentor, Herriot, twelve years earlier.

Auguste Isaac by contrast began a short-lived parliamentary career (1919–24) as a spokesman of Lyon business interests, becoming Minister of Industry and Commerce under Millerand and Leygues in 1920. Like his fellow Lyonnais and colleague, Edouard Aynard (see pp. 79–81), he felt that he could serve Catholicism best by avoiding too close an identity with confessional causes. But like Aynard, he was the father of eleven children and became closely associated with France's natalist policies – a cause that was as much national as Catholic. The Comte Charles de Lasteyrie du Saillant had similarly made his name in the world of commerce and finance, and had likewise entered parliament on the Bloc National ticket of 1919. He was an old boy of the Ecole Bossuet of Paris, a private school run by secular priests; and he had obtained his first taste of ministerial life when Denys Cochin employed him as his *chef de cabinet* during Briand's and Ribot's wartime governments. His financial flair prompted Poincaré to make him Minister of Finance in 1922, where his eventual success in dealing with the acute French crisis of payments helped to associate Poincaré in the public mind with stability and the courage to take unpopular decisions to achieve it. He remained a true-blue member of the Bloc National, 1936 finding him characteristically denouncing the Popular Front as an alliance of Masonry and Bolshevism. Edouard Lefebvre du Prey belonged to the same section of the Bloc National as Isaac and Lasteyrie. He came from a Catholic family of landowners and lawyers, and was appropriately Minister of Agriculture, then of Justice, in Briand's and Poincaré's governments of 1921 and 1924, before taking over the Quai d'Orsay in François-Marsal's five-day government of the same year.

These men owed their ministerial appointments to their competence in secular fields – and, Champetier apart, they were not primarily thought of as spokesmen of Catholic interests. Yet they were keen supporters of enfranchising women, which arguably was Catholicism's best hope for a political break-through in France – given the female preponderance in any church congregation. Secularists feared that a female vote would result in the election of a conservative majority, which would then set about repealing the anticlerical legislation of the pre-war era. It was this that left women without the parliamentary vote in France, Italy and Belgium until after the Second World War. Moreover the granting of the vote to Spanish women in 1931 had been followed by right-wing successes in the elections of 1933, all of which was invoked by French anticlericals as incontrovertible proof of the folly of enfranchising women. At the same time, however, any politician with pretensions to democratic principle felt increasingly embarrassed by the patent injustice of the situation. They looked uncomfortably at neighbouring countries such as Germany and Britain which had given women the vote following the First World War – admittedly without the deterrent of a clerical problem. Consequently Left-wing politicians in the Chamber of Deputies went through the motions of granting female suffrage, confident that any measure they passed on the subject would be rejected by the Senate with its old-style Radical majority. Even a Chamber vote of 488 to one in July 1936 cut no ice with the Senate, much to the relief of many of the deputies who had voted for it in the lower house.

Catholic education

The continuance of wartime tolerance towards the religious orders saw a steady increase in their clandestine re-establishment in private education during the inter-war years. The legal freedom they enjoyed in Alsace-Lorraine helped to underline the anachronistic nature of the Combist legacy. Even so, the Church still took the precaution elsewhere in France of placing the administrative and financial affairs of its schools in the hands of laymen; and a large proportion of the nuns, brothers and other members of religious orders who taught there wore a discreet if drab assortment of lay clothing.

In the late 'thirties about 17 per cent of the French primary-school population were taught in private schools, rising to well over 30 per cent in the strongly Catholic Massif Central and as much as 50 per cent and above in the Breton peninsula. The position of the private sector in secondary education was even stronger, despite the fact that the state schools in the 1930s now had the attraction of being free, an attraction that made surprisingly little difference to the ratio of pupils in the private and public sectors. In the lower forms, the private sector accounted for about two-fifths, but in the senior forms it dropped to little more than a quarter. This reflected the growing tendency of many Catholic parents to transfer their children to the state sector, once the *baccalauréat* began to loom large in their preoccupations. Only a few Catholic schools could match the academic record of the best state *lycées*, even if their attention to character formation and the pupils' overall welfare was considered superior in a number of respects.

Catholics and state employment

The slackening of anticlericalism between the wars does not appear to have given rise to a major increase in Catholic entry into the politicised sectors of the public services. The handful of Catholics who became ministers were men who inhabited a parliamentary world where their ability was sufficiently known for premiers to be able to take the political risk of appointing them to posts where their skills would be particularly useful. Senior civil servants on the other hand had to be more careful. With the reactions of superiors as well as junior staff to consider, they were less free to make unconventional 'imaginative' appointments – especially in a world where the particular abilities of individual candidates were far less publicly known than those of politicians. The increasing unionisation of the *fonctions publiques* obliged appointing committees to take more account of grass-roots opinion within each service. Unions of state employees were still denied the protection of the laws of 1884 and 1901; and for much of the 1920s they had a precarious existence, based on a collection of *ad hoc* administrative decisions.[11] The 1930s, however, found the Conseil d'Etat increasingly tolerant towards them – while still keeping a sharp distinction between the bread-and-butter services and those responsible for the maintenance of order, where rank-and-file pressure on government was still regarded as unacceptable. Despite these limitations, state employees' unions could afford to be much more vociferous than before the war. The militant suspicion of Left-wing unions towards committed Catholics in the public services saw a certain shift in the balance of traditional anticlerical animus from government level to that of the personnel themselves. This hostility among the membership had doubtless long been there – but the legal limitations on pre-war unionism among civil servants had curtailed its effective expression. At the same time the consciousness that pre-war governments were actively concerned to limit Catholic penetration gave grass-roots anticlerical pressure the critical but confident character of football supporters behind a winning team, whereas after the war it acquired something of the truculent tone of men who were no longer quite so sure of the team's determination to win. This was particularly true of the primary teachers' organisations, notably the Syndicat National des Instituteurs. Indeed these Left-wing professional bodies took over much of the watch-dog role of pre-war Masonry.

The lodges still remained active. Although Edouard Herriot was not himself a Mason, half his ministers were; and his anticlerical programme mirrored that of the Grand Orient. Not that Masonry dictated his policy. As noted earlier (see pp. 119–20), the heavy overlap between the Radical party and Masonry ensured much common ground, without one organisation being the creature of the other. And there were important items on Masonry's shopping list of anticlerical reforms that Herriot and his colleagues were not prepared to adopt. The Grand Orient wished to resurrect the *stage scolaire* that was examined but rejected in parliamentary committee in 1899 – the insistence that entrants to the *grandes écoles* and the civil service should be products of state secondary schools (see pp. 78–81). And it likewise favoured the abolition of the private sector of education. Herriot considered neither of these proposals politically viable.

The Grand Orient underwent remarkably little increase in the inter-war period, its membership rising from 33,000 in 1914 to 36,000 in 1936, despite the influx of a number of Socialist supporters. On the other hand, the Grand Lodge, which represented the other main strand of French Masonry, rose from 8,000 in 1914 to 15,000 in 1936.[12] Less tainted than the Grand Orient with the scandals of the pre-war era, it had acquired a more respectable image – while the Grand Orient itself had learnt the lessons of the past and was less importunate in seeking public appointments for its members. Ironically this newly assumed discretion made it less attractive to those whose only interest in Masonry was as a ladder to state employment. The stagnation of Grand Orient membership was matched by a certain softening of its anticlericalism in the late 1930s. The anti-Masonic measures of fascist dictatorships caused a number of its members to look to the Church as a possible ally against the mounting threat of totalitarianism in Europe. The Grand Orient's librarian and several of his associates sent a letter to Pius XI in the spring of 1937, urging closer co-operation; and although this appeal met with the disapproval of many Masons, it represented a significant crack in the traditional hostility of French Masonry towards the Church.[13]

But if *fonctionnaires'* associations were taking on some of Masonry's militant concern for the Republican purity of the public services, these associations were themselves split on what constituted a good Republican, particularly in a post-1917 France where Communism was rivalling clericalism as the *bête noire* to be kept at bay. Anti-Communism was even more marked at government level. Poincaré's Minister of the Interior, Albert Sarraut (July 1926 – November 1928), formally expressed the situation in his famous theft from Gambetta, 'Le communisme, voilà l'ennemi!' Addressing prefects in 1928 on the importance of their political neutrality, Sarraut added 'if you have correctly conformed to the instructions that I have given you, there is one issue on which you have always put neutrality on one side – and I congratulate you for this – you have, on my orders and instructions, fought Communism'. And the reasons he gave might have been uttered thirty years earlier against clericalism – 'we are dealing with a permanent conspiracy, under foreign guidance, against the laws, institutions and the very order of this country.'[14]

As demonstrated in earlier chapters, the most difficult area of public service for a committed Catholic to enter was the *corps préfectoral*; and the handful of former members interviewed in this enquiry can recollect having encountered only one among the prefects of the inter-war years. This was the future Gaullist deputy, Léon Noël, who was briefly transferred by André Tardieu from the Conseil d'Etat to the prefecture of the Haut-Rhin in August 1930, a strongly Catholic region of the former lost provinces where the government was anxiously trying to regain the goodwill of the population after the traumas of the Herriot fiasco (see pp. 155–8). Noël's presence at Sunday Mass raised many secular eyebrows in the nine short months he was there. Yet his departure, far from being a disgrace, was occasioned by his elevation to the Secretary-Generalship of the Ministry of the Interior under Pierre Laval – where the arrival of a staunch Catholic as factotum of the Place Beauvau caused far more astonishment than had his dominion over the arcades and winecellars of Colmar.[15] Generally speaking, however, not only would committed Catholics be unlikely to be appointed to the *corps préfectoral*, but it would not occur to them to seek to apply. Even so, government attitudes towards the Church had changed – and two survivors who entered the corps in the 1930s both remarked that the principle that was impressed upon them on their arrival at the Ministry of the Interior was that the attitude of the State and the *corps préfectoral* towards the Church was now one of neutrality rather than republican defence. The Republic was now secure from this quarter, and the prefect and his subordinates were no longer required to be watch-dogs against clerical subversion. And the golden rule of the *préfecture* was not to take sides. But precisely for this reason, it was still undesirable for a prefect to be seen going to Mass, even in his private capacity, since observers would draw conclusions about his personal inclinations and possible bias. Neither of these informants was a practising Catholic at the time of his entry into the corps, although both became so after the Second World War.

Reports on corps members for the mid-'twenties still carried questions on religion and politics, as in the pre-war period.[16] An important change, however, was the introduction of minimum formal qualifications for sub-prefects and *secrétaires généraux* (decree of 5 October 1928) – and this would eventually affect the quality of the prefects themselves, since they were largely recruited from these junior levels.[17] They were now expected to have a university degree or similar diploma – although there remained dispensations for men of established experience elsewhere in the public administration. In principle this limited the previous freedom of governments to appoint unqualified political supporters to sub-prefectures. But in practice many pre-war sub-prefects had held degrees – and the overwhelming majority of prefects had done so (see p. 104).

Until 1933, prefects were at perfect liberty to choose whom they liked as their *chef de cabinet*; and, like many ministers and politicians, they frequently chose their sons or nephews – who on eventually attaining prefectoral rank themselves, did likewise, thereby creating embryo dynasties.[18] This cosy world of father-to-son was in some ways an administrative counterpart of the family business in the private sphere of commerce, albeit with greater geographical displacement – making the French custom of *pantouflage* not such a *dépaysement* as it might seem to outsiders. But a decree of 12 October 1933 stipulated formal minimum requirements for *chefs de cabinet* in prefectures, as well as making their appointment subject to the approval of the Minister of the Interior.[19] If not already holding a degree or diploma, they were expected to be studying for one; and in 1935 a formal *concours d'entrée* was established.[20]

Catholics complained that these were cosmetic changes that made little difference to the composition of the corps between the wars. They were likewise sceptical when Sarraut told the prefects in 1928 that 'you should not be electoral agents; it is a task unworthy of you, in which the risks far outweigh the benefits'.[21] They pointed out that the advent of Herriot's Cartel des Gauches government had seen a major political reshuffle of prefects in August 1924, when a third of the prefectures saw new faces in command, with eight prefects leaving the corps altogether – some admittedly of an age ripe for removal.[22] Similarly the arrival of the Popular Front government saw the switch of nearly a quarter of the prefects in November 1936 and the permanent exit of nine, mostly of an age to go.[23]

Matters were much as they had been before the war. The life expectancy of a prefect in office remained about seven or eight years – and tenure of a particular post two to three years.[24] In fact the Popular Front had sought to democratise the higher echelons of the civil service, by proposing an Ecole Nationale d'Administration in August 1936 – a proposal which was eventually voted in an emasculated form by the Chamber of Deputies, only to rot in committee stage in the Senate.[25] Its aim was to sidetrack the moneyed elite whose parents could afford to send them to the private Ecole Libre des Sciences Politiques (see p. 82). But whether this democratised elite would have been a depoliticised elite is another matter.

As before the war, there appears to have been a modest trickle of Catholics into the Conseil d'Etat. The Collège Stanislas had at least one *maître de requêtes* and Ste Geneviève an *auditeur*, according to the casual information indirectly supplied by announcements of weddings, etc., in their respective old boys' magazines – and the number may have been considerably higher.[26] The son of the Catholic philosopher, Maurice Blondel, entered the Conseil d'Etat in 1922; and, as a *maître de requêtes* at the time of the Popular Front, Charles Blondel was a mentor in legal matters to the Catholic Confédération Française des Travailleurs Chrétiens (see pp. 167–8).[27] Blondel had three friends in the Conseil who also kept an eye on impending legislation that might have an adverse impact on the CFTC; but whether these were committed Catholics is not clear.

The passage of the years had made remarkably little difference to the sort of questions contained in the reports on candidates for the Conseil. A report from the Préfecture de Police in November 1936 covered the familiar ground of family and fortune.[28] 'He is of the Catholic religion [i.e. by baptism]; his political opinions are not known, since he does not display any.' It also reassured the council that the candidate did not have a police record and that he was 'equally unknown to the Service des Jeux, the Brigade Mondaine and the Section Financière' – a trio of services that challenges the imagination to speculate on the type of disguise that their inspectors affected: monocle and white tie for the gaming tables of Divonne-les-Bains, or eyeshades and shirt-sleeves for the smoke-filled backrooms of less salubrious establishments.

The judiciary was an area well infiltrated by committed Catholics before the war (see pp. 95–101), and continued to be so. At least a dozen old boys of the Collège Stanislas became magistrates between the wars, and one, possibly more, became a *commissaire de police*, always an important role in a France where political street violence was more widespread than before the war.[29] The gossip columns in the Jesuit alumni magazines of Ste Geneviève and Caousou also indicate several successful entrants into the magistracy.[30] Even so, the confidential reports on candidates for the judiciary in the 1930s still had spaces for their political attitudes and their religion. Yet the comments put there tended to be purely on the political aspects of their behaviour – the usual remark being 'attitude politique correcte', 'correcte' being a usefully guarded term that was later to be used to describe the behaviour of the German forces in the early months of the Occupation. But the comments on religion tended to be restricted to the mere notification that the candidate was a baptised Catholic – which of course was still true of the bulk of the population.[31]

As for other forms of public employment, Catholics appear to have been as free to enter as before the war – with probably even fewer eyebrows raised, except among the devotees of the Left-wing union news-sheets. From the engagement, marriage and change-of-address notices in the old boys' magazine of Ste Geneviève, a fairly familiar pattern of occupations emerges in the 'thirties. The armed services continued to be the dominant if a declining element in the public sector, while among civil posts Eaux et Forêts (eight), Ponts et Chaussées (nine) and other Public Works appointments (five) remained high. The development of communications in the inter-war period, however, brought the PTT to the head of the list (ten). There were also several *inspecteurs des finances*, and one or two other finance officers, as well as a member of the Cour des Comptes.[32]

The situation was broadly similar at the Collège Stanislas. A perusal of lists of weddings, etc., in the old boys' magazine likewise reveals much the same sort of employment pattern as before the First World War – with the Conseil d'Etat, the Cour des Comptes and the judiciary as the only warm to hot potatoes, other than a sub-prefect and a *commissaire de police.*[33] But the patchiness of the lists for both schools – restricted, as they were, to paid-up subscribers with happy events to announce – precludes the drawing of any clear conclusions.

A factor that needs investigating in the politico-religious composition of the *fonctions publiques* between the wars is the growing entry of women. Loss of life in the First World War resulted in a decree in 1919 opening the *concours des rédacteurs* to women.[34] The Ministry of Commerce took the lead, and was soon followed by others. So rapid were the consequences that, as early as 1928, women accounted for 23 per cent of *rédacteurs* in the Ministries of Commerce and War, 16 per cent in Pensions, 27 per cent in Agriculture, and no fewer than 36 per cent in the Préfecture de Police.[35] By the early 'thirties a number of women were *sous-chefs*, constituting 11 per cent of the total in the Ministry of War.[36] At a time when women were still without the vote and were to be absent from government until 1936, they were regarded as 'less political' than men, and thereby less in need of political screening than their male colleagues. On the other hand there was statistically a greater likelihood that they would be sympathetic to the Church; and it may not be entirely a coincidence that the ministries that were the first to recruit them in numbers were those where political vetting was relatively slight. Given the inaccessibility of personal dossiers for this period it is impossible to know the facts of the situation; but it is conceivable that the increasing number of women in the administration may have helped to blunt the surviving residue of political scanning by ministries. Otherwise a double standard for men and women would have resulted – compensating, one might argue, for the more serious differentials under which women *fonctionnaires* still laboured. The real test would come with the *corps préfectoral*, the Conseil d'Etat, the Cour des Comptes and the Inspection des Finances – all of which lay beyond the grasp of women in the interwar years.

At the humbler level of state employment, the growing self-confidence of committed Catholics was reflected in the foundation and expansion of the Confédération Française des Travailleurs Chrétiens. Although the bulk of its membership was in the private sector, its founder members in November 1919 included the Syndicat Professionnel Féminin des PTT.[37] By the mid 1920s the CFTC's state employees were grouped in the Fédération Française des Syndicats Professionnels des Fonctionnaires, their number rising from some 5,000 in 1934–5 to over 20,000 by 1939, many of them working for the PTT.[38] The CFTC maintained an ambivalent attitude towards the Popular Front, declaring sympathy for a number of its social aims but expressing resentment at the CFTC's exclusion from the Matignon negotiations of June 1936 which led to the implementation of some of the Front's most notable reforms in the workplace.[39] The parliamentary group with which the CFTC was most closely linked was an informal group of some seventy Catholic Deputies and Senators, calling itself the 'Groupe du Syndicalisme Chrétien', and variously drawn from the PDP (see p. 158), the UPR (see pp. 157–8) and disparate conservative elements, most of whom were hostile to Blum's government.[40] Although the CFTC developed more cordial relations with the Popular Front in the autumn of 1936, it greeted what it called Daladier's more 'national' government of 1938 with considerable warmth.[41]

State education was the field where the grass-roots anticlericalism of Left-wing unions was perhaps the principal concern for committed Catholics – arguably more irksome than the vestiges of political vetting perfunctorily practised by the Ministry, the Académies and the prefectures. The only solace was that the warning shouts of anticlerical unions were not always heeded by a government that was still in two minds about the legitimacy of unions in the public sector and which was increasingly inclined to regard Communism and the pacifist wing of Socialism as greater menaces than clericalism. Even so, the Chautemps circular of 25 September 1924 accorded a greater aura of legal respectability to the *fonctionnaires'* unions; and, following this, the de Monzie circular of 20 June 1925 advised *inspecteurs d'académie* to take account of the opinions of departmental-council delegates in the appointment of primary-school teachers. Although the de Monzie circular did not specifically introduce union members into the process, the practical outcome was that the Syndicat National des Instituteurs in particular had a growing voice in the selection of teachers. The impact of this development on the composition of the profession has still to be systematically studied, and assessment will have to await the release of the relevant dossiers. To keep the matter in proportion, it should be remembered that the selection bodies usually had only sparse information on the personal beliefs and opinions of young debutant teachers (see pp. 135–6); and as anticlericalism became less fashionable in the 1930s, union representatives increasingly felt obliged to strengthen their objections to Catholic candidates with non-sectarian arguments that were not always easy to find. Their simplest targets were the so-called Davidées – these were Catholic *institutrices* who periodically held meetings to discuss professional teaching methods and the lay apostolate, and who could therefore be portrayed as a potential threat to the secular ideals of state education. Many Catholic teachers, especially women, were made uneasy by the hostility of the largely Socialist Syndicat

National des Instituteurs and the partly Communist-inspired Fédération Unitaire. The SNI kept up a vigilant pressure on inter-war governments against what it saw as over-zealous Catholic teachers, particularly the *institutrices*.[42] Similarly the Fédération Unitaire in 1927 urged secondary-school teachers to report *lycée* chaplains whose comments to pupils might seem critical of the public education system – and it encouraged them to be equally vigilant concerning remarks by Catholic colleagues.[43] While recognising that in a free society these were difficult areas for the government to control, a leading spokesman of the primary-school anti-clericals, Rollo, deplored 'la carence laïque du Front populaire', which he implausibly attributed to the government's desire to secure Vatican support against fascism – an accusation that might have been directed with more credibility against those elements in the Grand Orient who were seeking just such a *rapprochement* (see pp. 162–3).[44] Nor was the *stage scolaire* issue of the 1890s completely dead – as exemplified by the Syndicat de la Haute-Savoie which demanded in November 1937 that entry to teachers' training colleges be restricted to products of the state system.[45]

But if Catholics were often the victims of the growth of public-sector syndicalism between the wars, they also resorted to it as a means of self-defence. The attacks on Catholic *institutrices* by the Syndicat National des Instituteurs were countered in 1925 by the formation of the Union Nationale des Membres de l'Enseignement Public, which based its defence of the Davidées on the principle of neutrality in philosophical–religious matters in the state sector.[46] By the 1930s its bulletin had a print-run of 30,000; and among its leading lights was Jacques Chevalier of the Grenoble Faculté des Lettres, later to achieve prominence as one of Vichy's Ministers of Education (see p. 179).[47] Catholic secondary teachers for their part had a vociferous mouthpiece in the Association des Professeurs Catholiques de l'Enseignement Public. It was unfortunate that from 1918 to 1929 its leadership was taken by Pierre Heinrich, a history teacher in Lyon with strong nationalist convictions. He and several of his colleagues were contributors to the *Revue de l'Ecole*, a journal with Maurassian overtones which supported the Bloc National in inter-war politics.[48] Heinrich was also active in the Cercle Fustel-de-Coulanges, a Maurassian group established in 1926–7, which had a modest following among Right-wing Catholic members of both higher and secondary state education, despite the Vatican's recent condemnation of Action Française.[49]

However significant the growing influence of the Left-wing unions on entry and promotion in the primary sector, these appointments were still a government matter. As before the war (see pp. 135–6), prefecture reports on primary-school teachers were restricted to those seeking appointment in another region, generally to some more senior post. The prefecture of the department of the Aude continued to use the same printed proforma throughout the inter-war years, with its questions on 'l'attitude et les opinions publiques de M—'.[50] The replies, however, became increasingly bland and more stereotyped as the period progressed. In the immediate post-war years, prefectures still thought it important to say 'Son attitude politique est républicaine' – and many continued to do so for a decade or so, even if 'il observe une attitude politique correcte' became more frequent in the late 'twenties and 'thirties. But this in turn was to be overtaken by the equally formalistic 'Meilleurs [or 'excellents'] renseignements à tous égards', with formalism reaching its apogée in the prefecture of the Nord in the 1930s, which literally rubber-stamped its replies to such enquiries, 'Bons renseignements à tous égards. Attitude politique correcte.'[51] Some prefectures, however, continued to take the task fairly seriously – even if the colour of their misgivings had changed. The reassuring resonance of 'bon républicain' of pre-war days could now become the exonerating 'Passe pour être républicain assez avancé, mais ne milite pas', or the cautious, bet-hedging 'Il ne se livrait à aucune activité politique . . . Il était inscrit comme membre à la section d'Argentin du parti radical-socialiste.'[52]

The archives of the Charente-Maritime have much to say on the power, but also the limitations, of political pressure on educational appointments in the inter-war years. They also exemplify the close connections between local grass-roots concerns and top-level ministerial activity in the Third Republic, and demonstrate that the familiar epithet, 'the regime of the provinces', had implications that cut both ways. The case of Emile Combes's granddaughter is a good illustration. Madeleine Martin-Combes had just emerged from training college, and her desire was to live with her parents in the family fief of Pons, life-long home of the recently deceased minister, still celebrated as Pons's most illustrious citizen. The Radicals were never short on loyalty to friends, and the newly appointed Minister of Education, Edouard Daladier, wrote to the prefect in December 1925, proposing her for a Pons primary school: 'Je m'intéresse tout particulièrement à cette jeune institutrice.'[53] The prefect lost no time in informing the Inspecteur d'Académie, only to receive the inconvenient reply that there were more senior applicants with stronger claims for the post, who moreover had husbands in public employment in Pons.[54] (The Roustan civil-service law of 1921 had favoured the appointment of working husbands and wives to the same localities.) Three years went by – with three more vacancies in Pons – but the

Inspecteur remained firmly wedded to the rule of law and equity, despite a plea from the Mayor of Pons and a bitter letter from the girl's mother to the prefect, attributing the 'mauvais vouloir de l'inspecteur à l'égard de ma fille' to 'les idées politiques de mon mari'.[55] By return of post the prefect protested his continued support for her daughter 'non seulement avec le désir de vous être agréable, mais aussi avec le sentiment d'accomplir comme un devoir envers la mémoire du Président Combes'.[56] The prefect had earlier taken the precaution of informing Daladier that his zeal on her behalf was all the stronger for his gratitude to the late-lamented Combes for having launched him on his career with a sub-prefecture in Charente-Inférieure.[57] Family and party loyalty eventually triumphed when Mlle Martin-Combes was appointed to a boys' primary school in September 1928, after much local bewilderment at the apparent lack of gratitude displayed by the Académie towards the great men of the recent past.[58]

Nor was this the only example of the Académie's insensitivity to the need for flexibility and deference to friends. The same prefect needed the help of a neighbouring departmental councillor in an awkward legal case, a councillor who happened to be currently seeking a post in a teachers' training college for 'ma petite cousine pour laquelle je nourris les sentiments les plus sympathiques et les plus affectueux'.[59] In reply to the prefect's solicitations, the Inspecteur d'Académie pointed out that with merely a year's service she could not expect to be successfully competing as yet for this kind of post.[60] Nothing daunted, the prefect promised to write to the Prime Minister, Edouard Herriot, 'who kindly honours me with his friendship'.[61] If the eventual outcome was not the coveted training-college post, the girl did at least become a *surveillante* at the Ecole Primaire Supérieure of La Rochelle, thereby demonstrating that the République des Camarades was still alive and well.

There were similar reassuring examples at secondary-school level. In 1918 Eugène Delaroue, Deputy for the Seine-et-Marne, wrote to the Director of Secondary Education, asking him to transfer Mlle Delgosse to a Paris *lycée* – and not neglecting to promise the Director 'a sign of his gratitude' in return.[62] The transfer was duly made. What is revealing is that the lady's dossier contains a report from the regional Inspecteur d'Académie written nineteen years earlier, complaining that she was the mistress of the deputy in question, then a philosophy teacher in the same town. Moreover they were seen going to the cold baths together, whether to indulge their ardour or to cool it down is not specified.[63] The case bears testimony not only to the lasting nature of the relationship but to the benign discretion of the post-war Director of Secondary Education, who, fully conversant with the sentimental contents of the dossier (which the deputy was not), acceded to Delaroue's request. No doubt his benignity was aided by the fact that Delaroue was a respected Radical-party spokesman on educational affairs, who in his time was to be President of the Association des Professeurs des Lycées et Collèges de France, as well as President of the Association des Maires des Villes de France.

The waning of state vigilance over Catholic penetration of public employment may have had some effect on the readiness of men to reveal their religious allegiance. Sporadic figures of church-attendance in the 1930s suggest that there may have been some increase in religious practice since the pre-war years, particularly in the case of men. The truth of this is hard to establish with any accuracy, since the age-groups surveyed and the criteria employed in the 1930s were often different from those that were used in the pre-war period. In the diocese of Chartres only 2 per cent of men and boys over the age of twelve took Easter Communion in 1898 and 1909 – and the proportion going to Mass every Sunday was probably lower than this. In 1931, however, 3.2 per cent of men and adolescents over the age of fifteen were regularly going to Sunday Mass – and the modest upward trend that these figures would seem to indicate was in all probability greater, given that the disparity in the methods of calculation would tend to minimise rather than inflate the difference. For women and girls the equivalent figures were 16 per cent in 1898 (dropping to 13 per cent in 1909), but still only 16.2 per cent in 1931.[64] In Nevers the proportion of men and adolescent boys taking Easter Communion was 9 per cent in 1909–10, but had risen to 12.6 per cent by 1933. The equivalent figures for women and girls were 41 per cent in 1909–10 but only 33.2 per cent in 1933.[65] These dioceses were areas of relatively low religious observance, and sufficiently close to the seat of national government to feel such winds of change that might come from there. In the diocese of Bourges, figures for a couple of localities showed the percentage of men and adolescent boys taking Easter Communion as 3.5 and 3.8 in 1909, rising to 5.5 and 5 in 1931.[66] In dioceses where the overall level of church-going was high, notably those situated at some remove from Paris, the fragmentary evidence for this period suggests that the direction of change in male attendance continued to be gently downwards rather than upwards.

It is obviously dangerous to hazard guesses as to why matters were thus – if indeed they were, given the shakiness of the figures. One factor that may have played a part in these movements is the modest but significant diminution in anticlericalism since the war, and a growing confidence among Catholic men that church-going was not going to prejudice their chances of promotion in public employment to the extent that it originally did – or was thought to do – in Combist times.

10   The leopard's spots: 1940–1960

Take the main road, even if it twists.

Bishop Martin of Le Puy, 'Lettre à un jeune catholique', 1943

The 1940s present the historian with a major paradox. The record of senior churchmen during the Occupation was not a heroic one – with certain remarkable exceptions. However much they may have felt that they were protecting church members from German repression, their readiness to profit from the benign attitudes of the Vichy government in its early days left them open to the obvious charge of opportunism – while the subsequent hostility of many senior clergy to the Resistance inevitably made them seem like counter-revolutionaries, seeking to preserve 'the Pétain miracle' against a return of the secular Republic of the pre-war years. Whether guilty of opportunism or naivety, their record would have seemed to invite a massive outbreak of anticlerical retribution when Vichy's victims and critics eventually triumphed at the Liberation. The whole history of the previous century would suggest that such an outcome was inevitable: the anticlerical outbursts of 1830, 1871 and the 1880s had all been the price paid for the Church's complicity with the Restoration, the Second Empire and the Ordre Moral of the 1870s.

Yet nemesis did not come. On the contrary the Church emerged strengthened, while committed Catholics had a greater share of ministerial portfolios in post-war France than they had had since the 1870s. Even Vichy at its most *bien pensant* had not invited so many Catholics to take Cabinet posts. Moreover the situation was to continue. This was not the case with the French Communists who, like the Catholics, had also been briefly welcomed into the comity of post-war coalitions. Although the stain of the Nazi–Soviet pact had been temporarily eclipsed by the Communists' impressive Resistance record, the advent of the Cold War soon exiled them from ministerial office. The Catholic Mouvement Républicain Populaire by contrast was to be represented in all but four of the twenty-six governments of the post-war

174

Fourth Republic, and was to provide the new regime with three of its nineteen prime ministers.

That such an apparent reversal of fortune could take place – and in the face of so much recent evidence of the Church's uncertain loyalty to Republican ideals – might seem extraordinary. That it happened was largely the result of two major changes in popular perceptions of the Church. On the one hand the public increasingly made a clear distinction between the accredited leaders of the Church and its rank-and-file adherents, whose professional and social lives bound them to the rest of the community and who were to provide post-war France with so many of its influential political figures. The distinction was centuries old; and in the so-called ages of faith it had been a basic presupposition of social and political life. But the anticlerical years of Republican consolidation had blurred the difference, as committed Catholics had been drawn into the lager of Church defence. The relaxed tension in Church–State relations that came with the inter-war years had loosened the tight discipline within the Catholic camp – to the extent that the conservative clergy feared that the Church was losing control over the disparate enthusiasms of the laity. The split was to reach crisis proportions during the Occupation when a small but influential minority of the Catholic laity became deeply involved in the Resistance, which although directed against the German occupation was inevitably critical of the Vichy regime and of those who continued to support it, including the bulk of the Catholic hierarchy. Though small in number they played important roles in what emerged as the winning side – with the leaders of both the internal and external Resistance, Georges Bidault and Charles de Gaulle, representing significant if very different strands of Catholic lay commitment. Not surprisingly their Resistance record and those of their sympathisers tended to overshadow the less glorious role of the much larger proportion of their co-religionists whose standpoint had been closer to that of the bulk of the bishops. As always, history justifies the side that wins – especially when it deservedly wins.

Yet the deference that was paid to the victorious minority and the place they were given in the New Jerusalem did not simply represent a generous impulse to forget the opportunism, pessimism and mis-calculations of the majority and their spiritual leaders. For what had been true of so many Catholics had also been true of a large section of the population as a whole; and in averting their gaze from the shortcomings of the Church they were also avoiding the uncomfortable recognition of their own passivity or acceptance of short-term advantage. They certainly had less reason than Catholics to welcome the *bien-pensant* paternalism of Vichy's initial image which was a poor substitute for the democratic

Republic of their ideals, whatever its deficiencies in practice. Yet they too saw the Armistice and Pétain's 'gift of his person' to shield France from further misfortune as the only realistic option available in the chaos and uncertainty of 1940. Most people assumed that Britain would be forced to come to terms with Hitler; and it was not until Russia and America were brought into the war in 1941 that hope arose that Germany would not necessarily be left as undisputed master of Europe. In these circumstances, and with ten million people on the road, it was easy enough for Marshal Pétain to obtain the full powers he sought, in the name of stabilising the situation and establishing a *modus vivendi* with Germany. Many of the Deputies and Senators who voted away the nation's democratic liberties assumed that it was a short-term measure, pending the establishment of peace in Europe and a return to normality – even if others saw in it a unique opportunity to rid France of an unstable parliamentary system that was not only inefficient but had let into power the Popular Front, despite the socio-demographic odds that were still stacked against Socialism. Democratic misgivings were also mollified by the fact that this temporary guardian of the nation's short-term destinies was the octogenarian Marshal Pétain – the man whom Léon Blum had called France's 'noblest and most humane soldier'. Many French bishops had served as soldiers in the First World War; and they like countless others remembered him not only as 'the victor of Verdun' but the constant champion of minimising hardship to the common soldier – a benevolent realist whose common sense seemed mirrored once more in his choice of an armistice rather than the bloody continuation of a hopeless war. Even so, there were at least five *catholiques avant tout* among the courageous eighty MPs who voted against granting him full powers – notably Senator (and ex-minister) Champetier de Ribes (see p. 159) and two of his Parti Démocrate Populaire colleagues in the lower house, Paul Simon and Pierre Trémintin, plus a couple of Jeune République adherents.

In the meantime the self-appointed leader of the French in London, Brigadier-General Charles de Gaulle, ten-day Under-Secretary of State for War in Reynaud's cabinet, was a committed Catholic, whose deep religious convictions were nonetheless linked with a firm resistance to clerical pressures in political matters, be it from Rome or the French episcopacy.[1] On his own admission, his initial following in London contained few Catholics: 'The synagogue sends me more than the cathedral.'[2] But his immediate entourage contained several Catholics of calibre who were later to achieve political prominence in the Fourth Republic. René Pleven was a former leader of the Association Catholique de la Jeunesse Française and a future prime minister, while de Gaulle's official spokesman with the BBC was Maurice Schumann of subsequent MRP fame. Schumann was to co-edit a monthly periodical, *Volontaire pour la cité chrétienne*, which in its first issue in October 1941 was to carry an article by Jacques Maritain and declarations by the independent-minded Archbishop Saliège of Toulouse (see pp. 228–9). Other Catholic colleagues of de Gaulle could almost have been invented by a French equivalent of Evelyn Waugh. Thierry d'Argenlieu had been provincial superior of the *déchaussé* Carmelite order in France; but the early months of the war found him serving as a naval officer. Captured by the Germans, he rapidly made his escape to London where he provided de Gaulle's followers with their rallying emblem, the Cross of Lorraine. By 1942, already a rear-admiral, he had become de Gaulle's National Commissioner for the Pacific, a happier prelude to his later disastrous spell as High Commissioner in Indo-China, where his heavy-handed treatment of a delicate situation was to contribute to Ho Chi Minh's successful bid for national independence. His Catholic colleague with responsibility for the Cameroons was Colonel Philippe Leclerc de Hautecloque, old boy of Ste Geneviève and later liberator of Paris in 1944, whose subsequent involvement in Indo-Chinese affairs was to show far more realism and sensitivity than that of Thierry d'Argenlieu.

The demoralising inactivity of the Phoney War and the speed and decisiveness of the German campaign of 1940 gave little scope for the clergy in uniform to recreate the reputation and respect that it had acquired in 1914–18, even if 2,800 of them subsequently found ample opportunity to do so behind the barbed wire of prisoner-of-war camps. As in the First World War, physical danger and imprisonment saw marked increases in religious observance among the armed services. Indeed a majority of officers in a number of prisoner-of-war camps regularly attended Sunday Mass; and although in many cases this assiduity did not survive release and the return of peace, periodic church-going at major Church festivals became a habit of a sizeable minority, aided no doubt by the more relaxed ethos that was to characterise Church–State relations in post-war France.[3]

The tradition of Union Sacrée, however, was to find its strangest expression at governmental level. A few days after the launch of the German onslaught on France in May 1940, Paul Reynaud's predominantly free-thinking government requested a service in Notre Dame de Paris to call on divine protection, a service which the premier attended in person, together with a large number of his ministers. Even in the worst days of the First World War, France had witnessed nothing of this kind; indeed those prefects who had attended local wartime services had been rapidly called to order. Five weeks later, on the day of the Armistice, Pétain's new government attended a similar service in Bordeaux cathedral, with Reynaud in tow and President Lebrun of the expiring Republic sitting enthroned in the sanctuary. The Archbishop publicly blamed the military defeat on the nation's neglect of 'trois grandes réalités – Dieu, la Patrie, la famille' – a trinity of ideas which coincidentally or not was to become Vichy's new motto for France, albeit with the prophetic substitution of 'travail' for 'Dieu'. A couple of days after the establishment of the new Vichy regime, the government celebrated Bastille Day by attending Mass in St Louis's church in Vichy – an example that prefects, sub-prefects and mayors followed all over France, bringing together in symbolic worship the largest collection of anti-clericals that France had ever seen in church.[4] It was perhaps only to be expected that many clergy interpreted these ambiguous expressions of community feeling as tokens of official penitence, with the result that retribution and expiation were to become a dominant theme of ecclesiastical discourse in the next few months.

There can be little doubt that the majority of committed Catholics, of both Left- and Right-wing sympathies, began with favourable expectations of Vichy. They welcomed its benevolence towards the Church, and many – by no means confined to the Right – saw it as an opportunity to set about tasks that had been beyond the powers of the Third Republic with its succession of weak ministers, constantly at the mercy of an impregnable parliament. There were socially progressive Catholics who naively envisaged a vigorous government of national solidarity, in which traditional class antagonisms would be subordinated to a common determination to get things done. Indeed both Vichy and its intellectual counterparts in the Resistance were anxious to recreate or discover the sense of community which each side felt was lost in France – hence Vichy's attention to the family and to youth organisations. For Right-wing Catholics, and those of the possessing classes who had been traumatised by the Popular Front, the attractions of Vichy were evident enough.

Pétain himself was not a practising Catholic. Married to a divorcée, even the expiatory piety that characterised the early months of Vichy did not find him at Sunday Mass except on official or special occasions, or when his advisers thought it expedient that he should make the gesture. 'A good Mass never did anyone any harm', he once remarked to a weary freethinker in his entourage on one of these sorties. Even then he did not take Holy Communion; and it was only in his final post-war captivity that he became a practising Catholic in a meaningful sense. Although the Vatican had granted the nullification of his wife's first marriage as early

as 1929, it was only in 1943 that he went through the formalities of a
religious marriage – and then by proxy.[5]

Pétain's ministers included very few *catholiques avant tout*, even if the
first year of the regime saw in government a number of the 'social and
political package' type of Catholic, equivalent to the routine but tepid
church-goers to be found in conservative governments in other countries
where the traditional church was respected as a buttress of the social
order.[6] There were also devotees of Action Française such as the
Minister of Justice, Raphael Alibert, who had become an enthusiastic
supporter of Church interests after Pius XII lifted the papal condemnation of Action Française in 1939, an enthusiasm he demonstrated by
legalising the long-standing clandestine presence of the religious orders
in Catholic schools (3 September 1940).[7] Jacques Chevalier, who was
Secretary of State for Education during Pierre-Etienne Flandin's brief
ministry (14 December 1940–9 February 1941), represented a much
more established Catholic commitment. A philosophy professor at
Grenoble, he had been an early mentor of Emmanuel Mounier and
a defendant of Catholic members of the state educational system (see
p. 169). His reintroduction of religious instruction as an optional subject
into state schools (6 January 1941) embarrassed even some of his
intended beneficiaries – so much so that the next head of government,
Admiral François Darlan (10 February 1941–17 April 1942), replaced
him with the straightforwardly secularist if professedly Catholic Jérôme
Carcopino who commuted the concession to simple time off for optional
instruction outside school (10 March 1941). Not only was Darlan, like
Laval, unsympathetic to the Church, but his ministry represented the
dominance of technocratic planning, dedicated to the mounting
imperatives of meeting Germany's economic demands. There was little
room for what he called 'the soft-cheeked altar-boys' who had hungrily
sniffed around the fringes of government in Vichy and whom the
German embassy staff in Paris accused of giving an undesirable clerical
tone to Vichy.[8] Indeed in the later stages of Vichy, the only prominent
Catholic at top level was Philippe Henriot, a leading radio propagandist
who became Laval's Secretary of State for Information from January
1944 until his assassination six months later.

It was largely at more junior level that *catholiques avant tout* were to be
found in government. The organisation of youth was put in the hands of
Georges Lamirand, a paternalistic Catholic of the Marshal Lyautey
stamp, who was entrusted with the task of lending conviction to the
National Revolution until Laval got rid of him in February 1943. While
Lamirand was in charge, there was a strong Catholic presence in the
various youth organisations. The *postard*, General Joseph de la Porte du

Theil, headed the Chantiers de la Jeunesse – a form of labour service for young men of conscript age – while Henri Dhavernas led the Compagnons de France, a youth movement for adolescents. The instructors of these organisations were themselves trained in special *écoles de cadres*, of which the best known was the Ecole Nationale des Cadres d'Uriage near Grenoble. Although Uriage was a non-confessional organisation, many of its staff and visiting lecturers were influenced by Emmanuel Mounier's Catholic Personalism – Mounier himself being one of the school's instructors, as was the future founder and editor of *Le Monde*, Hubert Beuve-Méry, who at one time had considered becoming a priest. Some 3,000 young people attended its courses; and when Admiral Darlan paid it a visit in July 1941, he was sufficiently impressed by what he found that he prescribed three weeks' residence at Uriage for all successful entrants into the Conseil d'Etat, the Cour des Comptes and the Ministries of Finance and Foreign Affairs. German suspicion, however, put an end to whatever potential Uriage might have had for being a formative influence on the future *fonctionnaires* of the leading *corps d'état*; and, after its dissolution, some of its staff eventually found their way into the Resistance – as did a number of former members of the Chantiers and the Compagnons.[9]

Vichy's nearest approximation to a political movement was the Légion des Combattants, in which a number of well-known Catholics played formative roles. Its vice-president was François Valentin who had been a regional organiser of the Association Catholique de la Jeunesse Française in the 'thirties. His strongly anti-German sentiments, however, led to his leaving the Légion in June 1942, and ultimately took him into the Resistance in the following year.[10] Very different was the career of his Catholic *légionnaire* colleague, Xavier Vallat, who like Philippe Henriot had moved sharply rightwards from Castelnau's Fédération Nationale Catholique in the 1920s (see p. 157) to Pierre Taittinger's strong-arm Jeunesses Patriotes in the 'thirties. His notorious antisemitism led to his appointment as France's first Commissioner-General for Jewish Affairs in March 1941, a post he held for a year until his Germanophobia led to his replacement by Louis Darquier de Pellepoix.[11]

In addition to these public office-holders, there were a number of Catholic hangers-on in the Marshal's entourage – men such as the *postard*, General Emile Laure – and a sizeable contingent of Action Française devotees who breathed once more the air of incense, now the papal ban had been lifted from their movement in 1939.[12] Many of them saw in the Marshal the ideal of monarchy that they found so singularly absent in the Royalist Pretender, the wheeling-and-dealing Henri Comte de Paris, who had not only disowned Action Française in December 1937 but was trying to strike a bargain with the Anglo-American Allies, after being turned down by Pétain in August 1942.[13] But such influence as these various cliques at Vichy exercised steadily declined, especially after 1942 when Pétain was progressively compelled by German pressure to leave decision-making to Laval and his ministers. Laval regarded Action Française as a political enemy, and he was increasingly irritated by the delicate consciences and ingratitude of many Catholics when faced with the dirty work that he saw himself performing on the nation's behalf.

Vichy's *fonctionnaires*

With Catholics in a variety of public posts, it might seem that the last bastions of secular purity in the civil service were theirs for the taking. Vichy certainly saw major changes of personnel – with Freemasons prominent among the early victims. Masonry had been proscribed along with other 'secret societies' (13–19 August 1940); and Bernard Fay, the obsessively anti-Masonic director of the Bibliothèque Nationale, headed a team that combed the archives of the Grand Orient, compiling lists of Masons that were subsequently published in the *Journal Officiel*.[14] Accounts vary as to the number of Masons who lost their jobs in the public sector – some claiming over 14,000, including 1,328 teachers.[15] Other targets of discriminatory action were former active members of Left-wing parties, while Jews began to suffer exclusion from responsible state employment and the teaching profession as early as October 1940. The continued captivity of conscripted soldiers in German prisoner-of-war camps likewise left vacancies in the civilian sectors from which they had been drafted. There were also defections of *fonctionnaires* to the Resistance, especially in the later stages of the Occupation when Germany's supremacy in Europe was being increasingly questioned. All of which potentially created opportunities for people whose opinions and beliefs had hitherto been considered a liability in pre-Vichy days.

Yet the impact of this situation on the *bien pensant* was less dramatic than is sometimes supposed. As shown in earlier chapters, politico-religious discrimination had ceased to be a significant factor in most sectors of public employment; and in the few branches where it still had some resonance in the 1930s, there was remarkably little influx of personnel from outside these branches under Vichy. One of the areas where most difference was felt was primary education. A circular of 22 July 1940 entrusted the nomination of probationary and supply teachers to the *inspecteurs d'académie*, thereby cutting out the vetting role of the *conseils départementaux de l'enseignement primaire* with their strong presence of anticlerical SNI delegates. And ten weeks later the SNI itself was to lose its legal status when unions at a national level were declared outlawed (10 October 1940).[16] The brevity, upheaval and uncertainty of the Occupation years make it impossible to gauge the effect of these changes on the profession, just as one cannot evaluate the impact of Vichy's Instituts de Formation Professionnelle which were substituted in September 1940 for the Republic's training colleges – 'these anticlerical seminaries', as Pétainists called them.

As far as the ministries and the *grands corps* were concerned, they had their jealously guarded ladders of promotion, which meant that vacancies in all but the lowest ranks would usually be filled by promoting existing members of the establishment who had already entered the service in the pre-war period and who would reflect whatever was *comme il faut* at that time. Admittedly those who knew how to trim with the new winds in France might be at an advantage in obtaining promotion – but this was of little satisfaction to those who had been or felt excluded in the 1930s and were now too old to want to compete for entry at the poorly paid bottom level. Even the judiciary remained remarkably stable in the Vichy period, despite the hard choices that faced it in a period when Frenchmen were hunting down Frenchmen. These conflicts of loyalty were rendered somewhat less acute by the government's establishment of special courts to deal with political opposition and certain categories of Resistance activity – otherwise defections among ordinary judges might have been greater.[17] Even so, many judges regarded the Resistance as terrorists, imperilling the *modus vivendi* with Germany that Vichy had established; and, like other senior civil servants, the majority preferred a flawed state of order to anarchy. Moreover it took courage to renounce a secure income in times of uncertainty.

The judiciary, however, had long since been open to Catholic infiltration; and a much more interesting area for investigation was the *corps préfectoral*. More than most regimes, Vichy needed to assure itself of the dedicated loyalty of its prefects, and it left them in no doubt as to the new tunes they would be required to sing. A circular of 15 October 1940 told them: 'You are the propagandists of truth, hope and liberating action, the defenders of a France that has been murdered by twenty years of error and folly.'[18] Lest any fell short of this ideal, the government had already accorded itself the power to shed unwanted civil servants by simple decree (17 July 1940); and the new Minister of the Interior, the renegade Socialist, Adrien Marquet, lost no time in making use of it. Thirty-five were sacked immediately, followed by others, while all but twenty-seven of the remainder were reshuffled to new departments within the first months of the regime. The process continued throughout the Occupation, with German demands for arrests and dismissals accelerating the pace; the result was that most departments saw new faces every eighteen months.[19]

Yet this did not bring about the collapse of the old Republican order in the *corps préfectoral*, still less a massive influx of the political pariahs of the past. Of the new prefects, 82 per cent had been sub-prefects under the Third Republic; and perhaps more astonishingly 87 per cent of Vichy's total complement of sub-prefects and prefectoral *secrétaires généraux* in 1943 had entered the service before the Occupation. Even the eighteen newly created regional prefects (19 April 1941) exhibited much the same career pattern; only a quarter had come from outside the *corps*.[20] What clearly emerges is that even in the most politicised branch of the civil service, the hard-won structures and career expectations of the profession were surviving the political pressures from outside. Not only were the one-time watchdogs of the Third Republic learning to bark at different enemies, but the small minority of outsiders whom Vichy appointed to prefectures turned out to be less satisfactory than the internal promotions. These new brooms, plucked from the armed services and the Right-wing pre-war parliaments, often had little under-standing of the adroit footwork that was traditionally required of a prefect, even in these much-changed times; nor were the transfers from the Conseil d'Etat, the Cour des Comptes and the Inspection des Finances all that better. Enthusiastic dedication to the aims of the new regime was no substitute for routine professionalism, however weary; and only a fifth of the outsiders survived in office until the last years of Vichy.[21]

Even so this modest incursion of outsiders might have seemed to have been the opportunity for committed Catholics, who were sympathetic to Vichy, to breach the secular citadel. Yet it is hard to demonstrate from printed sources the degree to which this may have happened. Putting aside common names with no clear means of identification, it would appear that none of Vichy's prefects was ever a pupil at the Ecole Ste Geneviève, Vaugirard or the Collège Stanislas.[22] This leaves open all the other Catholic schools – and indeed the state sector, which had many Catholic pupils. Among the half-dozen Vichy prefects who were former MPs, none of them was clearly associated with Catholic groups or causes in the inter-war period, whatever their private beliefs and opinions.[23] Thus, although Vichy would seem to have removed the barriers, it is far from clear how many committed Catholics actually became prefects. The presence of a prefect at Sunday Mass did not necessarily signify religious commitment, now that political and social expediency had changed camps; and it is even more difficult to ascertain the situation concerning sub-prefects and *secrétaires généraux*. Of the 13 per cent who entered the *corps* under Vichy, there is no unambiguous evidence that any of them had been at Ste Geneviève, Vaugirard or Stanislas.[24] But, as in the case of prefects, this leaves unexplored all the other possible sources of Catholic candidates.

The period 1941–2 found the French Ambassador to the Holy See vainly attempting to negotiate a concordat with the Vatican; but neither Rome nor the French episcopate thought it opportune to link the Church's fortunes with a regime of uncertain future, especially with Russia and America now in the war.[25] There was growing concern among the bishops over Vichy's increasing subservience to Germany; and in the autumn of 1942 their political spokesman privately advised Pétain to resign rather than become the mere tool of German policies.[26] The deportation of Jews likewise provoked a number of public protests from the more courageous bishops. But, despite these misgivings, episcopal loyalty to Pétain remained strong; and even as late as 17 February 1944 the assembly of cardinals and archbishops denounced Resistance activities as 'terrorism'.[27]

The Vatican, however, was more responsive to the changing fortunes of war. Occupying a position of theoretical neutrality, it could lean one way rather than the other with less displacement than the French hierarchy which was committed to a position of legal respect for the established government. The Archbishop of Lyon – 'Sa Réticence, le cardinal Gerlier', as Pétain drily described him – recalled in September 1941 how Pius XII had said to him, 'I believe that if Germany were to be victorious, it would be the greatest misfortune to befall the Church for centuries.'[28] But already in January 1943 the Pope indicated to Cardinal Suhard of Paris that he thought Hitler had lost the war; and when, eighteen months later, de Gaulle visited the Pope, the Vatican cautiously and ingeniously received him with the modest official honours which protocol prescribed for heirs to the throne as distinct from heads of government – for there was still a nuncio accredited to Vichy. But the papal Secretary of State, Cardinal Maglione, privately told de Gaulle that he was already regarded by the Vatican as the *de facto* head of government.[29] Maglione and his junior colleague Tardini were well versed in the tergiversations that were needed to survive in the modern world; and Tardini was later to remark with wry resignation that Vatican diplomacy first began with Peter's three-fold denial of Christ.

From de Gaulle to de Gaulle

The government that de Gaulle formed in liberated Paris was not only headed by a practising Catholic – the first for seventy years – but nearly a third of its principal portfolios were held by committed Catholics: men whose Catholicism went substantially further than the 'social package' variety that characterised some of Vichy's ministers. Three of them – Georges Bidault (Foreign Affairs), François de Menthon (Justice) and Pierre-Henri Teitgen (Information) – were to be leading figures in the Mouvement Républicain Populaire which came into formal existence two months later in November 1944. The other two, René Pleven (Colonies) and René Capitant (Education), who had likewise been deeply involved in Resistance activity, kept clear of the MRP – Pleven remaining part of the small UDSR, while Capitant was to be the social conscience of the Gaullist Rassemblement du Peuple Français when it eventually emerged in 1947.

The MRP was to continue to hold an average of four to five portfolios in the governments of the next ten years, with René Pleven as a frequent cabinet colleague. Bidault and Robert Schuman virtually monopolised the Quai d'Orsay in this period; Teitgen and Robert Lecourt dominated Justice in the first four years, while the sacking of the Communist ministers in 1947 and the gradual shift of government towards the Centre then the Right saw long periods of MRP tenure of Health, the Colonies, Industry and Labour, with a couple of successive tenancies of the Ministry of Information as well.[30] The party likewise provided the new republic with three prime ministers – Bidault and Schuman heading two governments each, with Pflimlin briefly presiding over the crisis of the regime in May 1958. De Gaulle's three premierships and Pleven's double innings brought the total of Catholic-headed governments to ten in the post-war republic – possibly twelve if one adds the less obvious claims of Pinay and Laniel.

Like the Radicals under the Third Republic or the Centre Party under Weimar, the MRP was to be a semi-indispensable make-weight in the creation of governments of both Left and Right – of the Left in its early years, and of the Centre and the Right thereafter. Its Resistance credentials and its initial commitment to social reform and a state-planned economy made it a viable if not particularly congenial bed-fellow for the Socialists and Communists in the euphoria of the Liberation, at a time when the conservatives were expiating their record under Vichy and the Radicals were tainted by memories of their mistakes in the 'thirties. But with the advent of the Cold War and the dropping of the Communists from government, the mathematics of coalition cabinets required compensation from the right of Centre, which gave the Radicals and then the conservatives the opportunity to come in from the cold. The pivotal position of the MRP in the spectrum of parliamentary politics made it a sought-after partner in the new game, just as it had been in the old.[31]

This flexible appeal was paradoxically aided by the disparity between the ideals of the MRP's founding fathers and the more conservative considerations of many of the electors who voted for it in the three elections of the mid-'forties. Its strong showing, a very close second to that of the Communists, was aided not only by the enfranchisement of women, but also by the votes of conservatives whose former leaders had been discredited by the events of the recent past. De Gaulle's RPF of 1947 had to await the 1951 elections before it could compete with the MRP for the Catholic vote; and despite its 120 seats in the new Assembly, its hostile attitude to the institutions of the Fourth Republic more or less excluded it from participation in government for the remaining short life of the regime. The solitary Gaullist mavericks who took occasional portfolios in the last years of the republic could not be regarded as representative of Catholic opinion, in the fashion of their MRP colleagues, despite their support for Catholic causes such as state aid for private education. Similarly the conservative ministers of the 1950s were first and foremost proponents of socio-economic aims rather than specifically Catholic objectives, even though they were prepared to speak on their behalf – especially if it won them Catholic votes at election time. An opinion poll of 1952 revealed that 79 per cent of those who voted MRP were regular Mass-goers. And if, conversely, 20 per cent of Mass-goers voted for conservatives and 18 per cent for the Gaullists, this still left 54 per cent who voted for the MRP. Had there been similar polls in the mid-'forties, before the launch of the RPF, they would certainly have revealed an even higher proportion – perhaps two-thirds to three-quarters. In these circumstances secular speculation as to what was likely to be the future political role of practising Catholics was inevitably heavily influenced by the behaviour and attitudes of the MRP.

The MRP had professed its dual aim of reconciling the working classes and the Church, and of reconciling the Church with the Republic. The Resistance record of its leaders lent credibility to its republican sentiments – although sceptics pointed out that Resistance did not guarantee Republicanism. A number of Catholic royalists had been active in the Resistance, while, more dangerously, the sort of republic wanted by the Gaullists was very different from what 'republic' meant in the ideology of the Left. Even so the MRP was given credit for keeping its distance from the bishops and from Rome. Unlike the Catholic parties of the Belle Epoque, neither the bishops nor the Vatican had been consulted in the negotiations that had brought it into being; and, although the hazardous circumstances of the Occupation would in any case have made consultation difficult, this distance reflected the low opinion that the MRP had of the political judgement and moral courage of the bulk of the episcopacy and Rome. It was likewise known that Bidault had pressed Rome for the removal of a dozen of the bishops – even if he eventually had to settle for four – while some MRP members were outbidding the Communists and demanding the mitres of thirty more.[32]

The initial appeal and influence of the MRP was also helped by the fact that neither the bishops nor the Vatican were tempted to reassert their authority at a time when their credit was so low. Like the conservative parties, the episcopate kept a low profile at the Liberation, waiting for the clouds of opprobrium to disperse before attempting to impose their traditional leadership over the faithful. The Vatican, too, emerged from the Second World War with its image tarnished in the eyes of the victors. It needed the development of the Cold War, and the reassuring domestic context of a strong Christian Democrat government in Italy, for Rome to resume its interventionist role in French Catholic affairs.

The democratic credentials of the MRP and the rehabilitation of Catholics as a political force in France inevitably coloured attitudes to the Catholic presence in the civil service. The fact that nearly a third of ministerial portfolios were now held by Catholics might have seemed to guarantee an end to any residual reluctance to appoint Catholics to the political pinnacles of *les fonctions publiques*. And, as in 1940, the purge of personnel expected of the new regime seemed to promise vacancies for those ready to take advantage of the *esprit nouveau*.

As it happened, the Liberation purges were modest as compared with those that occurred in other occupied countries where German rule had been direct. French civil servants made much of the fact that their loyalty had been to an indigenous French government that could point to the parliamentary vote of 10 July 1940 as a *de jure* if not a moral legitimation. At the same time de Gaulle was acutely conscious of the debilitating divisions in French society and of the need to present a united front to a hard competitive outside world, dominated by the superpowers. He was therefore anxious to keep reprisals to a minimum. The fact too that both the premier and the Minister of Justice were Catholic helped to ensure that retribution did not lead to a major anticlerical settling of scores – whatever might have happened unofficially at local level. Nearly 50,000 government employees were investigated, of whom 11,343 were sacked or subjected to lesser punishment, representing a mere 1.3 per cent of the total force. And of those dismissed, many were to be readmitted in the next five years.[33] Typically 98 per cent of the members of the Cour des Comptes who had been in office in 1942 were still *in situ* after the Liberation, and the same was true of 97 per cent of the *inspecteurs généraux des finances*.[34]

As always, the greatest changes were in the *corps préfectoral*. On the eve of the Liberation, de Gaulle's Committee of National Liberation in Algiers had compiled a list of eighty-seven new prefects for the promised land, only twenty of whom were members of the *corps*. But as in the case of Vichy's appointments of non-*corps* prefects, many of these outsiders proved unsatisfactory or chose to move to other occupations once order had been re-established. The result was that by 1947 about half the prefects were once more career *corps* members – sub-prefects and *secrétaires généraux* who had entered the *corps* in the inter-war period and many of whom had also served the Vichy regime.[35] Some had been prefects under Vichy, but had left the ship sufficiently early to count as bona fide opponents of the regime; indeed a number had been arrested by the Germans, while others had been active members of the Resistance, several while still in office. *Corps* experience under Vichy, coupled with arrest by the Germans, appears to have been a strong recommendation for a subsequent prefectoral career, as the 1947 list of prefects testifies. And among the sub-prefects and *secrétaires généraux* of the post-war period, an alphabetical sample of 114 in 1947 shows 52 per cent of them as having been *corps* members under Vichy.[36]

Given that a substantial proportion of the post-war prefects had first entered the *corps* in the inter-war period – as indeed had a number of the post-war sub-prefects and *secrétaires généraux* – there still existed in the *corps* something of the secular ethos of the Third Republic, whatever habits they might have temporarily picked up in the *bien pensant* interludes of Vichy. In any case the reaffirmation of the secular state – enshrined in the constitutional laws of the new republic – imposed on prefects the strict neutrality observed before the war. In practice Sunday Mass-going, even in a private capacity, was still regarded as something of a mild embarrassment which the Ministry of the Interior preferred not to happen. It was significant that no member of the MRP, or committed Catholic of any other party, was allowed to become Minister of the Interior under the Fourth Republic. None of the five Catholic premiers contemplated making such an appointment; and the portfolio was usually entrusted to a safely secular Socialist or Radical who knew what the Republic expected of him.

After the departure of many of the Liberation prefects into other occupations, the more stabilised *corps* of the remaining years of the Fourth Republic seems to have contained few committed Catholics who can be easily identified as such. One estimate of the personal political sympathies of the *corps préfectoral* during the Fourth Republic put the proportions as one half radical, a quarter socialist, and the remaining quarter *modérés*, with a small sprinkling of MRP supporters – 'ces derniers ont toujours été très peu nombreux'.[37] It would seem that no old boy of Ste Geneviève, Vaugirard, Caousou or the Collège Stanislas became a prefect in the post-Liberation years of the Fourth Republic – although Ste Geneviève provided a *secrétaire général* and Stanislas at least a couple of sub-prefects.[38]

It was nevertheless claimed – if only by the *corps* and its masters – that the prefects of the Fourth Republic now represented what Edgard Pisani called 'les formes techniques du gouvernement' rather than the particular attitudes of the ministry currently in power.[39] Henri Queuille, when Minister of the Interior, instructed his prefects, 'To govern, to administer, is essentially to seek out the common ground between people, to avoid contentious issues; it is a continual attempt to lay bare the unity of the nation that lies beneath the diversity of spiritual views that divides public opinion.'[40] But while this might seem a world away from the ethos of the Combes era, some argued that the search for consensus and common ground was itself a good reason for being wary of committed Catholics in the prefectures.

It was widely hoped that the establishment of the Ecole Nationale d'Administration (9 October 1945) would eliminate what remaining scope there was for political favouritism in the public services. While ENA undoubtedly brought a much greater degree of homogeneity to the recruitment of the senior civil service, it did not bring a unity to the various *concours* which were still the fortified portals of the central administration of the various ministries.[41] Its creation did at least ensure that intending candidates for these various *concours* had been sifted beforehand and the weaker aspirants effectively eliminated by the ENA entrance requirements. This in turn reduced the opportunity for the ministerial selection committees to favour candidates of their choice; their favourites had at least to be good enough to have passed through ENA. At the same time the institutionalising of early career-patterns, which ENA helped to reinforce, reduced the power of the *piston* and lessened without eliminating the volleys of MPs' letters that had traditionally accompanied promotions and transfers. Even so, it was not until 1964 that ENA acquired a monopoly of entry into the *corps préfectoral*; and in the meantime none of the *énarques* who entered the *corps* under the Fourth Republic was of an age and experience to obtain a prefecture before the fall of the regime in 1958.[42] Even under the Gaullist presidency there were to be only seven *in situ* by 1967.[43] There was piquancy in the fact that the driving force behind the creation of ENA was the Gaullist jurist, Michel Debré, a Jew who became a Catholic during the Second World War. Although his commitment to the idea of ENA dated back to the 1930s, he was to discuss it at length with his Resistance colleague, François de Menthon, a future luminary of the MRP.

The ordinance that created ENA also brought the old Ecole Libre des Sciences Politiques under the state umbrella – which many idealistically hoped would indirectly help to democratise the senior ranks of the civil service. It is true that in its private days the considerable expense of attending the school had guaranteed it a clientele that was *bien bourgeois* – and thus, to some modest degree, *bien pensant* as well (see p. 82). But in a grant-starved society, the cost of attending its state-run successor was still considerable, especially for students whose families lived in the provinces; and the newly created replicas in other university centres were little match for the Rue Guillaume when it came to grooming successful entrants for ENA. Thus while all Catholics stood to gain by the growing depoliticisation of the civil service, those of 'good family' still enjoyed the traditional advantages that social privilege conferred in a world of unequal opportunities.

If the *corps préfectoral* was still a contentious area in post-war France, so was education. Like the Ministry of the Interior, Education was a portfolio that no MRP member was allowed to have under the Fourth Republic. Although the Catholic Gaullist, René Capitant, held it in de Gaulle's first government, that was in the pre-parliamentary days of the Liberation. As soon as the First Constituent Assembly came into existence in October 1945, de Gaulle gave the Education portfolio to a tried-and-true Radical, Paul Giacobbi; and thereafter, like the Interior, it was handed backwards and forwards between Radicals and Socialists for the remaining years of the regime. Even so, Catholics could take a sly satisfaction in the fact that one of the Radicals, René Billères, was a regular if inconspicuous Mass-goer who was given the ministry by the Socialist leader, Guy Mollet, in February 1956 and held it under the two Radical premiers who followed.

The contentious nature of Education was evident from the early days of the Liberation. Teachers, like journalists, were performers, who left a memorable impact on their public that could be recalled, embellished or distorted, when retribution was meted out in the purges. Taking all levels of state education, some 680 teachers were sacked outright, while

320 others were suspended or obliged to take early retirement – this representing about 0.7 per cent of the total.[44] Attitudes to the Germans were the decisive criteria; and, as elsewhere in the public services, it would be very hard to demonstrate these punishments as in any way an anticlerical backlash.

Even so the Left-wing parties were determined not to allow Vichy's breaches in secular neutrality to be re-opened. The MRP had already aroused their vigilance by including in its manifesto of 1944 the principle that the State should subsidise private as well as public schools, provided they observed comparable academic standards.[45] Indeed the MRP members of the Second Constituent Assembly attempted to get the principle incorporated in the constitution; and, given the support of the Right-wing parties, they nearly succeeded – falling short by the narrow margin of 272 votes to 274 (28 August 1946). When the RPF was launched in 1947, the Gaullists saw the schools issue as a salutary method of wooing the Catholic vote; and the MRP, scared of being upstaged by this newcomer, yielded to the temptation of returning to the issue, despite the attendant risk of breaking its coalition with the Socialists. The MRP Health minister, Madame Poinso-Chapuis, issued a decree (23 May 1948) which proposed modest funds to help educate the children of needy families, including those at private schools. Although it was never implemented, it helped to turn the Socialists towards the Radicals as their future allies, thereby accelerating the MRP's drift from its initial reformist ideals and encouraging its growing tendency to seek friends on the Right. This unhealthy development gathered pace after the 1951 elections, when the Gaullist capture of many former MRP voters drove the MRP to try to regain lost Catholic support. With a Catholic once more in the Matignon – this time, René Pleven of the UDSR – the MRP yielded to the same temptation as in 1948, and sacrificed goodwill on its Left in return for the inclusion of private-school pupils in the State's meagre financial help to families (21 September 1951).

All this revived anti-Catholic feeling in the state teachers' unions, even if it had relatively little impact on the entry of Catholic teachers into the state sector – a number of whom shared the misgivings of their secular colleagues. The financial concessions, though small, were seen as the thin end of a wedge inserted into a basic tenet of Republican principle. In fact the imagined consequences were as nothing compared with the thick end of the wedge that was to come after the collapse of the regime in 1958. Yet ironically the consummation of this process with the Debré law of 1959 was eventually to quench the quarrel rather than inflame it – even if this effect was far from obvious at the time.

The extent of the Debré law's concessions was the outcome of the political difficulties facing de Gaulle's government in 1959. Many of the men who had brought de Gaulle to power in the previous year had assumed that de Gaulle would save France from the humiliation of a Vietnamese-style withdrawal from Algeria; but de Gaulle was increasingly convinced that independence was inescapable and that the Right in parliament would have to be cajoled into accepting it. While the Gaullists since 1947 had consistently courted the Catholic electorate with proposals for financial help to private schools, de Gaulle held no particular political brief for the Church, despite the sincerity of his own religious convictions; and his prime minister, Michel Debré – although a convert to Catholicism – typified the Jacobin étatist strand of Gaullism. On the other hand de Gaulle believed that tax-paying parents with children in the private sector – whose education cost the nation nothing – had a right to some return on their contribution to the education budget, provided that the schools of their choice came up to state standards. The existence of a large Right-wing majority in parliament made this a propitious moment for having done with this issue – especially while potential opposition in the country at large was distracted by the Algerian war and the general upheaval of assimilating the new institutions of the Fifth Republic. But the need to propitiate a Right, increasingly uneasy about de Gaulle's handling of the Algerian question, resulted in concessions to private education that were far larger than the government had originally envisaged: so much so that the Minister of Education, André Boulloche, resigned in protest. Neither Charles X nor Vichy at their most clerical had contemplated such generosity; and the bishops, scarcely believing their luck, kept a prudent reticence throughout the affair.

The majority for the bill in the Assembly, 427 to 71 (24 December 1959), broadly reflected the Right–Left strength of the parties, and inevitably fuelled Left-wing accusations that the Catholic leopard had once more shown its spots. When in a minority and politically vulnerable, Catholics were ready enough to profess their loyalty to the Republic, but as soon as a temporary advantage came their way, as with Vichy or the Gaullist victory of 1958, they did not hesitate to seize whatever benefits they could – even if they directly violated basic Republican principles. Catholics replied that the Debré law merely brought them closer to the position of their co-religionists in a number of neighbouring countries. Even Britain, where there existed an established Protestant Church, paid the salaries and running costs of Catholic schools – and a growing proportion of their capital expenditure as well. Secularists replied that British Catholics had bought these concessions by conceding that their schools should be an integrated part of the state system, subject to its control in secular matters; schools that did not accept these terms received in most cases next to nothing from the British government. French Catholics by contrast had been given many of the advantages of the British bargain, but had refused to pay the price of submitting to state control; vetting of appointments and parity of standards was all that they had conceded.

Within four years, two-thirds of French private schools had entered into contracts with the State. Initially, all but 5 per cent of these contracts were *contrats simples*, under which the State paid the salaries and an increasing proportion of the national insurance of those teachers whose qualifications and teaching were on a par with those in the state schools. But in the years that followed, a growing number of private secondary schools opted for the *contrat d'association* which provided for state contributions to the running costs of the school as well, in return for a greater degree of state supervision.

Despite the initial furore in secular circles, the very size of these concessions paradoxically gave them an air of semi-finality which discouraged a continuing fight against them – until such time as the Left should itself enjoy a majority in parliament. A lot was to happen in the meantime. As the next chapter will show, the Catholic leopard, for all its spots, was to become a somewhat emaciated beast in the intervening years; and the spots themselves began to fade, causing many old anti-clericals to conclude that a person's Catholicism no longer had much relevance to his or her acceptability for positions of public trust.

11 Croquet through the looking glass: rules and identity in question, 1960–1994

For much of the twentieth century, constitutional and religious issues played a more prominent role in French politics than in most of the democracies of north-western Europe. In countries such as Britain and the Scandinavian kingdoms, politics have tended to be bipolarised on matters of social and economic policy and the distribution of income, whereas in France it is only in the last thirty years that socio-economic issues have not had to share public attention with major differences over the constitution and the place of religion in society. Hitherto, as Philip Williams said of the Third and Fourth Republics, 'three issues were fought out simultaneously: the eighteenth-century conflict between rationalism and Catholicism, the nineteenth-century struggle of democracy against authoritarian government, and the twentieth-century dispute between employer and employed'.[1] The Second World War and its aftermath saddled French politics with a fourth issue – a crisis of national self-esteem arising from the disintegration of empire. Over-burdened, the Fourth Republic collapsed beneath the divisive weight of these four problems, each of which cut across opinion in a different direction – thereby making coherent governmental majorities increasingly difficult to find.

The following decades, however, saw these debilitating issues virtually reduced to one – or so it seemed to many contemporaries. What is often called 'the social contest over the distribution of the national income' now dominated the stage; and observers claimed that French politics had belatedly come of age. France had taken her place among the advanced democracies, where power could be expected to alternate between the disciplined forces of Right and Left, taking their stance mainly on socio-economic matters. There remained sceptics, however, who claimed that the religious issue was far from dead – and a number of them sought to explain current French voting patterns in terms of deep-rooted religio-cultural differences. They pointed to the schools dispute of the early 1980s, where the champions of Catholic private education participated in the largest public demonstration in French history – and indirectly

194

brought about the resignation of the government. Nor were they convinced by the argument that the dispute fundamentally concerned the nature of private education, rather than Catholic education, and that it was a matter of social privilege and state control, rather than a resurgence of religious issues.

Debates of this kind beg many questions. Those who claim that religious problems in politics are largely a relic of the past concede their reality in under-developed or totalitarian societies. They assert that under-developed societies are still living in the past, while the all-embracing claims of totalitarian government are bound to come into conflict with the private, inner world of religious belief. They also recognise the political importance of religious matters for immigrant communities, reflected in the recent conflict between Muslim conventions and the French Ministry of Education. But they are embarrassed by the recrudescence of religious issues among the indigenous populations of advanced, western democracies. They prefer to see them as secular issues in clerical dress, owing more to social, ethnic or political factors.

The Gaullist Republic not only inaugurated twenty-three years of unbroken Right-wing government, but it gave France a succession of three presidents who openly professed to be practising Catholics. The prime ministers of the period were a more varied bunch, hard to pin down. Future presidents apart, Debré was a Jewish convert to Catholicism (see p. 190), Chirac spoke of himself as a Catholic and Barre behaved like one. With the rest it was difficult to say – and, more importantly, it did not seem to matter. Indeed the question was rarely put, except in interviews for glossy magazines, which made what they could of their subjects' suavely ambivalent replies. Even the self-proclaimed Catholics did not pursue policies or adopt styles and tactics that were observably any different from their freethinking or Protestant colleagues. Symptomatically, abortion and contraception made their greatest legal headway under President Giscard d'Estaing, a publicly church-going Catholic.

Outside the Elysée and the Matignon, distinctions were even harder to discern. The first four years of the Gaullist presidency had seen a cluster of MRP ministers in the cabinet, until de Gaulle's dismissive comments on the future of western European union led to their resignation in May 1962; and taking de Gaulle's and Pompidou's presidencies together, it has been claimed that as many as 54 per cent of their ministers were practising Catholics.[2] However wary one may be of such a figure, six of their ministers were products of the Collège Stanislas, including the tough-minded Roger Frey at the Ministry of the Interior (May 1961–April 1967); and whatever Frey's personal beliefs may have been, there was no doubting the Catholic convictions of Joseph Fontanet, one-time secretary-general of the MRP, who at long last planted the now-defunct party's flag on the Ministry of Education (July 1972–May 1974). As under the Ordre Moral or Vichy, the presence of a fair number of 'social package' Catholics in Gaullist government circles made identification of the significantly committed Catholic more difficult than was the case in Left-wing governments where a practising Catholic became the subject of journalistic curiosity. When the Left eventually came to power in 1981, the Finance Minister, Jacques Delors, was confidently identified as the only practising Catholic in Mauroy's government; and there was little speculation about the possible religious predilections of the others. But significantly it was widely agreed both inside and outside the cabinet that Delors's Catholicism was not a matter of political interest – except to people wishing to understand his personal development. For them it was obviously enlightening to know that his attitudes to social issues were strongly influenced by his early admiration for Mounier and by his involvement in Left-wing Catholic activity; but the past odyssey of his social conscience was seen as no more of an asset or encumbrance than those of his cabinet colleagues who had risen through the chequered channels of secular Socialism. It was his professional expertise in financial and economic matters that made him the focus of political attention. And in his later European role, even the anti-Brussels neo-anticlericals have made little of his Catholic commitment, despite its influence on the evolution of his ideas on European social welfare.

This growing indifference to the religious beliefs of French politicians owed much to developments in the 1960s. It was true that Catholic complaisance towards de Gaulle's dismantling of the Fourth Republic in 1958 had reawakened accusations that Catholic acceptance of Republican democracy was a mere cloak of convenience – just as Catholic complaisance towards Vichy had aroused similar and more virulent claims in the early 'forties. But the fact remained that other segments of opinion had also accepted Vichy, albeit with less initial expectation and reward. Similarly, and more obviously, most people had come to accept the virtues of the Fifth Republican constitution by the end of the 1960s – some more grudgingly than others. Even the Communists fielded a presidential candidate in 1969, if only to spite the Socialists; and once the 1980s demonstrated that the system could work in the interests of the Left as well as the Right, there was little nostalgia for the institutions of the Third and Fourth Republics. Even the shortening of the presidential seven-year term of office seemed less compelling when one's own man was in power.

There were additional factors, however, that helped to reduce traditional fears of Catholics in high places. It was increasingly realised in the late 'sixties and early 'seventies that religious practice was undergoing a marked numerical decline. This was a phenomenon that in varying degrees affected all the Christian churches in the developed economies, especially in western Europe.[3]

Yet it was preceded by a sharp if short-lived boom in church-going. The Second World War, like most wars, had temporarily increased religious observance, especially in the sections of society most at risk – soldiers and their families, and populations near to the battle-zones or subject to bombing and sudden deprivation. Even in non-belligerent countries, uncertainty as to what the future might bring had a similar if much less marked effect. Although peace saw a fall once more, it did not simply restore the status quo: the wartime resumption of church-going lingered in many families, especially in the generations that most clearly remembered the danger and hardship.[4] In the case of France, post-war religious observance was further strengthened by the political rehabilitation of the Church that took place in the mid-'forties (see pp. 185–7). With Catholics holding ministerial portfolios, including the premiership, *bien-pensant* civil servants could scarcely feel the nervousness about being seen at Mass that many of their predecessors had claimed to feel in the earlier years of the century.

Moreover Catholicism had acquired a certain intellectual as well as political respectability. The low profile adopted by the Vatican and the bishops in the Liberation years (see p. 187) gave laymen a louder voice in Catholic debate and contributed to the rich diversity that characterised Catholic writing and thought in post-war France – all of which temporarily awakened interest among the reading and theatre-going public. And even when the East–West divide came to the Vatican's rescue and restored its readiness to resort to anathemas in the 1950s, its reprimands were never treated with quite the same respect by the laity as they had been before the war. Indeed the Second World War had encouraged in France a Catholic anticlericalism that had hitherto been largely confined to an intellectual elite. It now became an attitude of mind that kept many middle-class Catholics within the Church – posing the question 'Why should I abandon my faith on account of the literal-minded fundamentalism of a few celibate geriatrics in Rome?' These and other factors saw a marked increase in religious observance among the professional classes, compared to pre-war years. Indeed in the early 1960s a sample poll of medical doctors revealed that nearly half claimed to be practising Catholics – a remarkable figure for a profession which had produced so many leading apostles of secular and materialist thought in the nineteenth century and which was sharply at odds with the Church's pronouncements on medical ethics.[5]

Figures of church-attendance and Easter communion in the 1950s and early 'sixties had indicated a significant rise in many dioceses since the 1930s, especially among men. This was especially evident in areas where government anticlericalism had been a potent factor before the First World War, and where traces of it had still existed in the inter-war years. Thus in the diocese of Chartres, where male Mass-going had shown some improvement between 1909 and 1931 (see pp. 172–3), the proportion had more than doubled by 1959, albeit to a modest 8 per cent. The level of women, by contrast, had risen much less spectacularly from 16.2 per cent in 1931 to 20.6 per cent in 1959 – suggesting that fear of anticlerical disapproval in earlier decades had kept the level of male attendance artificially low.[6] This pattern of difference was also true – but much less markedly so – of a number of dioceses where government anti-clericalism had been less stringently enforced during the Belle Epoque. This would seem to indicate that the decline of anticlericalism was only one of several factors accounting for the rise in male church-going since the 1930s.

Whatever encouragement the Church could draw from these trends was to be rapidly overturned in the 1960s. Regular Mass-going dropped from well over 20 per cent of the adult population (both sexes combined) in the early 'sixties to less than 15 per cent by the end of the decade – while the next twenty years were to see it fall to 10 per cent.[7] The dramatic fall in the 'sixties was undoubtedly part of the broader rejection of traditional forms of constraint and authority that swept developed countries in the later part of the decade. The generation that was coming of age at that time was the first which had not known the uncertainties and anxieties of the Second World War. It was maturing moreover in a period of unparalleled material prosperity and optimism when almost anything seemed possible. The development of the contraceptive pill had greatly increased sexual freedom and was putting women on a closer par with men. The only obstacles to this pursuit of the millennium were the hesitations and constraints of those in authority, people of an older generation which lacked the imagination to exploit the unrivalled opportunities of the present – and which had, moreover, involved mankind in a succession of wars (including Vietnam). The churches were just one form of traditional authority that came under scrutiny; and criticism by the young was increasingly paralleled by that of older people.

The crisis was particularly evident in the Catholic Church where the personal price of observing its teaching was greater – regular Mass-going, no artificial contraception, celibacy for the clergy, etc. At the same time the Second Vatican Council (1962–5) was creating expectations of major change and liberal reform which in many respects failed to materialise. Marginal Catholics, who had been delaying departure to see whether the Council would make the Church a more congenial haven, had no further reason to stay, while the bitter disappointment of progressives added to the exodus. The greatest blow was the papal encyclical *Humanae vitae* of 25 July 1968, which reasserted traditional Catholic teaching on birth control. It was widely known that a majority of the Pope's advisory committee on the matter favoured change, and change was widely expected. Many practising Catholics had long been using methods that the Church officially condemned; and others, anticipating a liberalising of Church teaching, had started to adopt them. Not only did Paul VI's rejection of change have a direct and serious bearing on family life but it posed enormous problems for the Third World where the efforts of relief agencies were constantly being negated by the rise in population. Of the Catholics who stayed – and they were still a large majority of the previous practising population – a sizeable number ignored the encyclical, taking as their justification the majority opinion of the Pope's advisory committee, which they saw as condoning what many of them had been doing for decades. Indeed by the early 1990s sample polls were to suggest that only a fifth of regular Mass-going women in France were heeding the encyclical's precepts.[8]

In this way the Church not only lost members, but it lost authority among those it retained. The laity became increasingly selective in the prescriptions it chose to follow, not only in sexual matters but in sacramental and liturgical issues as well. Some replaced the regular attendance of Sunday Mass with a more easy-going alternate Sunday formula, and a large number ceased to go to confession altogether, claiming that few priests had much understanding of the realities of married life or of the subtle psychological issues that effective moral guidance often involved. Whereas in 1952, a fifth of adult practising Catholics in France went to confession at least once a month, by 1983 the proportion had fallen to 1 per cent.[9] Indeed many priests began to question their own competence in a professional world where qualified counsellors, social workers and psychiatrists were much better equipped to deal with the problems that came their way. This was but one of many factors that saw the number of secular priests in France fall from about 40,000 in the mid-'sixties to 27,000 in 1986 – with the prospect of a mere 16,000 by the millennium.[10] Even their relatively unchallenged role of dispensers of the sacraments was being gently eroded at the edges by lay enthusiasts with their kitchen-table liturgical innovations,[11] while their more general role of benign dispensers of consolation and common sense was increasingly undermined by the rift they perceived between the Vatican rulings on sexual issues and the desperate family problems of many of those who sought their guidance. Although the French bishops advised priests to be extremely cautious in the confessional when dealing with matters of birth control, lest they precipitate further defections from confession and from the Church in general, this deepened still further the suspicion between Rome and the French Church, especially when John Paul II (1978–) embarked on a renewed offensive to assert Vatican views in this area. Faced with the embarrassment of a charismatic travelling pope, preaching uncongenial precepts, Catholic progressives made the best of an unpromising situation by resorting to a dialectical view of the Church, with the Vatican as thesis and the theological *avant garde* as antithesis – which, they bravely suggested, would allow a happy if precarious synthesis to emerge in God's good time. They would nod appreciatively when *avant garde* notions met with Roman anathemas – pointing out that this was the creation of dialogue which would eventually result in progress, however acrimonious the exchange: reaction had its vital place in the divine economy, as well as vision.

Faced with a Catholic laity that was increasingly selective in what it accepted from its spiritual leaders, governments of both Right and Left felt little concern at the committed Catholics who made their way into the secular recesses of state service. Their beliefs were not a matter for comment; rightly or wrongly they were largely seen as irrelevant. What even a prefect did with his Sunday mornings was his own affair – unless it clashed with functions that he was expected to attend. Indeed, in the new-fangled Church, *une messe d'anticipation* on a Saturday evening might be his choice. There was in fact a noticeable growth in the number of prefects whose roots lay in the Catholic west of France. The proportion had slowly grown from a mere 7 per cent during the Belle Epoque to 15 per cent by the Fourth Republic – with the upheaval of 1944–7 seeing a substantial part of this change. But the first decade of the Fifth Republic saw a rapid rise to 20 per cent, despite the fact that demographically these regions were in relative decline.[12] This did not necessarily mean, of course, that a significant number of these spray-spattered westerners were Catholic – either then or in earlier life – but they were symptomatic of the change in personnel brought about by the arrival of a Right-wing establishment, imbued with a top-down ethos and determined to make itself felt at local level. For the first time in the twentieth century, the Collège Stanislas could boast at least one prefect, while the Jesuit Vaugirard at last made a breach into the ranks of sub-prefects.[13] The degree of change was reflected in the fact that the first decade of the Fifth Republic saw the departure from the *corps* of 101 prefects, as compared with only 59 in the previous ten years; and, should anyone doubt what was still expected of a prefect, there was a prefectoral reshuffle in three-quarters of the departments where governmental candidates were beaten in the 1962 election.[14]

Yet the replacements for those prefects who left the *corps* altogether mostly came from existing sub-prefects – indeed a decree of 1 October 1959 stipulated that 80 per cent of prefects should be so chosen. It must therefore be conceded that, insofar as the Fifth Republic saw a change in their political colour, it was largely by dint of promoting the more congenial elements in a body of men initially appointed by earlier regimes, albeit to junior posts.

As for the other *grands corps*, a third of the Inspection des Finances belonged to the Catholic-inspired Confédération Française des Travailleurs Chrétiens in the early 'sixties.[15] But in many cases this was no more proof of Catholic commitment than would be the counterclaim that membership of the CGT was proof of Communist commitment. Indeed the local controller of the CFTC at that time was the free-wheeling Protestant, Michel Rocard. Choosing a union was often a matter of opting for the least uncongenial of an unattractive bunch, with the protection of one's material and professional interests taking precedence over the display of political or religious loyalties. In fact the CFTC was to split in 1964, the minority struggling on under the old Catholic banner, while the majority took the secular title of the Confédération Française Démocratique du Travail and developed links with the Socialist SFIO and PSU. This reflected the leftward inclinations of a significant section of committed Catholics – people whose intellectual evolution had affinities with that of figures such as Jacques Delors.

All these developments reflected the decline of religion as a divisive political force in French politics. Not only were committed Catholics a smaller proportion of the population, but their political allegiance was increasingly split between parties whose leading concerns were not religious. The demise of the MRP exemplified the trend. With the Gaullists in power and responsible in 1959 for what were the greatest financial concessions to Catholic education since the *ancien régime*, the MRP no longer seemed necessary for the defence of Catholic interests – even if MRP and conservative pressures were important factors in persuading Debré to be much more generous to Catholic education than he originally intended. Increasingly the MRP became identified first and foremost with agricultural interests and the European idea. Its transformation into the Centre Démocrate in the mid-'sixties more or less signified the end of its career as the accredited defender of confessional interests. Thereafter what was left of this role was split up and parcelled out to other parties with a record of Catholic support.

The disintegration of a principal focus for Catholic political loyalty was also accelerated by the constitutional changes that de Gaulle brought to France in 1958 and 1962. The creation of a popularly elected presidency in 1962 obliged voters and parties temporarily to put on one side their differences and rally behind the two competing finalists in the decisive stage of each presidential contest; and, given the power of the presidency in the new republic, this increasingly tended to colour the character of French parliamentary politics in general. The indirect outcome was that the Assembly became gradually bipolarised in the 1960s into two large opposing alliances, clustered around the dominant issues of public order and the distribution of wealth. Not only did this development work to the detriment of centre parties like the MRP and its successor, but it tended to push to the side-lines secondary issues such as religion, which in the past had created such disastrous divisions within the alliances of both Right and Left, thereby contributing to the governmental instability of the Third and Fourth Republics.

Many observers claimed, however, that religious issues were still a major element in French political life; and they pointed in particular to the schools question, arguing that here lay one of the great geological fault-lines that continued to cut across the opposing rock faces of class interest. This, they asserted, made nonsense of the notion that French politics had now come of age and were like those of Britain and Scandinavia, simply and securely composed of two confronting blocks based primarily on differences of socio-economic policy. They made much of the monster rally in Paris on 24 June 1984 which drew over a million participants – the largest gathering of protest ever seen in France. This was organised by private-school parents and the Right-wing parties as a protest against the Mauroy government's proposals to tighten state supervision over private schools that were in receipt of state funding under the Debré law of 1959 and subsequent legislation.[16] Not only did the size of the demonstration intimidate the government into an anodyne compromise, but it led indirectly to a change of prime minister. The government's opponents chose to present it as a bid to protect religious freedom; yet the issues involved were not primarily religious – even if religious factors were undoubtedly present. The government's proposals would still have left the state-subsidised private schools with a greater measure of independence than state-funded Catholic schools in Britain; and the government was principally concerned to ensure that government money in the private sector was well spent. Many of the French bishops were privately disposed to accept the proposals – with certain modifications that the government was prepared to make. In fact only a fifth of the parents with children at Catholic private schools were themselves practising Catholics. Of the rest, most chose the private sector for much the same reasons as British parents: they might be in the catchment area of a state school with social problems or where there was a large immigrant population with language difficulties. And, as in Britain, parents with a child at a state school might disagree with the school's assessment of how their child should be streamed – and therefore saw the private sector as a means of obtaining the level of education they sought. Although the government's proposals, as they stood, did not directly threaten either of these considerations, many parents feared that increased state involvement could lead in that direction.

Nor was religion the prime issue in the counter-demonstration that took place ten years later on 16 January 1994 when nearly half a million supporters of state education protested against a Right-wing government's proposals to allow local authorities to provide increased funding to the private sector – a government, moreover, that was headed by a practising Catholic, Edouard Balladur. While there were undoubtedly secularist elements that deplored further public expenditure on what were predominantly Catholic schools, the main concern of the protesters was the donation of funds that might otherwise have been available for the cash-starved public sector. Once again the principal axis of contention was an issue of public versus private education, rather than of secularism versus religion, even though the religious issue was unquestionably present.

It was also widely asserted that religious affiliations still remained a dangerous factor in determining the outcome of elections. When 1981 saw the presidency and the Assembly pass to the Left for the first time in the Fifth Republic, opinion polls indicated that there were at least three practising Catholics supporting Giscard d'Estaing's Right-wing coalition for every one supporting Mitterrand's Left. This therefore indicated that Catholicism was a force that favoured the Right rather than the Left.[17] Old-style anticlericals claimed that in these circumstances there was still a case for vigilance in appointing *catholiques avant tout* to positions of trust where strict neutrality was an essential requirement. Catholics replied that anticlericals were in danger of assimilating *catholiques avant tout* with the 'social package' type of Catholic. What the opinion polls left unanswered was whether the Catholicism of Giscard's supporters was what determined their overall attitude to the political programme of the Right, or whether their Catholicism was merely a product of the socio-cultural milieu to which they belonged – in which case it was arguably their milieu, not their Catholicism, that drew them to the Right, with its congenial financial and economic policies. While there is always an element of 'the chicken and the egg' in such discussions, anticlerical warnings left unexplained the behaviour of the substantial minority of practising Catholics who voted for the Socialists. Left-wing Catholics naturally resented the unspoken implication in many of these electoral analyses that they were somehow or other 'less intrinsically Catholic' than those who voted for the Right.

Commentators are much divided on how they see the future of the Church in French society and politics. Some interpret the various explosions of religious enthusiasm in the 1980s as the start of a brave new period of expansion. Yet it is uncertain how many of these new currents of religious feeling will continue to accept the tight hierarchical control of the Catholic Church in its traditional form. The devotees of *les nouvelles vagues religieuses* insist that individuals have the freedom and duty to make their own independent decisions on moral issues, provided that they accept the responsibility for the consequences of these decisions. This often results in a highly selective attitude to current Church teaching and discipline. *Bricolage* – a do-it-yourself eclecticism – is perhaps the dominant feature of these dynamic areas of French religious life; and it is here that the main chances of significant growth are often said to lie, rather than in the familiar forms of disciplined adherence to the Church.

Yet this vibrant individualism is not as yet the prevailing feature of the 10 per cent of French adults who still go regularly to Mass each week. What goes on in the bulk of French parishes today is not so very different from the familiar routines of neighbouring countries. Anglo-American Catholics, excited by what they have read about the intellectual ferment of the French Church, arrive in Paris, assuming that 'this is where the action is' and demanding to be taken 'to a way-out Mass' – in much the same spirit as hedonists arrive in the Rue St Denis, expecting *nouveautés inouïes*. Dreary disappointment is usually the lot of both bands of seekers. Not only is what they find depressingly familiar, but – if visiting Catholics look hard enough – they will find surviving expressions of the Right-wing Catholicism of a century earlier. The Comtesse de Paris, when interviewed in 1986, still spoke the language of the milieux described in the opening chapter of this book; and if her description of a typical day in her life is that of an endangered species, its later parts contain dispiriting echoes of what *le gratin du bon vieux temps* was saying in the 1890s.

I usually get up at seven-thirty but sometimes wake as early as seven. If that's the case I just quietly say my rosary in bed . . . Then around eight I'm ready for breakfast with those of my nine surviving children . . . who may be staying with me . . . At ten o'clock my trusted secretary . . . comes in and helps me with any correspondence connected with the charities I support, such as the work of the Knights of Malta for African lepers. Then I may go shopping . . . Recently my daughter and I went on an expedition to buy things for the castle where she now lives in Austria . . . yards and yards of linen to make sheets – she'll give them to the nuns in the nearby convent to embroider . . . In the afternoon I may knit blankets or bandages for the lepers . . . I follow French politics and always vote. I was very pleased when the Socialists lost. We had bandits at the head of the country for five years . . . The politician who best expresses what everybody really thinks is Jean-Marie Le Pen, the National Front leader – a true, great French patriot, although I find it a pity when his party sometimes votes with the Socialists . . . Cardinal Lustiger, the Archbishop of Paris, has overcome the handicap of his origins – he is a converted Jew – and is doing a really splendid job.[18]

Charles Maurras would not have been so accommodating. He would doubtless have greeted Lustiger's appointment with the same words as he greeted his own trial and conviction in 1945 – 'c'est la revanche de Dreyfus!' For anyone seeking to disentangle the legacy of the past, France is indeed *le pays des merveilles.*

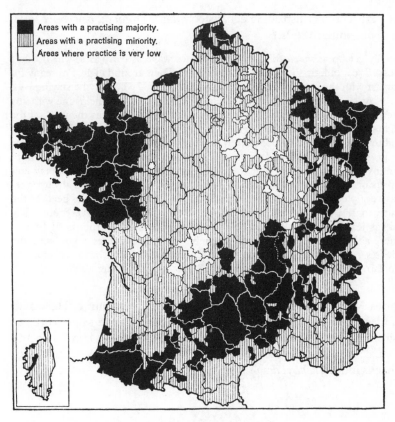

Religious observance in France, c. 1960.
Source: Fernand Boulard and Jean Rémy, *Pratique religieuse urbaine et régions culturelles* (Paris, 1968), by kind permission of Editions Ouvrières.

Notes

1: RALLIÉS AND *DÉRAILLEURS*: CATHOLICS AND SUBVERSION

1 Michel Lagrée, 'Exilés dans leur patrie (1880–1920)', in François Lebrun (ed.), *Histoire des catholiques en France du XV siècle à nos jours* (Toulouse, 1980), pp. 407–53.

2 The Archives Nationales (cited as 'A.N.') hold the political papers of both the Orleanist and Bonapartist pretenders, Philippe, Duc d'Orléans and Prince Victor Napoléon, as well as the personal letters received by Paul Déroulède. These are classified as 300 AP, Archives de la Maison de France (branche d'Orléans), III 795–811 (subject to authorisation by the Comte de Paris); 400 AP, Archives Napoléon, 174–214; 401 AP, Papiers Déroulède (subject to authorisation by Monsieur Yves Barbet-Massin). The Jesuit archives (cited as 'Jes. Rom.') are held by the Curia Generalizia PP Gesuiti, and the Assumptionist papers (cited as 'Assumpt.') in the Archivio dei Padri Assunzionisti. The principal Vatican holdings are in the Archivio Segreto Vaticano (cited as 'A.S. Vat.') and the Segretaria di Stato (cited as 'Stat. Vat.').

3 A.N., 401 AP, 17103, 8730. Peter Rutkoff likewise found Déroulède's papers of limited interest on the subversive activity of 1898–9, when he consulted them prior to their donation to the Archives Nationales. Rutkoff, *Revanche and revision: the Ligue des Patriotes and the origins of the radical right in France, 1882–1900* (Athens, Ohio, 1981). The older but lively account contained in Zeev Sternhell, *La Droite révolutionnaire, 1885–1914: les origines françaises du fascisme* (Paris, 1978) is heavily reliant on the reports of police informers, who often gave undue credence and importance to the hearsay and gossip they picked up, in the hope of convincing their paymasters that their money was well spent.

4 6 Nov. 1906, A. N., 401 AP, 28157.

5 *Gazette des Tribunaux*, 19 Nov. 1899.

6 *Journal Officiel* (1891), p. 2012.

7 Declaration at the High Court trial, reported in *L'Eclair*, 22 Feb. 1900.

8 *L'Univers*, 25 Feb. 1899.

9 E.g. letter of 24 Dec. 1913, A.N., 401 AP, 493621.

10 Chapon papers. Archives Historiques du Diocèse de Nice.

11 *Mémoires de Boni de Castellane, 1867–1932* (Paris, 1986).

12 On his early theological aspirations and his assessment of Anna Gould, see the MS diaries of the Abbé Arthur Mugnier, entries for 5 Feb., 2 and 21 Aug. 1906, A.N., 258 AP. A brief selection of Mugnier's comments, mainly on literary figures, has been published as *Journal de l'Abbé Mugnier (1879–1939)* (Paris, 1985).

13 On Vatican reactions, see the reports of the Belgian Minister Plenipotentiary to the Holy See, Baron Maximilien d'Erp, for 1906. Archives du Ministère des Affaires Etrangères et du Commerce Extérieur, Brussels (cited as 'Belg. SS'). On American Catholic reactions, see Georges Goyau's diary, 20 May 1906, 'Journal inédit de Georges Goyau', *La Pensée Catholique*, No. 33 (1954), 77–91.

14 On the Assumptionists' involvement in French politics in the 1890s, see the account, based on the Assumptionist archives, in Maurice Larkin, *Church and State after the Dreyfus Affair: the Separation issue in France* (London, 1974), pp. 65–79. See also Pierre Sorlin, *'La Croix' et les juifs, 1880–1899* (Paris, 1967).

15 On the political, non–religious aspects of the question, see Maurice Larkin, '"La République en danger"? The Pretenders, the Army and Déroulède, 1898–1899', *English Historical Review*, C (1985), 85–105. See also Bertrand Joly, 'Le Parti royaliste et l'affaire Dreyfus (1898–1900)', *Revue historique*, CCLXIX (1983), 311–64.

16 Lur-Saluces to Orléans, 6 Feb. 1899, A.N. 300 AP, III 806.

17 E.g. Jacques Cailly, 25 Feb. 1899, cited in *Journal Officiel: Haute Cour*, hearing of 18 Sept. 1899, p. 5.

18 Robert Le Texier, *Le Fol Eté du Fort Chabrol* (Paris, 1990), p. 110.

19 Letter of 9 April 1897, reproduced in *ibid.*, unnumbered illustration.

20 The signature is illegible, and could conceivably be that of an associate; Guérin (?) to Orléans, 20 Jan. 1899, A.N., 300 AP, III 806.

21 Notes of Gen. de Charette, Mar. 1897, A.N., 300 AP, III 803.

22 Spoken to Alexandre Maupetit and related in Maupetit's letter to Léon Harmel, 29 Mar. 1900, Assumpt., PZ 53.

23 Letter of 21 Dec. 1898, A.N., 300 AP, III 805.

24 These plans, with explanatory maps and photographs, are contained in A.N., AP, III 804–7.

25 See account, based on Assumptionist archives, in Larkin, *Church and State*, pp. 67–70.

26 Platel to General, 25 Oct. 1896 and 7 May 1898, Jes. Rom., Franc. 16, fo. II, 67 and 96.

27 J. Ehrman to General, 6 Oct. 1896, Jes. Rom., Franc. 16, fo. III, 2.

28 Matignon to General, 6 Oct. 1896, Jes. Rom., Franc. 16, fo. III, 2a.

29 See, *inter alia*, report of the Comité central électoral royaliste to the Duc d'Orléans, 24 May 1898, A.N., 300 AP, III 804.

30 Undated cutting in the archives of the Ecole Ste Geneviève.

31 'Jesuits hit by Dreyfus Affair: the alleged machinations of the disciples of Loyola in the Great French Scandal', undated cutting (probably 16 or 17 Aug. 1899) in Jes. Rom., Franc. 16, fo. III.

32 A.N., 300 AP III, 804–6.

33 Undated report by du Lac (probably early 1901, or late 1900), Jes. Rom., Franc. 20, fo. IV, 38.

34 See note 30 above.

35 These and other colourful rumours are listed in Louis Capéran, *L'Anticléricalisme et l'Affaire Dreyfus, 1897–1899* (Toulouse, 1948), pp. 263–76.

36 See note 33 above.

37 See note 22 above.

38 E.g. Ollivier to Victor, 11 Feb. and 28 July 1893, 27 Oct. 1899, 8 May 1910, 14 June 1911, A.N., 400 AP, 205 (O).

39 On these fears, see the unsigned reports from numbered Royalist agents: No. 121bis, 18 and 25 June, 18 July 1899; No.12, 30 July 1899, A.N., 300 AP, III 806–7.

40 Ollivier to Victor, 11 Feb. 1893, A.N., 400 AP, 205 (O).

41 *Ibid.*

42 Déroulède to Louis, 1 Dec. 1900. Déroulède was replying to Louis's letter of condolence on his exile. There had earlier been an amicable exchange of letters between Déroulède and Victor on the virtues of the plebiscitary principle: Déroulède to Victor, 10 Dec. 1895, A.N., 400 AP, 184 B (Dec-Div).

43 E.g. Cuneo d'Ornano to Victor, 20 Jan. 1897, 19 Mar. 1899, 19 Jan. and 31 Dec. 1900; and Cuneo d'Ornano to Blanc, series of letters, 1897, A.N., 400 AP, 183 (Cue-Cuv).

44 On their attitude to Dreyfus, see Joseph Reinach, *Histoire de l'Affaire Dreyfus*, 7 vols. (Paris, 1901–8), vol. III, pp. 53–4, vol. IV, p. 306.

45 Police report, 2 Jan. 1900, Archives de la Préfecture de Police (cited as 'A. Préf. Pol.'), Ba 70.

46 Cuneo d'Ornano, probably to E. Blanc, Jan.(?) 1904, A.N., 400 AP, 183 (Cue-Cuv).

47 See Morny to Victor, 23 Mar. 1899, A.N., 400 AP, 203 (Mon-Mor), for the following points.

48 On Drumont, see *inter alia*, *Libre Parole*, 4 Jan. 1899. On his Bonapartist sympathies, see Jousselin to Victor, 3 Mar. 1901, A.N., 400 AP, 193 (I-J); and veiled allusion in police report, 24 Oct. 1898, A.N., F7 12717.

49 Police report of 22 Feb. 1899, A. Préf. Pol., Ba 70.

50 17 Aug. 1899, A.N., 401 AP, 48968.

51 G. de Beauregard to Blanc, 1 Jan. 1899, A.N., 400 AP, 175 (Bas-Bea).

52 Lur-Saluces to Orléans, 6 Feb. 1899, A.N., 300 AP, III 806.

53 Lavigerie to Victor, 8 Jan. 1886, A.N., 400 AP, 196.

54 Geay to Leo XIII, 3 Jan. and 13 June 1898, copies sent to Prince Victor, A.N., 400 AP, 190.

55 See Henry to Victor, 23 Nov. 1900, A.N., 400 AP, 193.

56 See Victor to Reille, 1 Aug. 1902, and Reille to Victor, 23 July 1903, A.N., 400 AP, 208, B.70.

57 On the documents, see Pierre Sorlin's excellent *Waldeck-Rousseau* (Paris, 1966), pp. 415–16. Those that currently survive in Waldeck-Rousseau's papers (notably MS 4578–80) and in Commissaire Hennion's report of 30 Sep. 1899 (revealed in the Nationalist *Echo de Paris*, 4 Nov. 1899)

represent a highlighting of the information contained in existing police informers' reports rather than the fabrication of new evidence, as later writers have claimed. The premier's fault, apart from his spurious dating, is to assert a faith in the accuracy of the police informers' reports that no police chief or Minister of the Interior could seriously have held, given the notorious shortcomings of such reports (see note 3 above). The reports were at their most fanciful in speculating on what was happening in the summer of 1899.

Beginning in 1976, several general histories of the period have misrepresented Sorlin's argument as a demonstration that the Déroulède affair was little more than an invention by the government to incriminate potential subversives. Waldeck-Rousseau's papers are held in the Bibliothèque de l'Institut (cited as 'Bib. Inst.').

58 Thuret to Orléans, 20 Jan. 1899, A.N., 300 AP, III 806. Thuret was a member of the Duke's *service d'honneur*.

59 Personal dossier, Archives du Service Historique de l'Armée de Terre (cited as 'Armée'), GD G3 165.

60 'D'un correspondant', 11 Feb. 1899, A.N., F^7 12451: 'Nothing has been decided as yet.'

61 André Galabru (Paris, 1988).

62 *Mistinguett* (London, 1954), pp. 64–5. At least one newspaper made the traditional lament, 'Ainsi est mort un grand président dans la pleine exercice de ses fonctions.'

63 Card. Richard to Rampolla, 17 Feb. 1899, A.S. Vat., S. Stato 1899, Rubr. 248, Fasc.1, pp. 64–5; Armand Nisard to Rampolla, 18 Feb. 1899, *ibid.*, p. 74.

64 Ramel to Orléans, 21 Feb. 1899, A.N., 300 AP, III 806.

65 See the undated, unsigned account in Waldeck-Rousseau's papers, based on police reports and seemingly compiled by a senior member of the administration at some time after Feb. 1900, Bib. Inst., MS 4578.

66 A.N., 300 AP, III 806.

67 Gramont to Orléans, 20 Feb. 1899, A.N., 300 AP, III 806.

68 De Luynes to Orléans, 28 Mar. 1899; Lur-Saluces to Orléans, 26 June 1899, A.N., 300 AP, III 806.

69 Reinach, *Affaire Dreyfus*, vol. IV, pp. 588–92. Reinach partly based his claim on 'certain conversations with Déroulède which were reported to me': vol. IV, p. 588, n. 4; Maurice Barrès, *Scènes et doctrines du nationalisme*, 2 vols. (Paris, 1925), vol. I, pp. 247–9. Barrès emulated Déroulède's refusal to accuse Castellane specifically by name in his public account of the episode in 1901.

70 See note 65 above.

71 *Ibid.*

72 *Ibid.* This account ('our correspondents are unanimous on this point') cites an admission by Guérin that Castellane had told him of Déroulède's plan, including his hopes in Pellieux. Castellane was basically a Nationalist with moderate Orleanist sympathies. Guérin later claimed that Castellane had indeed visited him on the eve of the funeral to sound him out on his intentions towards Déroulède's proposed *tentative*; but he denied that

Castellane had mentioned the name of Pellieux or any other general. Jules Guérin, *Les Trafiquants de l'antisémitisme* (Paris, 1905), pp. 202–3.

73 Letter of 17 Feb. 1899, Assumpt., Picard TS, VIII, no. 3964.

74 Account in Vincent Bailly's letter to Emmanuel Bailly, 26 Feb. 1899, Assumpt., Bailly TS, XII, no. 3301.

75 'Le Moine', 'L'Emeute', *La Croix*, 23 Feb. 1899.

76 See note 74.

77 This episode is treated in Le Texier, *Fort Chabrol*, which unfortunately is sparing in its citation of sources.

78 On Royalist funding, see A.N., 300 AP, III 807, notably Lur-Saluces to Orléans, 27 Aug. 1899. On Castellane and Archdeacon, see Le Texier, *Fort Chabrol*, pp. 138 *et seq.*

79 *Ibid.*, pp. 168–78.

80 Account in Bailly's letters to Picard, 19 and 25 Sep. 1899, Assumpt., Bailly TS, XII, nos. 3283 and 3285.

81 See account in René Querenet to Victor, 27 June 1906, A.N., 400 AP, 208 (Qu-Ru).

82 Querenet to Victor, 8 Aug. 1907, A.N., 400 AP, 175 (Bas-Bea).

83 See account in Victor to Gauthier de Clagny, 19 Nov. 1911, A.N., 400 AP, 205 (0). Prince Victor's views may well have been influenced by a series of conversations between one of his political agents and several ecclesiastics in the summer of 1911, notably Archbishop Dubourg of Rennes, Bishop (auxiliary) Déchelette of Lyon, Bishop Meunier of Evreux, the vicars-general of Montauban and Nîmes, and the secretaries-general of Agen, Valence, Avignon and La Rochelle, deputising for their absent masters. Studiously avoiding the issue of their personal attitudes to a Bonapartist restoration, the bulk of expressed opinions favoured a negotiated settlement with Rome that would leave the Church complete freedom in the matter of ecclesiastical appointments, even at the price of receiving only limited material support from the State. Several also agreed that there should be legal restraints on the proliferation of the religious orders in France under any future regime. Undated and unsigned report, intercepted by the Préfecture de Police, A.N., F⁷ 12868.

84 Described in Victor to Odelin, 2 Jan. 1912, A.N., 400 AP, 205 (0).

85 Baudrillart to Victor, 12 Feb. and 20 Mar. 1914, A.N., 400 AP, 175 (Bas-Bea).

86 Herscher to Victor, 5 June 1914, A.N., 400 AP, 193.

87 See his 'sentiments de fidélité' in Dansette to Victor, 23 May 1914, A.N., 400 AP, 184 (Da-De).

88 24 Nov. 1909, A.N., 300 AP, III 809.

89 Gramont to Orléans, 9 Jan. 1898, A.N., 300 AP, III 804.

90 Interview with Theillier de Poncheville, Jan. 1910, Assumpt., QG 81.

2: *LE SABRE ET LE GOUPILLON*: CATHOLICS AND THE ARMY

1 These and the following statistics on education are based on Antoine Prost, *Histoire de l'enseignement en France 1800–1967* (Paris, 1968), notably p. 45,

and Françoise Mayeur, *Histoire générale de l'enseignement et de l'éducation en France*, vol. III: *De la Révolution à l'école républicaine* (Paris, 1981), notably p. 472.

2 'Journal', VIII 100, Bibliothèque Nationale (cited as 'Bib. Nat.'), N.A.F., 12,711.

3 *Bulletin du Grand Orient de France*, vol. LIV (1898–9).

4 See note 2 to chapter 1, p. 207.

5 See note 65 to chapter 1, p. 210; Déroulède's remarks cited by Barrès, *Scènes et doctrines*, vol. I, pp. 248–9; and Reinach, *Affaire Dreyfus*, vol. IV, pp. 591–2, note 4.

6 Unsigned report in an envelope dated 9 Oct. 1898, A.N., 300 AP, III 805.

7 Orléans to Lur-Saluces, 9 Oct. 1898, A.N., 300 AP, III 805.

8 Lur-Saluces to Orléans, 5 June 1899, A.N., 300 AP, III 806.

9 Pellieux's personal army file sheds no light on the matter, Armée, GB 3 572. The ostensible reason for this transfer was his unsatisfactory handling of the Esterhazy enquiry: Reinach, *Affaire Dreyfus*, vol. V, p. 238.

10 Lur-Saluces to Orléans, 6 Feb. 1899, A.N., 300 AP, III 806; lady's report cited in note 6 above.

11 Thuret to Orléans, 7 Oct. 1898, A.N., 300 AP, III 805.

12 Lur-Saluces to Orléans, 6 Feb. and 5 June 1899, A.N., 300 AP, III 806. His source for the last opinion was General François Montaincourt.

13 Police report, 6 Aug. 1899, A.N., F⁷ 12870. His personal file is uninformative on the issue: Armée, GD 3 53. (He is not to be confused with General François Marie de Négrier.)

14 Hervé to Déroulède, 17 July 1897 (?), A.N., 401 AP, 23788. Déroulède's papers also contain coded information on the functioning of some items of military equipment, e.g. a Westinghouse brake: 49289.

15 Lur-Saluces to Orléans, 5 June 1899, A.N., 300 AP, III 806. His wife's remark was made after Hervé testified in Déroulède's favour at the Cour d'assises trial in May 1899.

16 Report of 9 Oct. 1898, A.N., 300 AP, III 805. The information on their marital and educational background is drawn from their personal dossiers: Armée, GD 3 series. Many generals' dossiers, however, are silent on their secondary education.

17 Lur-Saluces to Orléans, 5 June 1905, A.N., 300 AP, III 806. See also Reinach, *Affaire Dreyfus*, vol. V, p. 74.

18 A scribbled list of numbers on a piece of squared paper, possibly in Thuret's hand, A.N., 300 AP, III 806. The list is too consistent with the other evidence on corps commanders to permit alternative explanations as to its significance.

19 The principal sources are report of 9 Oct. 1898, A.N., 300 AP, III 805; list of Jan. (?) 1899; and Thuret to Orléans 20 Jan. and 15 Feb. 1899, and an undated report probably of late Jan. 1899, A.N., 300 AP, III 806. For a complete source list for each general, see Larkin, 'République en danger?', p. 103. The family details are drawn from their personal dossiers, Armée, GD 3 series, and from the sources listed for the pages of cross-references shown in brackets.

20 Thuret to Orléans, 20 Jan. 1899 and undated second report of same period, A.N., 300 AP, III 806.

21 Lur-Saluces to Orléans, 1 Feb. 1899, A.N., 300 AP, III 806.

22 Thuret to Orléans, 20 Jan. 1899, A.N., 300 AP, III 806. A former Minister for War, Mercier was now in the reserve.

23 Boussenard was supporting Garnier des Garets (1895), Coiffé recommended Metzinger (1898), Hervé supported Monard (1896) and Kessler (1897) who was also recommended by Jamont (1897–8), while de France supported Sonnois (1898). See dossiers of protégés, Armée, GD 3 series.

24 See sample in Christophe Charle, 'Intellectuels et élites en France (1880–1900)', Thèse de doctorat (Univ. Paris I, 1985), p. 141. Caution is needed, however, in using the statistics of Catholic generals in Walter Barge, 'The Generals of the Republic: the corporate personality of high military rank in France, 1889–1914', Ph.D. dissertation (University of North Carolina, 1982), where insufficient distinction is made between practising Catholics and merely baptised Catholics. See also William Serman, Les Officiers français dans la nation (1848–1914), (Paris 1982).

25 John W. Bush, 'Education and Social Status: the Jesuit collège in the early Third Republic', French Historical Studies, IX (1975), 136.

26 Ibid., p. 130.

27 On the Jesuit schools in general, see Bush, 'Jesuit collège', and Pierre Delattre, Les Etablissements des Jésuites en France, 1540–1900, 5 vols. (Paris, 1940–57). On the Ecole Ste Geneviève and the Collège de l'Immaculée Conception ('Vaugirard'), see the valuable work of John W. Langdon in 'Social implications of Jesuit education in France: the schools of Vaugirard and Sainte-Geneviève', Ph.D. dissertation (Syracuse University, 1973) and 'Whither the Postards? Graduates of the Ecole Sainte-Geneviève, 1914–1954' in Donald N. Baker and Patrick J. Harrigan (eds.), The making of Frenchmen: current directions in the history of education in France, 1679–1979 (Waterloo, Ontario, 1980) pp. 429–39.

28 Langdon, 'Jesuit education', p. 110.

29 Ibid., pp. 116 and 172. See also information in the Archives de la Société de Jésus, Province de Paris, Chantilly (cited as 'Jes. Chant.') and the school archives of the Ecole Ste Geneviève (cited as 'A. Ste Gen.'). These include a number of uncatalogued but informative lists and press-cuttings.

30 Archives of the Ecole Polytechnique (cited as 'A. Ec. Pol.'), VI 2a (1891–2).

31 Jes. Chant. and A. Ste Gen., cuttings.

32 Ibid., and Langdon, 'Jesuit education', pp. 131, 181–4 and 211.

33 The school archives of the Ecole Ste Geneviève and the Marianist Collège Stanislas (cited as 'A. Stan.') contain not only lists of former pupils, but also various publications designed to keep old boys in touch with each other. The most valuable of these are the Annuaire des Anciens Elèves of Ste Geneviève and the Diptyques du Collège Stanislas, which were published at infrequent intervals – with less comprehensive newsletters appearing in the interim. Although the Annuaire of Ste Geneviève was not published until the middle decades of the twentieth century, it has the inestimable advantage of including deceased members as well as living.

34 Mémoires, pp. 43–4.

35 Report cited in note 33 to chapter 1, p. 209.
36 This and subsequent Stanislas information is drawn from A. Stan.
37 A. Ec. Pol., VI 2 series.
38 Private papers of Emile Combes, Archives Départementales de la Charente-Maritime (cited as 'Combes MSS, A.D. Char.-Mar.'), 13 J 14.
39 For a discussion of the various explanations, see Sorlin, *Waldeck-Rousseau*, p. 484, and Larkin, *Church and State*, pp. 90–1.
40 Labrosse to General, 4 Aug. 1901, Jes. Rom., Franc., 20, fo. 1, 19.
41 Report of 15 Feb. 1904, Jes. Rom., Franc., 20, fo. 1, 68bis.
42 Langdon, 'Jesuit education', pp. 58–9.
43 Douglas Porch, *The march to the Marne: the French Army, 1871–1914* (Cambridge, 1981), p. 76.
44 Letter to Combes, 4 Nov. 1904, in response to Combes's request for information, Combes MSS, A.D. Char.-Mar., 13 J 24.
45 André did not become War Minister until 29 May 1900.
46 A.D. Char.-Mar., 13 J 24, pp. 28–42. These reports predated Combes's arrival in government by two years, yet subsequently found their way into his private papers.
47 Letter cited in note 44 above.
48 François Vindé, *L'Affaire des Fiches, 1900–1904: chronique d'un scandale* (Paris, 1989), p. 34.
49 *Ibid.*, p. 36.
50 *Ibid.*, p. 37.
51 *Ibid.*, p. 41.
52 *Ibid.*, p. 93.
53 Reported in Vadecard to Président du Conseil de l'Ordre, 27 Dec. 1900, Archives du Grand Orient, Bibliothèque Nationale, Cabinet des Manuscrits (cited as 'G.O. Bib. Nat.'), FM[1] 541.
54 Vindé, *Fiches*, pp. 45–6.
55 *Ibid.*, p. 106.
56 *Ibid.*, p. 56.
57 *Ibid.*, p. 106.
58 *Ibid.*, pp. 54–5.
59 *Ibid.*, p. 61.
60 *Ibid.*, p. 70. The surviving *fiches* were those that Bidegain handed over to Guyot de Villeneuve (see following pages) and which Vindé uses in *Fiches*.
61 *Ibid.*, pp. 61–3.
62 *Ibid.*, p. 69.
63 *Ibid.*, p. 71.
64 Combes MSS, A.D. Char.-Mar., 13 J 24 43.
65 Vindé, *Fiches*, p. 120.
66 *Ibid.*, pp. 79–82.
67 29 Dec. 1904, A.N., F[7] 12476.
68 Vindé, *Fiches*, p. 198.
69 *Ibid.*, p. 184.
70 *Ibid.*, pp. 59 and 205, note 21.
71 *Ibid.*, p. 205, note 22.
72 *Ibid.*, p. 181.

73 E.g. Prefect of the Meuse to Minister of the Interior, 8 Dec. 1904, Combes MSS, A.D. Char.-Mar., 13 J 24.
74 Vindé, *Fiches*, pp. 186–7.
75 *Ibid.*, pp. 187–8.
76 *Ibid.*, pp. 196–7. See also J. K. Tannenbaum, *General Maurice Sarrail, 1856–1929* (Chapel Hill, 1974).

3: *RAISON D'ÉTAT, RAISON D'ÉGLISE:* THE ROMAN DIMENSION

1 The bulk of the relevant holdings, including much of the correspondence between the Secretary of State and the various nuncios, is in A. S. Vat.; but more sensitive material, notably the documents and minutes of the meetings of the Sacra Congregazione degli Affari Ecclesiastici Straordinari, are still held by the Seconda Sezione of the Segretaria di Stato in its own administrative archives (Stat. Vat.).
2 6 Nov. 1901 (wrongly dated '1900'), N. 941, A. S. Vat., S. Stato 1901, Rubr. 248, Fasc. 1. For a more detailed examination of the issue during Leo XIII's reign, see Maurice Larkin, 'The Vatican, France and the Roman Question, 1898–1903: new archival evidence', *The Historical Journal*, XXVII (1984), 177–97.
3 Reported in d'Aubigny to Delcassé, 30 Jan. 1902, Archives du Ministère des Affaires Etrangères, 'Saint-Siège – relations avec l'Italie', II, 211–13.
4 Examples and evidence in Larkin, *Church and State*, pp. 40–4.
5 Lorenzelli to Rampolla, 9 May 1902, N. 1214, A. S. Vat., S. Stato 1902, Rubr. 248, Fasc. 10; and Nunz. Lor., Busta 3.
6 Described in Lorenzelli to Rampolla, 2 Apr. 1902, N. 1154, A. S. Vat., Nunz. Lor., Busta 3.
7 Letter of 21 Feb. 1902, Assumpt., MM 137.
8 Labrosse to Assistant General, 27 Dec. 1900, Jes. Rom., Franc. 20, fo. IV, 17.
9 8 Apr. 1900, N. 264, A. S. Vat., S. Stato 1902, Rubr. 248, Fasc. 7.
10 Lorenzelli's reports to Rampolla in A. S. Vat. on his protests to Delcassé are too numerous to list individually. De Mun's suggestion was made in a letter to Leo XIII, 15 Feb. 1900, A. S. Vat., S. Stato 1902, Rubr. 248, Fasc. 8.
11 Reported in Lorenzelli to Rampolla, 26 May 1901, N. 747, A. S. Vat., S. Stato 1902, Rubr. 248, Fasc. 8. Ill-health obliged de Mun to ask Piou to assume the leadership of Action Libérale.
12 Rampolla to Lorenzelli, 14 Feb. 1901, N. 61612 and 4 June 1901, N. 63633, A. S. Vat., S. Stato 1902, Rubr. 248, Fasc. 8.
13 Lorenzelli to della Chiesa, 16 July 1901, N. 821, A. S. Vat., Nunz. Lor., Busta 4; decoded, S. Stato 1902, N. 64483, Rubr. 248, Fasc. 9.
14 Telegram, 20 July 1901, A. S. Vat., S. Stato 1902, Rubr. 248, Fasc. 9; Nunz. Lor., Busta 4.
15 On these developments, see Larkin, *Church and State*, pp. 120–6, 182–4, 215–16.
16 Letter to Colonel Keller, 19 June 1909, cited in Adrien Dansette, *Histoire religieuse de la France contemporaine*, vol. II (Paris, 1951), pp. 381–2.

17 The Abbé J. Belorgey, report of 19 Mar 1902, attached to Lorenzelli's letter to Rampolla, 23 Apr. 1902, N. 1188, A. S. Vat., S. Stato 1904, Rubr. 248, Fasc. 3, pp. 81–104.

18 Letter cited in note 17 above.

19 Meeting of 12 July 1906. Stat. Vat., Segretaria della Sacra Congregazione degli Affari Ecclesiastici Straordinari (cited as 'A.E. Straord.'), Sess. 1076.

20 Stat. Vat., A.E. Straord. On Ecuador, see meetings of 9 Mar. 1905, Sess. 1055; 12 Oct. 1905, Sess. 1061; 22 Nov. 1906, Sess. 1082. On Bolivia, 28 Oct. 1906, Sess. 1080. On Venezuela, 28 Oct. 1906, Sess. 1080; 22 Nov. 1906, Sess. 1082.

21 Stat. Vat., A.E. Straord., Sess. 1076 and 1077.

22 19 July, Sess. 1077.

23 Merry del Val to Montagnini, 26 Aug. 1906, Montagnini MSS, A.N., C.D., c. 1027–1036, Sc. 25 p. 76.

24 As well as the original MS papers, the archives hold the printed copies and extracts that were circulated to the members of the Congregation for Extraordinary Ecclesiastical Affairs prior to its meeting on 12 July 1906 (Francia: associazioni cultuali, June 1906), Stat. Vat., A.E. Straord., Sess. 1076.

25 On Pressensé's insufficiently recognised contribution to the Separation Law, see Larkin, Church and State, pp. 108–93. Although he died in 1914, his amendment to Article 4, seeking to guarantee the Catholic orthodoxy of the associations cultuelles, did much to reduce clerical fears of the alleged schismatical dangers inherent in the Law.

26 Undated note to Merry del Val, Nov.–early Dec. 1905, discussed and approved at meeting of Congregation for Extraordinary Ecclesiastical Affairs, 25 Jan. 1906, Stat. Vat., A.E. Straord., Sess. 1066.

27 See his undated note discussed by the Congregation on 18 Oct. 1905, Stat. Vat., A.E. Straord., Sess. 1062; and his letter of 5 Dec. 1905 to Mgr. Pietro Gasparri.

28 18 Oct. 1905, Sess. 1062.

29 Archives Historiques de l'Archevêché de Paris (cited as 'Archiepisc. Paris'): this letter was uncatalogued at the time of consultation.

30 Stat. Vat., A.E. Straord., Sess. 1076.

31 Ibid. Touchet wrote three reports on what happened at the assembly: a twenty-four page document for the Pope, a shorter one for Merry del Val, and a brief résumé for the papal chargé d'affaires in Paris which he composed several months later. The twelve veteran opponents of the associations, whom he listed, were de Cabrières of Montpellier, Turinaz of Nancy, Dubillard of Quimper, Andrieu of Marseille, Bonnet of Viviers, Carsalade du Pont of Perpignan, Foucault of St Dié, Dubois of Verdun, de Briey of Meaux, Douais of Beauvais, himself and the titular Bishop of Lydda (presumably an auxiliary bishop, unnamed in the report). His guesses on the identity of the twelfth were Fiard of Montauban, or Delamaire of Périgueux, or Laborde of Blois – although in his shorter report for Merry del Val he also hazarded Guérard of Coutances or Renouard of Limoges.

32 Interviews with Fathers Ernest and Franc, 20 Dec. 1906, Assumpt., PZ 64, p. 11.

33 Mugnier, MS diaries, entries of 14 Jan. and 26 June 1906, A.N., 258 AP.

34 Interview with Emile Ollivier, reported to Mugnier, *ibid.*, entry of 29 June 1906.

4: PROBLEMS AND PRINCIPLES

1 *France*, 2nd edn (London, 1899), p. 117.
2 There are disappointingly large gaps in the runs of issues retained in school archives and in the Bibliothèque Nationale.
3 A number of the leading French private schools have succeeded in adopting modern technology without succumbing to the rapacious ethos that often accompanies it in Anglo-American private schools.
4 Christophe Charle, *Les Elites de la République (1880–1900)*, (Paris, 1987). See also his *thèse de doctorat* on which it is based, 'Intellectuels'.
5 Charle, 'Intellectuels', pp. 151–2.
6 *Ibid.*, p. 153.
7 Combes MSS, A.D. Char.-Mar., 13 J 14.
8 Vindé, *Fiches*, p. 17.
9 *Ibid.*, pp. 18 and 45.
10 Parliamentary complaints came notably from members of the Union Républicaine of the Senate, 10 Nov. 1898, reported in J.D., 'Les Elèves des congréganistes', *Radical*, 12 Nov. 1898. The Seine council plea echoed similar demands from Masonic lodges.
11 See minutes and papers of the Commission de l'Enseignement, 7th Legislature, vol. III. A. N., C.D., c 5663.
12 *Ibid.*, for this and subsequent paragraphs.
13 His report to the Chamber, containing the following arguments, is available in *Chambre des Députés. Documents parlementaires. Annexe No. 1490. Session ordinaire. Séance du 6 mars 1900.*
14 Source as in note 11 above.
15 Langdon, 'Jesuit education', p. 172.
16 Jes. Chant. and A. Ste Gen.
17 *Ibid.* and A. Stan., for this and subsequent paragraph.
18 Jean-François Sirinelli, *Génération intellectuelle: Khâgneux et Normaliens dans l'entre-deux-guerres* (Paris, 1988), pp. 160 and 633; Régis Ladous, *Monsieur Portal et les siens (1855–1926)* (Paris, 1985), p. 319.
19 Marie-Christine Kessler, 'Historique du système de formation et de recrutement des hauts fonctionnaires', *Revue française d'administration publique*, No. 1 (Jan.–Mar. 1977), pp. 28–32.
20 *Ibid.*, p. 35.
21 A. Stan.; and cumulative lists in later issues of the *Annuaire de la Société des Anciens Elèves et Elèves de l'Ecole Libre des Sciences Politiques.*
22 A. Ste Gen.
23 Kessler, 'Recrutement', p. 28.
24 Guy Thuillier, *Bureaucratie et bureaucrates en France au XIXe siècle* (Geneva, 1980), p. 355.
25 *Ibid.*, p. 361.
26 Kessler, 'Recrutement', p. 38.
27 *Ibid.*, p, 33.

28 *Ibid.*, p. 34.
29 Guy Thuillier, *La Bureaucratie en France aux XIXe et XXe siècles* (Paris, 1987), pp. 696 *et al.* (not to be confused with the similarly titled book cited in note 24 above).
30 Thuillier, *Bureaucrates XIXe siècle*, p. 385.
31 *Ibid.*, p. 398.
32 *Ibid.*, p. 399.
33 Laurent Amodru to Minister of Education, 27 Jan. 1897, A.N., F[17] 24132.
34 E.g. Paul Thierry-Delanoue to Minister of Education, received 13 Nov. 1899, A.N., F[17] 24132.
35 A.N., F[1b] I 637.
36 Georges Ermant to Director of Secondary Education, 2 Sept. 1899, A.N., F[17] 24135.
37 Letters of 6 Nov. 1893 and 14 Nov. 1899, A.N., F[1b] I 638.
38 Letter of 28 Apr. 1913, A.N., F[1b] I 637.

5: PATTERNS OF PREFERMENT: SECTORS WITH TEETH

1 A.N., F[1d] I 106.
2 Combes MSS, A.D. Char.-Mar., 13 J 24.
3 *Ibid.*
4 18 April 1901, *ibid.*
5 Bib. Inst., MS 4579.
6 *Ibid.*
7 Combes MSS, A.D. Char.-Mar., 13 J 24.
8 26 Nov. 1902, *ibid.*
9 Combes MSS, A.D. Char.-Mar., 13 J 24.
10 Louis Fougère (ed.), *Le Conseil d'Etat: son histoire à travers les documents d'époque, 1799–1974* (Paris, 1974), pp. 597 and 652.
11 A. Stan.; and archives of the Conseil d'Etat (cited as 'A. Con. d'Et.'). The reports on candidates in A. Con. d'Et. do not carry catalogue numbers.
12 11 Nov. 1894, A. Con. d'Et.
13 14 Nov. 1894, A. Con. d'Et.
14 19 Nov. 1897, A. Con. d'Et.
15 Letter of 28 Feb. 1902, A. Con. d'Et.
16 Police report, 6 Nov. 1901, A. Con. d'Et.
17 A. Con. d'Et.
18 Charle, *Elites de la République*, pp. 66–7.
19 A. Con. d'Et.
20 18 Nov. 1894, A. Con. d'Et.
21 Trarieux's circular of 27 Sep. 1895 and Cruppi's report of 1901, both cited in Jean-Pierre Machelon, *La République contre les libertés: les restrictions aux libertés publiques de 1879 à 1914* (Paris, 1976), p. 93, n. 140, and p. 94.
22 Speech in the Chamber of Deputies, 13 Dec. 1906, cited in Machelon, *République*, p. 96.
23 *Ibid.*, pp. 93–4.
24 *Ibid.*, p. 93.

25 Vincent Wright, 'L'Epuration du Conseil d'Etat en juillet 1879', *Revue d'histoire moderne et contemporaine*, XIX (1972), 650–1.

26 Machelon, *République*, pp. 297–9.

27 *Ibid.*, p. 83.

28 Charle, *Elites de la République*, p. 200.

29 Machelon, *République*, pp. 90–1.

30 A. Stan.

31 Langdon, 'Jesuit education', pp. 143, 206–7, 210–11. Langdon's concerns in his valuable study are primarily socio-occupational rather than political (unlike this book), with the result that his figures cover broad chronological sweeps from the 1850s to the First World War, without having need to distinguish between the easy and difficult periods of Catholic entry into state employment. This obviously limits their utility for the very different purposes of this particular book.

32 Letter of 8 Sep. 1877, A.N., BB⁶ II 980 3631.

33 Letter of 9 Sep. 1877, *ibid.*

34 Letter of 25 Nov. 1902, *ibid.*

35 Prefect of the Gard to Minister of Justice, 21 July 1917, *ibid.*

36 Letter to Minister of Justice, 9 Aug. 1917, *ibid.*

37 Proc. gen. of Rennes, 2 Mar. 1885 and 30 April 1891, A.N., BB⁶ II 1002 3828.

38 Machelon, *République*, p. 102.

39 *Ibid.*, p. 100.

40 *Ibid.*, pp. 86–7.

41 Speech in Chamber of Deputies, 13 Nov. 1905, cited in Machelon, *République*, p. 93.

42 Machelon, *République*, pp. 86 and 89.

43 E.g. dossier of Isaac Ada, report of 1887, A.N., BB⁶ II 435.

44 Undated letter of Louis Blanc (Senator, 1902–14) on behalf of Pariat, A.N., BB¹⁰ 2427ᴬ.

45 Reports on François Heitz, 4 Jan. 1896, and Jean-François Bobichon, 26 Mar. 1896, A.N., BB¹⁰ 2291ᴬ.

46 Reports on Jules Buffin, 3 Oct. 1903, and Joseph Cettier, 25 May 1904, A.N., BB¹⁰ 2429ᴬ and 2427ᴬ.

47 7 July 1904, *ibid.*

48 Prefect of the Drôme on Joseph Avignon, 29 Nov. 1904, A.N., BB¹⁰ 2427ᴬ.

49 A. Stan.

50 Information in the Caousou school newsletters for old boys, now held in the Jesuit archives in Toulouse (cited as 'Jes. Toulouse').

51 A. Stan.; Langdon, 'Jesuit education', pp. 206 and 210.

52 Wright, 'L'Epuration', p. 650.

53 Jeanne Siwek-Poudyesseau, *Le Corps préfectoral sous la Troisième et la Quatrième République* (Paris, 1969), p. 117.

54 *Ibid.*, pp. 34–5, 60 and 62.

55 Thuillier, *Bureaucratie en France*, p. 180, n. 19.

56 *Ibid.*, pp. 179–81.

57 Siwek-Poudyesseau, *Corps préfectoral*, p. 78.

58 *Ibid.*, p. 78; Charle, *Elites de la République*, p. 206.

59 Charle, *Elites de la République*, p. 209.
60 Siwek-Pouydesseau, *Corps préfectoral*, p. 78.
61 A. Stan., and relevant annual issues of *Almanach National* (Paris).
62 See the different samples examined in Siwek-Pouydesseau, *Corps préfectoral*, p. 32, and Charle, *Elites de la République*, p. 109.
63 Recollections of Chaumié's niece, June 1956.
64 A. Stan., and relevant annual issues of *Almanach National*.
65 *Ibid.*
66 *Ibid.*
67 *Ibid.*
68 A.N., F^{1d} I 106.
69 A.N., F^{1d} I 112–15.
70 A. Stan.

6: *RONDS-DE-CUIR, GENOUX-DE-CHAMEAU*: OTHER SECTORS

1 Thuillier, *Bureaucrates XIXe siècle*, p. 355, n. 100.
2 *Ibid.*, p. 393.
3 *L'Eglise catholique et l'Etat en France sous la Troisième République*, vol. II (Paris, 1909), 8.
4 A. Stan.
5 Jes. Toulouse. Langdon's much longer periods include sixteen tax men and twelve other finance officials for Ste Geneviève (1854–1913) and six tax men and nine finance officials for Vaugirard (1852–1908), 'Jesuit education', pp. 143, 206–7, 210–11.
6 Letter to Déroulède, 3 Oct. 1898, A.N., 401 AP, 43001.
7 Emmanuel Chadeau, *Les Inspecteurs des finances au XIXe siècle (1850–1914)* (Paris, 1986), pp. 29 and 58.
8 Sample in Charle, *Elites de la République*, pp. 66–7.
9 A. Stan., and *Annuaire de l'Ecole Polytechnique pour l'an 1896* (Paris).
10 Charle, *Elites de la République*, p. 434.
11 Time, the great healer, allowed mention of his subsequent premiership in the school's centenary publications in the 1950s; but Caillaux's peace moves in the First World War were an added embarrassment to a nursery of generals.
12 Chadeau, *Inspecteurs des finances*, p. 45.
13 *Ibid.*, pp. 43 and 133–4.
14 *Ibid.*, p. 9.
15 *Ibid.*, p. 31.
16 *Ibid.*, p. 30. A sample study of Jews in state employment under the Third Republic indicates surprisingly little Jewish penetration of the Inspection des Finances or the Cour des Comptes. Pierre Birnbaum, *Les Fous de la République: histoire politique des Juifs d'Etat de Gambetta à Vichy* (Paris, 1992).
17 Victor Turquan, cited in Thuillier, *Bureaucratie en France*, p. 699.
18 E.g. Letter on Georges Leclerc, 17 June 1891, A.N., F^{12} 7633^2.
19 The relevant correspondence, too protracted and complicated to be individually itemised here, is to be found in A.N., F^{12} 7633^2.
20 On the central administration, A.N., F^{14} 11638.

21 A. Stan.
22 *Annuaire Polytechnique 1896*; and Langdon, 'Jesuit education', pp. 143 and 211.
23 On Vaugirard, see Langdon, 'Jesuit education', p. 207. On Caousou, see Jes. Toulouse.
24 E.g. Jean Lesage, 1885, A.N., F^{10} 5906.
25 A. Stan.
26 *Annuaire Polytechnique 1896*; and Langdon, 'Jesuit education', pp. 210–11.
27 E.g. see A.N., F^{10} 1898.
28 Victor Turquan's *Guide pratique de jeunes gens dans le choix d'une carrière* (Paris, 1893), cited in Thuillier, *Bureaucratie en France*, p. 700.
29 A. Stan.; Langdon, 'Jesuit education', pp. 210–11.
30 A.N., F^{90} 20434.
31 Letter of 26 Jan. 1899, A.N., 401 AP, 42914.
32 On the changes of personnel, Wright, 'L'Epuration', p. 650.
33 Kessler, 'Recrutement', p. 28.
34 Cited by Thuillier, *Bureaucratie en France*, p. 695.
35 A. Stan.
36 Langdon, 'Jesuit education', pp. 178, 207 and 211; *Almanach National*, relevant years.
37 A. Stan.; Langdon, 'Jesuit education', pp. 143, 206–7, and 210–11.
38 Siwek-Pouydesseau, *Corps préfectoral*, p. 24.
39 Charle, 'Intellectuels', p. 141.
40 *Ibid.*
41 *Ibid.*
42 Siwek-Pouydesseau, *Corps préfectoral*, p. 27.
43 Charle, 'Intellectuels', p. 141.
44 *Ibid.*
45 See the very full treatment of this issue in Thuillier, *Bureaucrates XIXe siècle*, pp. 423–52.

7: THE BROTHERHOOD AT WORK

1 E.g. Bergère to Humanité lodge of Nevers, 22 Jan. 1897, G.O. Bib. Nat., FM^1 485.
2 These and the following statistics are drawn from Mildred J. Headings, *French Freemasonry under the Third Republic* (Baltimore, 1949), Daniel Ligou, *Frédéric Desmons et la Franc-maçonnerie sous la Troisième République* (Paris, 1966), and Pierre Chevallier, *Histoire de la franc-maçonnerie française*, vol. III (Paris, 1975).
3 This is evident from the archives of the provincial lodges, G.O. Bib. Nat., FM^2, Boîtes Oranges.
4 Letter of 4 Mar. 1897, G.O. Bib. Nat., FM^1 487.
5 E.g.. Letter to. Bro. Dagouès, 6 Feb. 1897, G.O. Bib. Nat., FM^1 485.
6 Letter cited in note 1.
7 Letter of 9 Feb. 1897, G.O. Bib. Nat., FM^1 485.
8 *Bulletin officiel du Grand Orient de France*, LIII, 23.
9 Chevallier, *Franc-Maçonnerie*, vol. III, p. 20.

10 27 Jan. 1897, G.O. Bib. Nat., FM¹ 485.
11 See notably the outgoing post for 6 Feb. 1897 alone, G.O. Bib. Nat., FM¹ 485.
12 E.g. letters of 6 Feb. 1897 to Bros. Dagouès and Ragon, G.O. Bib. Nat., FM¹ 485.
13 Letter to Loégaux, 30(?) Jan. 1898, G.O. Bib. Nat., FM¹ 497.
14 Letter of 25 Jan. 1898, G.O. Bib. Nat., FM¹ 497.
15 Letter to Bro. Dupuy, 7 Jan. 1901, G.O. Bib. Nat., FM¹ 541.
16 E.g. see Vadecard to Fraternité Provençal lodge of St Auban, 3 Jan. 1901, G.O. Bib. Nat., FM¹ 541.
17 Letter to Bro. Combieu, 14 Dec. 1900, G.O. Bib. Nat., FM¹ 540.
18 Letter to Bro. Bernard of Annecy lodge, 28 Dec. 1900, G.O. Bib. Nat., FM¹ 541.
19 Letter to Rabier, 4 Jan. 1901, G.O. Bib. Nat., FM¹ 541.
20 On complaints against the minister, Georges Leygues, see letter of 30 Nov. 1900, G.O. Bib. Nat., FM¹ 539. On Vadecard's petitioning for favours in education, see in one week alone his letters of 25 and 29 Jan. 1900 to three provincial lodges, FM¹ 524.
21 Vadecard to Perezas, 22 Jan. 1900, G.O. Bib. Nat., FM¹ 524.
22 12/18 Jan. 1900, G.O. Bib. Nat., FM¹ 524.
23 Letter to Bro. Eugène Etienne, 27 Dec. 1900, G.O. Bib. Nat., FM¹ 541.
24 E.g. letters of 24 Nov. 1900 to Triple Union et Amitié lodge and 4 Jan. 1901 to Doumer, G.O. Bib. Nat., FM¹ 539 and 541.
25 E.g. Vadecard's letters of 14 Dec. 1900 to Lafferre and of 10 Jan. 1901 to Massé, G.O. Bib. Nat., FM¹ 540 and 541.
26 See Vadecard to Conseil de l'Ordre, 28 Dec. 1900, G.O. Bib. Nat., FM¹ 541.
27 Letter to Bro. Mollin, 13 Dec. 1900, G.O. Bib. Nat., FM¹ 540.
28 Letter to Amédée Knight, 8 Jan. 1901, G.O. Bib. Nat., FM¹ 541.
29 E.g. Frédéric Desmons to Directeur de l'Enseignement de la Seine, 26 Nov. 1900, soliciting the headship of a primary school for a Mason, who is simply described as 'ce fonctionnaire républicain'. G.O. Bib. Nat., FM¹ 539.
30 Reported by Vadecard to Bro. Bernard of Annecy lodge, 28 Dec. 1900, G.O. Bib. Nat., FM¹ 541.
31 Letter of 27 Dec. 1900. G.O. Bib. Nat., FM¹ 541.
32 Letter of 28 Dec. 1900. G.O. Bib. Nat., FM¹ 541.
33 12 Dec. 1900, G.O. Bib. Nat., FM¹ 540.
34 Letter to Bro. Lignier, 28 Dec. 1900, G.O. Bib. Nat., FM¹ 541
35 G.O. Bib. Nat., FM¹ 541.
36 13 May 1902, G.O. Bib. Nat., FM¹ 541.
37 Bergère to Bro. Brousse, 29 Mar. 1898, G.O. Bib. Nat., FM¹ 497.
38 Bergère to Belisaire lodge, Algiers, 18 Jan. 1898, G.O. Bib. Nat., FM¹ 497.
39 Letter of 19 Jan. 1900, G.O. Bib. Nat., FM¹ 524.

8: MARIANNE AT SCHOOL

 1 Report on Maurice Croiset, 11 Aug. 1868, A.N., F¹⁷ 24131.
 2 12 July 1890, A.N., F¹⁷ 24131.
 3 A. Stan. and Jes. Toulouse.

4 Charle, 'Intellectuels', p. 151.
5 Charle, *Elites de la République*, pp. 66–7.
6 Paul Gerbod cites examples in *Les Enseignants et la politique* (Paris, 1976), pp. 12 and 20, and in Gerbod *et al.*, *Les Epurations administratives, XIX*^e *et XX*^e *siècles* (Geneva, 1977), p. 89.
7 A. Stan.
8 Jes. Toulouse.
9 Gerbod, *Enseignants*, p. 20.
10 Françoise Mayeur, *L'Enseignement secondaire des jeunes filles sous la Troisième République* (Paris, 1977), p. 370.
11 *Ibid.*, p. 364.
12 *Ibid.*, pp. 364–5.
13 *Ibid.*, p. 367.
14 Charles Dumont, 25 Sep. 1898, A.N., F^{17} 24135.
15 Undated reply to Eugène Fagot's request of 18 Aug. 1902, A.N., F^{17} 24132.
16 Gerbod, *Epurations*, p. 92.
17 E.g. Jean Faury, *Cléricalisme et anticléricalisme dans le Tarn 1840–1900* (Toulouse, 1980), p. 475.
18 *Ibid.*, p. 472.
19 Cited in Gerbod, *Enseignants*, pp. 21–2.
20 Jacques and Mona Ozouf, *La République des instituteurs* (Paris, 1992), p. 205.
21 *Ibid.*, pp. 341–56.
22 Request of 24 Sep. 1909, reply 8 Oct. 1909, Archives Départementales de l'Aude (cited as 'A.D. Aude'), W 334.
23 E.g. Ecole Normale d'Auteuil, Archives Départementales de la Seine (cited as 'A.D. Seine'), DIT^1 166.
24 E.g. A.D. Seine, DIT^1 166.
25 *Ibid.* The same situation was reflected in the departmental archives of the Aude, the Charente-Maritime and the Tarn.
26 E.g. A.D. Seine, DIT^1 153.
27 *Inspecteur primaire* to Directeur de l'Enseignement Primaire, 17 Nov. 1885, A.D. Seine, DIT^1 345.
28 Mayor of Asnières to Directeur de l'Enseignement Primaire de la Seine, 23 Nov. 1899, and similar letter from Alexandre Millerand, 21 Sep. 1903 on behalf of same candidate, A.D. Seine, DIT^1 166.
29 Undated letter of early July 1905, A.D. Seine, DIT^1 166.
30 E.g. *inspecteur primaire* to Directeur de l'Enseignement Primaire, 30 Apr. 1908, A.D. Seine, DIT^1 345.
31 Faury, *Tarn*, pp. 472 and 475. This excellent departmental study does not make use of the personal dossiers of teachers, which were presumably not accessible at the time of writing.
32 *Ibid.*, p. 475.
33 *Ibid.*, pp. 475–6.
34 Letter of 20 July 1903, Archives Départementales du Tarn (cited as 'A.D. Tarn'), IT2 80.
35 *Inspecteur primaire* to Inspecteur d'Académie, 18 Sep. 1898, A.D. Tarn, IT2 82.
36 Letter of 12 Dec. 1892, A.D. Tarn, IT2 81.

37 A.D. Tarn, IT2.
38 Letter of 8 Aug. 1901, A.D. Tarn, IT2 86.
39 Letter to Inspecteur d'Académie, 27 May 1904, A.D. Tarn, IT2 85.
40 Letter to Inspecteur d'Académie, 7 May 1902, A.D. Tarn, IT2 85.
41 Letter to Inspecteur d'Académie, 8 Feb. 1904, A.D. Tarn, IT2 83.
42 See letter of Inspecteur d'Académie to Prefect, 3 Nov. 1892, A.D. Char.-Mar., IT 135.
43 Letter of 11 Aug. 1899, A.D. Char.-Mar., IT 137.
44 Letters of 3 Oct. and 3 Nov. 1892, A.D. Char.-Mar., IT 135.
45 Recounted in letter of *inspecteur primaire* to Inspecteur d'Académie, 26 Mar. 1900, A.D. Char.-Mar., IT 136.
46 Recounted in Inspecteur d'Académie to prefect, 27 May 1892, A.D. Char.-Mar., IT 137.
47 Recounted in letters of *inspecteurs d'académie* to prefects, 31 Mar. and 30 Sep. 1902, A.N., F17 11619.
48 Report of Inspecteur d'Académie, 3 Apr. 1902, A.N., F17 11619.
49 Report of Inspecteur d'Académie, 29 Mar. 1902, A.N., F17 11619.
50 Combes MSS, A.D. Char.-Mar., 13 J 32.
51 E.g. A.D. Seine, DIT1 554.
52 E.g. A.D. Seine, DIT1 567.
53 Former acquaintance of Alan Boase.

9: *LA GRANDE ILLUSION?* 1914–1939

1 Recent publications concerning French Catholics during the First World War include Gérard Cholvy and Yves-Marie Hilaire, *Histoire religieuse de la France contemporaine*, vol. II: *1880–1930* (Toulouse, 1986), pp. 235–61; Jacques Fontana, *Les Catholiques français pendant la Grande Guerre* (Paris, 1990); Michel Lagrée, 'Exilés dans leur patrie', pp. 440–51; Nadine-Josette Chaline (ed.), *Chrétiens dans la première guerre mondiale* (Paris, 1994), especially Jean-Marie Mayeur, 'Les Catholiques français et Benoît XV en 1917', pp. 153–65.
2 In addition to the books cited in note 1 above, the role of committed Catholics in government can be followed in the biographical entries in Jean Jolly (ed.), *Dictionnaire des parlementaires français (1889–1940)*, 8 vols. (Paris, 1960–77).
3 The broad outline of the politico-religious history of the inter-war years is given in Cholvy and Hilaire, *Histoire religieuse*, vols. II and III, and in Lebrun (ed.), *Histoire des catholiques*. See also Harry W. Paul, *The Second Ralliement: the rapprochement between Church and State in France in the twentieth century* (Washington, 1967) and Eugen Weber, *Action Française: royalism and reaction in twentieth-century France* (Stanford, 1962).
4 In February 1906 the two newly appointed archbishops were both leading choices of their respective regions; and of the fourteen bishops, six were arguably the most favoured candidates in their provinces, two had some support, and only four had no apparent support for the particular see. Even then, some of the disregarded suggestions were given sees elsewhere. Moreover the Congregation for Extraordinary Ecclesiastical Affairs informed the

French bishops that they should confine their suggestions to 'candidats attachés aux directions que le Siège Apostolique a tracées dans ces dernières années, relativement aux institutions civiles que la nation française s'est données' – in other words supporters of the Ralliement. They should likewise confine their recommendations to the secular clergy – prudently avoiding members and ex-members of the religious orders. See in particular the papers and minutes of the Congregation for Extraordinary Ecclesiastical Affairs, meeting of 25 Jan. 1906, Stat. Vat., A.E. Straord., Sess. 1066. But it later became Merry del Val's policy to look to the French seminary in Rome for future bishops; these young men were nurtured in salutary isolation from Gallic influences and could be relied upon to be tough in times of crisis. The head of the seminary, Father Le Floch, was a malign influence on the Consistorial Congregation, responsible for these appointments, as was Cardinal de Lai; and it was only when these duties were transferred to the Congregation for Extraordinary Ecclesiastical Affairs in 1921 that a more conciliatory type of nominee started to emerge. This partly explains why a number of Benedict XV's appointments in the war years were as unwelcome as those of Pius X.

5 MS notes and oral recollections of the Abbé Ferdinand Renaud, Nov. 1956.

6 On Gamelin and the broad issue of relations between the high command and the regime in the 1930s, see Martin Alexander, *The Republic in danger: General Maurice Gamelin and the politics of French defence, 1933–1940* (Cambridge, 1992). On his attitudes while in prison, p. 394.

7 See notably Christian Baechler, *Le Parti catholique alsacien, 1890–1939: du Reichsland à la République jacobine* (Paris, 1982).

8 See Jean-Claude Delbreil, *Centrisme et Démocratie-Chrétienne en France: le Parti Démocrate Populaire des origines au M.R.P., 1919–1944* (Paris, 1990). The Sillon's quasi-successor, Jeune République, had decided not to form a parliamentary group, although several of its members were elected to the Chamber as members of other parties.

9 Paul Christophe, *1936: les catholiques et le Front Populaire* (Paris, 1979); Agnès Rochefort-Turquin, *Front Populaire: 'socialistes parce que chrétiens'* (Paris, 1986).

10 See note 2 above.

11 Michel Launay, *La C.F.T.C.: origines et développement, 1919–1940* (Paris, 1986), pp. 249–50. On the question in general, see Jeanne Siwek-Pouydesseau, *Le Syndicalisme des fonctionnaires jusqu'à la guerre froide* (Lille, 1989). The Chautemps circular of 25 Sep. 1924 was an important step.

12 See works listed in note 2 to chapter 7 (p. 221), notably Headings, *French Freemasonry*.

13 Chevallier, *Franc-Maçonnerie*, vol. III, pp. 290–2.

14 Siwek-Pouydesseau, *Corps préfectoral*, p. 118.

15 Information on his reception in Colmar kindly supplied by Jean-Marie Mayeur. See also Pierre-Henry, *Histoire des préfets: cent cinquante ans d'administration provinciale, 1800–1950* (Paris, 1950), pp. 307–9.

16 E.g. report on Lamy-Boisroziers, 16 Apr. 1925, A.N., F[1b] I 638.

17 Siwek-Pouydesseau, *Corps préfectoral*, p. 48.

18 *Ibid.*, p. 30.
19 *Ibid.*, p. 47.
20 *Ibid.*, p. 31.
21 *Ibid.*, pp. 128–9.
22 *Ibid.*, p. 79.
23 *Ibid.*, p. 79.
24 *Ibid.*, pp. 60 and 62.
25 Kessler, 'Recrutement', pp. 41–4.
26 A. Stan. and A. Ste Gen.
27 Launay, *C.F.T.C.*, p. 343.
28 Report on Gaston Pinet, 19 Nov. 1936, A. Con. d'Et.
29 A. Stan.
30 A. Stan. and Jes. Toulouse.
31 E.g.. A.N., BB⁶ II 999, 1002 and 1004.
32 See issues of *Servir* in A. Ste Gen. and Bib. Nat. On the growing preference of *postards* for civil rather than military careers, see Langdon, *'Postards'*. The percentage of *postards* choosing to enter St Cyr dropped from 40% in 1914–24 to 34% in 1925–34 – but much more markedly to 15% in 1945–54, *ibid.*, p. 434.
33 A. Stan.
34 Thuillier, *Bureaucratie en France*, p. 715.
35 Guy Thuillier, *Les Femmes dans l'administration depuis 1900* (Paris, 1988), p. 50.
36 *Ibid.*, p. 70.
37 Launay, *C.F.T.C.*, p. 28.
38 *Ibid.*, pp. 250–1 and 302; Siwek-Pouydesseau, *Syndicalisme des fonctionnaires*, pp. 184–5.
39 Launay, *C.F.T.C.*, p. 338.
40 *Ibid.*, p. 339.
41 *Ibid.*, p. 340.
42 Gerbod, *Epurations*, p. 88.
43 Gerbod, *Enseignants*, p. 45.
44 *Ibid.*, p. 84.
45 *Ibid.*, p. 84.
46 Gerbod, *Epurations*, pp. 88–9.
47 Gerbod, *Enseignants*, p. 75.
48 *Ibid.*, p. 34.
49 *Ibid.*, p. 41.
50 A.D. Aude, T W 334.
51 E.g. report from the prefecture of the Nord on Terras, candidate for the Ecole Pratique of Narbonne, 17 Sep. 1936, A.D. Aude, T W 334.
52 Prefecture of the Nièvre on Brunel, 18 Aug. 1930; prefecture of the Indre on Suire, 26 Oct. 1936, A.D. Aude, T W 334.
53 31 Dec. 1925, A.D. Char.-Mar., IT 137.
54 Inspecteur d'Académie to prefect, 15 Apr. 1926, A.D. Char.-Mar., IT 137.
55 Letter of Mme Martin-Combes, 29 Mar. 1928, A.D. Char.-Mar., IT 137.
56 30 Mar. 1928, A.D. Char.-Mar., IT 137.
57 Letter of 5 Jan. 1927, A.D. Char.-Mar., IT 137.

58 Prefect's letter to her mother, Mme Germaine Martin-Combes, 26 Sep. 1928, A.D. Char.-Mar., IT 137. Mme Martin-Combes was to have a fine Resistance record in the Second World War, helping shot-down American airmen escape to safety. When President de Gaulle congratulated her in 1963, he also commented that her father, Emile Combes, was a great Frenchman. (Information kindly supplied by her family and the Mairie of Pons.) While making allowances for the required courtesies of such occasions, Combes's *étatisme* may well have struck a responsive chord in de Gaulle, despite his own family's vicissitudes as a result of the Combes laws on Catholic education (see p. 44).

59 Léon Lartet to prefect, 9 Sep. 1926, A.D. Char.-Mar., IT 137.

60 Letter of 19 Jul. 1927, A.D. Char.-Mar., IT 137.

61 Letter to Lartet, 24 Dec. 1927, A.D. Char.-Mar., IT 137.

62 12 Aug. 1918, A.N., F^{17} 24132.

63 24 Oct. 1899, A.N., F^{17} 24132.

64 For 1898 and 1909, see Larkin, *Church and State*, p. 8, based on information supplied by Canon Fernand Boulard; for 1931, see Cholvy and Hilaire, *Histoire religieuse*, vol. III, p. 188.

65 Cholvy and Hilaire, *Histoire religieuse*, vol. III, p. 193.

66 Fernand Boulard and Yves-Marie Hilaire, *Matériaux pour l'histoire religieuse du peuple français*, vol. I (Paris, 1982), p. 581.

10: THE LEOPARD'S SPOTS: 1940–1960

1 Jean-Marie Mayeur, 'De Gaulle as politician and Christian', in Hugh Gough and John Horne (eds.), *De Gaulle and Twentieth-Century France* (London, 1994), pp. 95–107. Emmanuel de l'Astier de la Vigerie, *postard*, pro-Communist fellow-traveller and early Resister, claimed to see in de Gaulle's Catholicism an element of stoical monism or pantheism. Philip G. Cerny, *The Politics of Grandeur: ideological aspects of de Gaulle's foreign policy* (Cambridge, 1980), pp. 19–20.

2 Jacques Duquesne, *Les Catholiques français sous l'Occupation* (Paris, 1966), p. 113. Duquesne remains the best general account of the attitudes of French Catholics during the Occupation years. There is also much useful material in Xavier de Montclos (ed), *Eglises et chrétiens dans la deuxième guerre mondiale: la France* (Lyon, 1982) and William D. Halls, *The Youth of Vichy France* (Oxford, 1981). See also Cholvy and Hilaire, *Histoire religieuse*, vol. III: *1930–1988*, pp. 67–125.

3 Examples cited in Cholvy and Hilaire, *Histoire religieuse*, vol. III, p. 100.

4 On these services, Duquesne, *Catholiques*, pp. 9–17.

5 On Pétain's attitudes to religion, *ibid.*, pp. 17–19.

6 Historians disagree as to who of these should be classified as 'Catholic'. Paul Baudouin described himself as a Catholic anticlerical. Other Catholic ministers, such as General Weygand and the Stanislas old boy and 'thirties *ligueur*, Michel Ybarnegaray, did not survive the cabinet reshuffle of 6 Sep. 1940.

7 Other sympathisers with Action Française, grateful to Pius XII, were the early Secretaries of Education, Albert Rivaud, Emile Mireaux and Georges

Ripert. Halls, *Youth*, pp. 16–20; Nicholas Atkin, 'The challenge to laïcité: Church, state and schools in Vichy France, 1940–44', *Historical Journal*, XXXV (1992), p. 157.

8 Duquesne, *Catholiques*, p. 90.

9 On Uriage, see in particular Bernard Comte, *Une Utopie combattante: L'Ecole des cadres d'Uriage, 1940–1942* (Paris, 1991). On Mounier, John Hellman, *Emmanuel Mounier and the New Catholic Left, 1930–1950* (Toronto, 1981). Hellman's *The Knight-monks of Vichy France: Uriage 1940–1945* (Montreal, 1993), appeared after the completion of this chapter.

10 Cholvy and Hilaire, *Histoire religieuse*, vol. III, p. 82.

11 On the horrendous treatment of the Jews during the Occupation, see M. R. Marrus and R. O. Paxton, *Vichy France and the Jews* (New York, 1981).

12 Duquesne, *Catholiques*, p. 22; and A. Ste Gen. Other Catholic hangers-on included Captain Feat and André Lavagne.

13 On Action Française and the Pretender during the Occupation, see Weber, *Action Française*, pp. 435–76, and Samuel M. Osgood, *French Royalism under the Third and Fourth Republics* (Hague, 1960), pp. 160–81.

14 On the whole episode, see Dominique Rossignol, *Vichy et les francs-maçons: la liquidation des sociétés secrètes, 1940–1944* (Paris, 1981).

15 Halls, *Youth*, p. 115.

16 Montclos, *France*, pp. 173–4.

17 Robert O. Paxton, *Vichy France: Old Guard and New Order, 1940–1944* (London, 1972), p. 339. This remains the best single-volume analysis of the period as a whole.

18 Sonia Mazey and Vincent Wright, 'Les Préfets', in J.-P. Azéma and F. Bédarida (eds.), *Vichy et les français* (Paris, 1992), p. 272.

19 Siwek-Pouydesseau, *Corps préfectoral*, pp. 79–80; Paxton, *Vichy France*, p. 342; Mazey and Wright, 'Les Préfets', p. 276.

20 Paxton, *Vichy France*, p. 342; Mazey and Wright, 'Les Préfets', pp. 274 and 277; the percentage for sub-prefects and *secrétaires généraux* is based on information in Ministère de l'Intérieur, *Annuaire du Corps préfectoral et de l'administration centrale* (Paris, 1943).

21 Mazey and Wright, 'Les Préfets', p. 277.

22 A. Ste Gen. and A. Stan.; *Annuaire des anciens de Franklin et Vaugirard* (Paris, 1977). The old Jesuit Vaugirard school was amalgamated with the Franklin school.

23 See individual biographies in Jolly, *Dictionnaire*.

24 For sources see note 22 above and Min. Intérieur, *Annuaire* (1943).

25 Cholvy and Hilaire, *Histoire religieuse*, vol. III, p. 78.

26 Duquesne, *Catholiques*, pp. 274–5.

27 Archbishop Saliège of Toulouse, unable to attend the assembly, angrily denounced the declaration in a private letter to Cardinal Liénart of Lille (24 Feb. 1944). Cholvy and Hilaire, *Histoire religieuse*, vol. III, p. 111. During the first two years of the Occupation, Saliège had affirmed his loyalty to the established government, even when becoming increasingly critical of Vichy's policies; but in 1943 he informed de Gaulle of his adherence to his cause. Duquesne, *Catholiques*, pp. 334–5. Saliège was the most outspoken opponent of Vichy's treatment of the Jews; and only his physical infirmities

saved him from imprisonment when the Gestapo came to fetch him in June 1944. In the early days of Vichy, Saliège's friend, the rector of the Institut Catholique de Toulouse, Mgr. de Solages, was rumoured to have said to a fashionable preacher at Vichy's quasi-*chapelle royale*, St Louis, 'I would sooner have a victorious France governed by Léon Blum and the Freemasons than a defeated France ruled by the Marshal.' *Ibid.*, pp. 162–3. Very different was the attitude of the former rector of the Institut Catholique de Paris, the ageing Cardinal Baudrillart, one-time Bonapartist and Germanophobe, who now welcomed the German connection as a resurrection of medieval Christendom against the new infidel, Bolshevism.

28 Duquesne, *Catholiques*, pp. 174 and 276.

29 *Ibid.*, pp. 276 and 336.

30 Other ministries that were fleetingly held by Catholics included the Economy, the Army, Ex-Servicemen and Defence.

31 On the MRP in general, see Cholvy and Hilaire, *Histoire religieuse*, vol. III, pp. 127–37; Duquesne, *Catholiques*, pp. 367–456; Ronald E.M. Irving, *Christian Democracy in France* (London, 1973); Jean-Marie Mayeur, *Des partis catholiques à la démocratie chrétienne* (Paris, 1980), pp. 161–74.

32 The four removed were Archbishop Du Bois de la Villerabel of Aix (not to be confused with the former Archbishop of Rouen and devotee of Action Française), Bishop Auvity of Mende, Bishop Dutoit of Arras and the auxiliary Bishop Beaussart of Paris. All four had made public comments that were regarded as either supportive of Franco-German co-operation or hostile to its critics. Idle speculators may savour the fact that Beaussart had taught the young Charles de Gaulle at the Collège Stanislas four decades earlier – for there were to be many teachers shopped by ungrateful pupils at the Liberation. The negotiations for the bishops' removal are treated in André Latreille, *De Gaulle, la Libération et l'Eglise catholique* (Paris, 1978). Apart from the four French Bishops, the Apostolic Vicars of Rabat, St Pierre et Miquelon and Dakar were obliged to resign.

33 See Peter Novick, *The Resistance versus Vichy: the purge of collaborators in liberated France* (London, 1968); Paxton, *Vichy France*, pp. 330–52.

34 Paxton, *Vichy France*, pp. 335–8.

35 *Ibid.*, p. 342.

36 The 52% includes eight Vichy *corps* members who had either been subsequently arrested by the Germans or who had joined the Resistance. Based on information in Ministère de l'Intérieur, *Annuaire du Corps préfectoral et de l'administration centrale* (Paris, 1947).

37 Siwek-Pouydesseau, *Corps préfectoral*, p. 40.

38 Sources as in note 22 above.

39 Siwek-Pouydesseau, *Corps préfectoral*, pp. 132–3.

40 *Ibid.*, p. 121.

41 Kessler, 'Recrutement', pp. 50–2. See also her authoritative study, *L'Ecole Nationale d'Administration: la politique de la haute fonction publique* (Paris, 1978).

42 Siwek-Pouydesseau, *Corps préfectoral*, pp. 52 and 97.

43 *Ibid.*, pp. 33 and 152.

44 Gerbod, *Epurations*, p. 94.

45 The bishops had tried hard to obtain from the Vichy government some sort of financial assistance for private schools. But despite persistent lobbying, all they got was a temporary annual grant, which was supposedly intended for schools with particular problems (2 November 1941). The government had nevertheless permitted sympathetic municipalities to give help, if they were so minded; but this became a reality only in areas where Catholicism was a strong force in the local population. Even so these various tokens of government favour had encouraged more Catholic parents to resort to the private sector, with the result that its share of the primary-school population rose from 18% to 23% by 1943. These various favours to private schools were swept away at the Liberation, leaving Catholics worried as to how the expansion achieved under Vichy could be kept in being during the economically hard times ahead.

11: CROQUET THROUGH THE LOOKING GLASS: RULES AND IDENTITY IN QUESTION, 1960–1994

1 *Crisis and Compromise: Politics in the Fourth Republic*, 4th edn (London, 1972), p. 4.

2 Pascale and Jean-Dominique Antoni, *Les Ministres de la Ve République* (Paris, 1976), p. 18. On the number of Collège Stanislas old boys among ministers, see *ibid.*, p. 24.

3 Compiling comparable figures of religious practice for different denominations in various countries is extremely difficult. Not only is weekly church-going taken much less seriously in some denominations than in others, but the methods of collecting and classifying data vary enormously. Chronological and geographical comparisons in France are further bedevilled by the fact that information for the last two decades is largely based on nation-wide sample polls, using oral questionnaires put to approximately 1,500 people – with all the deficiencies that this method entails. Information for the 1960s and earlier, however, was based on head counts, which enabled regional differences to be charted, something which current methods make no attempt to tackle. There are no successors – or predecessors – to the excellent maps of Catholic Mass-going and ordinations in western Europe during the 1950s and early 'sixties, contained in Fernand Boulard and Jean Rémy, *Pratique religieuse urbaine et régions culturelles* (Paris, 1968), maps F and G *hors-texte*. For a general discussion of secularisation in the late twentieth century, see *inter alia* David Martin's *A General Theory of Secularisation* (Oxford, 1978) and *The Religious and the Secular* (London, 1969). For France in particular, see Danièle Hervieu-Léger, *Vers un nouveau christianisme?* (Paris, 1986) and Guy Michelat *et al.*, *Les Français sont-ils encore catholiques?* (Paris, 1991).

4 In the immediate post-Liberation weeks, nearly a third of the adult French population went to Sunday Mass. Michelat, *Français*, p. 28. This represented perhaps a high tide, combining a residue of wartime apprehension and Vichy habits, together with Liberation euphoria and gratitude.

5 Cholvy and Hilaire, *Histoire religieuse*, vol. I, p. 313.

6 *Ibid.*, vol. III, p. 188.

7   *Ibid.*, pp. 167–208; Michelat. *Français, passim.* Yet even in 1986, 81% of the respondents to the poll described themselves as 'Catholics', despite the fact that only one in eight followed the Church's directives on Mass-going. 84% of the French population in the mid-'eighties had been baptised, as were 64% of the children born in the period – despite the statistical impact of post-war non-Catholic immigration. See René Rémond, 'Un chapitre inachevé (1958–1990)', in *Histoire de la France religieuse*, vol. IV (Paris, 1992), p. 367.

8   Rémond, 'Un chapitre inachevé', p. 388.

9   *Ibid.*, p. 417.

10 *Ibid.*, p. 377.

11 Ironically the liturgical experiments of lay enthusiasts were being paralleled by the official expedients of the Church to provide for the spiritual needs of parishes that no longer had a priest of their own. From 1967 the laity in such parishes could hold services with pre-consecrated hosts. *Ibid.*, p. 381.

12 Siwek-Pouydesseau, *Corps préfectoral*, pp. 148–9.

13 A. Stan. and Association des Anciens Elèves, *Franklin et Vaugirard* (1977).

14 Siwek-Pouydesseau, *Corps préfectoral*, p. 150.

15 Hervé Hamon and Patrick Rotman, *La Deuxième Gauche: histoire intellectuelle et politique de la C.F.D.T.* (Paris, 1982), p. 133, n. 2.

16 Notably the Guermeur law of 25 November 1977 which had given private schools under *contrat d'association* much greater control over the appointment of their staff. For a narrative of the 1984 episode, see Gérard Leclerc, *La Bataille de l'école: 15 siècles d'histoire, 3 ans de combat* (Paris, 1985); for a judicious, well-informed interpretation of its significance, see Antoine Prost, *Education, société et politiques: une histoire de l'enseignement en France de 1945 à nos jours* (Paris, 1992), pp. 169–87.

17 In 1986, when the Socialists lost the legislative elections and much of their popularity, a sample poll revealed that only 10% of weekly Mass-goers supported the Socialists and Communists, while 60% favoured the parties of the Right. Michelat, *Français*, p. 81. On the general question, see Guy Michelat and Michel Simon, *Classe, religion et comportement politique* (Paris, 1977).

18 Interviewed by Anne-Elisabeth Moutet, *Sunday Times*, 7 Sep. 1986.

Sources

ARCHIVAL SOURCES

ECCLESIASTICAL ARCHIVES

Archivio Segreto Vaticano (cited as 'A.S. Vat.'): documents are not available for the period after 1922.

Segretario di Stato (cited as 'Stat. Vat.'): the Seconda Sezione archives, likewise subject to the 1922 rule, contain sensitive material such as the papers of the Sacra Congregazione degli Affari Ecclesiastici Straordinari (cited as 'A.E. Straord.').

Archivio dei Padri Assunzionisti (cited as 'Assumpt.'), Rome.

Curia Generalizia PP Gesuiti (cited as 'Jes. Rom.'), Rome.

Archives de la Société de Jésus, Province de Paris, Chantilly (cited as 'Jes. Chant.').

Bibliothèque de la Société de Jésus, Province de Toulouse (cited as 'Jes. Toulouse').

Archives Historiques de l'Archevêché de Paris (cited as 'Archiepisc. Paris').

Archives Historiques du Diocèse de Nice

FRENCH PUBLIC ARCHIVES

Archives Nationales (cited as 'A.N.'):
Série F: main ministerial archives.
Série BB: Ministère de la Justice.
Série C: parliamentary archives.
Série AP: private letters and papers of various political and other figures. (Those principally consulted were: 258 AP, MS diary of the Abbé Arthur Mugnier; 300 AP, Archives de la Maison de France (branche d'Orléans), III 795–811 (subject to authorisation by the Comte de Paris); 400 AP, Archives Napoléon, 174–214; 401 AP, Papiers Déroulède (subject to authorisation by Monsieur Yves Barbet-Massin).)

Archives du Conseil d'Etat (cited as 'A. Con. d'Et.').

Archives du Ministère des Affaires Etrangères.

Archives du Service Historique de l'Armée de Terre (cited as 'Armée'), Vincennes.

Archives de la Préfecture de Police (cited as 'A. Préf. Pol.'), Paris.

Archives Départementales de l'Aude (cited as 'A.D. Aude'): primary-school and training-college personnel.

Archives Départementales de la Charente-Maritime (cited as 'A.D. Char.-Mar.'): private papers of Emile Combes; primary-school personnel.

Archives Départementales de la Seine (cited as 'A.D. Seine'): primary-school personnel.

Archives Départementales du Tarn (cited as 'A.D. Tarn'): primary-school personnel.

Archives de l'Ecole Polytechnique (cited as 'A. Ec. Pol.').

Bibliothèque de l'Institut (cited as 'Bib. Inst.'): private papers of René Waldeck-Rousseau.

Bibliothèque Nationale, Cabinet des Manuscrits (cited as 'Bib. Nat.'):

  FM. Central and provincial archives of the Grand Orient de France (20th-century material subject to authorisation by the Grand Orient)

  N.A.F. Papers of Bishop Lucien Lacroix of Tarentaise, Albert Houtin and Auguste Scheurer-Kestner (diaries).

OTHER ARCHIVES

L'Ecole Ste Geneviève, Versailles (cited as 'A. Ste Gen.').

Le Collège Stanislas, Paris (cited as 'A. Stan.').

Archives du Ministère des Affaires Etrangères et du Commerce Extérieur, Brussels (cited as 'Belg. SS'): despatches of Baron Maximilien d'Erp, Belgian Minister Plenipotentiary to the Holy See.

MS notes on the associations cultuelles, kindly lent by the late Canon Ferdinand Renaud.

PUBLISHED SOURCES

This alphabetical list is confined to publications that are either cited in the notes or proved useful for backgound reading and reference. Much fuller and thematically classified lists of secondary works are to be found in the excellent bibliographies in Gérard Cholvy and Yves-Marie Hilaire, *Histoire religieuse de la France contemporaine*, vols. II and III (Toulouse, 1986–88) and in Christophe Charle, *Les Elites de la République (1880–1900)* (Paris, 1987).

Alexander, Martin. *The Republic in danger: General Maurice Gamelin and the politics of French defence, 1933–1940*. Cambridge, 1992.

Almanach National. Annual publication. Paris.

Antoni, Pascale and Jean-Dominique. *Les Ministres de la Vᵉ République.* Paris, 1976.

Association Amicale des Anciens Elèves de l'Ecole Sainte-Geneviève. *Annuaire des Anciens Elèves de l'Ecole Sainte-Geneviève.* Paris; then Versailles.

  Servir. Periodical. Paris; Alençon; Versailles.

Association Amicale des Anciens Elèves du Collège Stanislas. *Annuaire des Anciens Elèves de Stanislas.* Paris.

  Dyptiques du Collège Stanislas. Irregular publication. Paris.

Association des Anciens Elèves de Franklin et Vaugirard. *Annuaire des Anciens de Franklin et Vaugirard.* Paris.

234   Sources

Atkin, Nicholas. 'The challenge to laïcité: Church, state and schools in Vichy France, 1940–44', *Historical Journal*, XXXV (1992), p. 157.
   Church and schools in Vichy France, 1940–1944. New York, 1991.
Aubert, Jacques, *et al. Les Préfets en France (1800–1940).* Geneva, 1978.
Avril, Pierre, *et al. Personnel politique français, 1870–1988.* Paris, 1989.
Baechler, Christian. *Le Parti catholique alsacien, 1890–1939: Du Reichsland à la République jacobine.* Paris, 1982.
Barge, Walter. 'The Generals of the Republic: The corporate personality of high military rank in France, 1889–1914'. Ph.D. dissertation. Univ. North Carolina, 1982.
Barrès, Maurice. *Scènes et doctrines du nationalisme.* 2 vols. Paris, 1925.
Bell, David S., Johnston, Douglas, and Morris, Peter. *A Biographical dictionary of French political leaders since 1870.* London, 1990.
Birnbaum, P. *Un Mythe politique: 'La République juive', de Léon Blum à Pierre Mendès France.* Paris, 1988.
   Les Fous de la République: Histoire politique des Juifs d'Etat de Gambetta à Vichy. Paris, 1992.
Bodley, J. E. C. *France.* 2nd edn. London, 1899.
Bosworth, William. *Catholicism and crisis in modern France: French Catholic groups at the threshold of the Fifth Republic.* Princeton, 1962.
Boulard, Fernand, and Rémy, Jean. *Pratique religieuse urbaine et régions culturelles.* Paris, 1968.
Boulard, Fernand, Hilaire, Yves-Marie, and Cholvy, Gérard. *Matériaux pour l'histoire religieuse du peuple français.* 3 vols. Paris, 1982–92.
Brunot, André, and Coquand, Roger. *Le Corps des ponts et chaussées.* Paris, 1982.
Bush, John W. 'Education and social status: The Jesuit *collège* in the early Third Republic', *French Historical Studies*, IX (1975), 127–40.
Buttoud, Gérard. *Les Conservateurs des eaux et forêts sous la Troisième République, 1870–1940.* Nancy, 1981.
Camus, Michel. *Histoire des Saint-Cyriens 1802–1980.* Paris, 1980.
Capéran, Louis. *L'Anticléricalisme et l'Affaire Dreyfus, 1897–1899.* Toulouse, 1948.
Castellane, Boni de. *Mémoires de Boni de Castellane, 1867–1932.* Paris, 1986.
Cerny, Philip G. *The politics of grandeur: Ideological aspects of de Gaulle's foreign policy.* Cambridge, 1980.
Chadeau, Emmanuel. *Les Inspecteurs des finances au XIXᵉ siècle (1850–1914).* Paris, 1986.
Chaline, Nadine-Josette (ed.) *Chrétiens dans la première guerre mondiale.* Paris, 1994.
Charle, Christophe. *Les Hauts Fonctionnaires en France au XIXᵉ siècle.* Paris, 1980.
   'Intellectuels et élites en France (1880–1900)'. Thèse de doctorat. Univ. Paris I, 1985.
   Les Elites de la République (1880–1900). Paris, 1987.
Charle, Christophe, and Ferré, Régine. *Le Personnel de l'enseignement supérieur en France aux XIXᵉ et XXᵉ siècles.* Paris, 1985.
Charle, Christophe, *et al. Prosopographie des élites françaises, XVI–XXᵉ siècles: Guide de recherche.* Paris, 1980.

Charmasson, T. (ed.). *L'Histoire de l'enseignement XIX–XX siècles. Guide de chercheur.* Paris, 1986.

Chevallier, Pierre. *Histoire de la Franc-Maçonnerie française.* Vol. III. Paris, 1975.

Cholvy, Gérard, and Hilaire, Yves-Marie. *Histoire religieuse de la France contemporaine.* 3 vols. Toulouse, 1985–8.

Christophe, Paul. *1936: Les catholiques et le Front Populaire.* Paris, 1979.

Clark, James M. *Teachers and politics in France: A pressure group study of the Fédération de l'Education Nationale.* New York, 1967.

Cohen, Paul M. *Piety and politics: Catholic revival and the generation of 1905–1914 in France.* New York, 1987.

Comte, Bernard. *Une Utopie combattante: L'Ecole des cadres d'Uriage, 1940–1942.* Paris, 1991.

Cour des Comptes, La. Paris, 1984.

Coutrot, A., and Dreyfus, F. *Les Forces religieuses dans la société française.* Paris, 1965.

Dansette, Adrien. *Histoire religieuse de la France contemporaine.* Vol. II. Paris, 1951.

Debidour, Antonin. *L'Eglise catholique et l'état en France sous la Troisième République.* Vol. II. Paris, 1909.

Delattre, Pierre. *Les Etablissements des Jésuites en France, 1540–1900.* 5 vols. Paris, 1940–57.

Delbreil, Jean-Claude. *Centrisme et démocratie-chrétienne en France: Le Parti Démocrate Populaire des origines au M.R.P., 1919–1944.* Paris, 1990.

Dictionnaire des parlementaires français, 1940–1958. 2 vols. Paris, 1988–92.

Donegani, Jean-Marie, and Lescanne, Guy. *Catholicismes de France.* Paris, 1986.

Duquesne, Jacques. *Les Catholiques français sous l'Occupation.* Paris, 1966.

Encrevé, André. *Les Protestants en France de 1800 à nos jours.* Paris, 1985.

Estèbe, Jean. *Les Ministres de la République, 1871–1914.* Paris, 1982.

Faury, Jean. *Cléricalisme et anticléricalisme dans le Tarn, 1840–1900.* Toulouse, 1980.

Fontana, Jacques. *Les Catholiques français pendant la Grande Guerre.* Paris, 1990.

Fougère, Louis (ed.) *Le Conseil d'Etat: Son histoire à travers les documents d'époque, 1799–1974* (Paris, 1974).

Freyssinet-Dominjon, Jacqueline. *Les Manuels d'histoire de l'école libre, 1882–1959.* Paris, 1969.

Galabru, André. *L'Assassinat de Félix Faure.* Paris, 1988.

Gerbod, Paul. *Les Enseignants et la politique.* Paris, 1976.

Gerbod, Paul, et al. *Les Epurations administratives, XIXᵉ et XXᵉ siècles.* Geneva, 1977.

Gibson, Ralph. *A social history of French Catholicism, 1789–1914.* London, 1989.

Goyau, Georges. 'Journal inédit de Georges Goyau', *La Pensée Catholique*, No. 33, 1954.

Grand Orient. *Bulletin officiel.* Paris.

Guiral, Pierre, and Thuillier, Guy. *La Vie quotidienne des députés en France de 1871 à 1914.* Paris, 1980.

La Vie quotidienne des professeurs en France de 1870 à 1940. Paris, 1982

Halls, William D. *The youth of Vichy France.* Oxford, 1981.

Hamon, Hervé, and Rotman, Patrick. *La Deuxième Gauche: Histoire intellectuelle et politique de la C.F.D.T.* Paris, 1982.

Headings, Mildred J. *French Freemasonry under the Third Republic.* Baltimore, 1949.

Hellman, John. *Emmanuel Mounier and the New Catholic Left, 1930–1950.* Toronto, 1981.

The Knight-monks of Vichy France: Uriage 1940–1945. Montreal, 1993.

Hervieu-Léger, Danièle. *Vers un nouveau christianisme?* Paris, 1986.

Hood, Ronald C. *The French naval officer corps 1919–1939: A social and political history of France's naval dynasties between the world wars.* Ann Arbor, 1979.

Howorth, Jolyon, and Cerny, Philip G. (eds.). *Elites in France: Origins, reproduction and power.* London, 1981.

Inglehart, Ronald. *The silent revolution: Changing values and political styles among western publics.* Princeton, 1977.

Irving, Ronald E.M. *Christian Democracy in France.* London, 1973.

Isambert, François-André. *De la religion à l'éthique.* Paris, 1992.

Isambert, François-André, and Terrenoire, J.-P. *Atlas de la pratique religieuse des catholiques en France.* Paris, 1980.

Jolly, Jean (ed.). *Dictionnaire des parlementaires français (1889–1940).* 8 vols. Paris, 1960–77.

Joly, Bertrand. 'Le Parti royaliste et l'affaire Dreyfus (1898–1900)', *Revue historique*, CCLXIX (1983), 311–64.

Kessler, Marie-Christine. 'Historique du système de formation et de recrutement des hauts fonctionnaires', *Revue française d'administration publique*, No. 1 (Jan.–Mar. 1977), pp. 9–52.

L'Ecole Nationale d'Administration: La politique de la haute fonction publique. Paris, 1978.

Kok-Escalle, Marie-Christine. *Instaurer une culture par l'enseignement de l'histoire: France 1876–1912.* Berne, 1988.

Ladous, Régis. *Monsieur Portal et les siens (1855–1926).* Paris, 1985.

Lagrée, Michel. 'Exilés dans leur patrie (1880–1920)' in François Lebrun (ed.), *Histoire des catholiques en France du XVᵉ siècle à nos jours.* Toulouse, 1980.

Lanfrey, André. *Les Catholiques français et l'école (1902–1914).* 2 vols. Paris, 1990.

Langdon, John W. 'Social implications of Jesuit education in France: The schools of Vaugirard and Sainte-Geneviève'. Ph.D. dissertation, Syracuse Univ., 1973.

'Whither the *Postards*? Graduates of the Ecole Sainte-Geneviève, 1914–1954', in Donald N. Baker and Patrick J. Harrigan (eds.), *The making of Frenchmen: Current directions in the history of education in France, 1679–1979.* Waterloo, Ontario, 1980.

Laprévote, Gilles. *Les Ecoles normales primaires en France, 1879–1979: Splendeurs et misères de la formation des maîtres.* Lyon, 1984.

Larkin, Maurice. *Church and State after the Dreyfus Affair: The Separation issue in France.* London, 1974.

'Loubet's visit to Rome and the question of Papal prestige', *The Historical Journal*, IV (1961), 97–103.

'The Vatican, French Catholics, and the *associations cultuelles*', *The Journal of Modern History* XXXVI, (1964), 298–317.

'The Church and the French Concordat, 1891 to 1902', *The English Historical Review*, LXXXI (1966), 717–39.

'The Vatican, France and the Roman Question, 1898–1903: New archival evidence', *The Historical Journal*, XXVII (1984), 177–97.

'"La République en danger"? The Pretenders, the Army and Déroulède, 1898–1899', *English Historical Review*, C (1985), 85–105.

Latreille, André. *De Gaulle, la Libération et l'Eglise catholique*. Paris, 1978.

Launay, Marcel. *L'Eglise et l'Ecole en France XIXᵉ–XXᵉ siècles*. Paris, 1988.

Launay, Michel. *La C.F.T.C.: Origines et développement, 1919–1940*. Paris, 1986.

Le Texier, Robert. *Le Fol Eté du Fort Chabrol*. Paris, 1990.

Leclerc, Gérard. *La Bataille de l'école: 15 siècles d'histoire, 3 ans de combat*. Paris, 1985.

Leveau, Rémy, and Kepel, Gilles. *Les Musulmans dans la société française*. Paris, 1988.

Ligou, Daniel. *Frédéric Desmons et la Franc-Maçonnerie sous la Troisième République*. Paris, 1966.

Machelon, Jean-Pierre. *La République contre les libertés: Les restrictions aux libertés publiques de 1879 à 1914*. Paris, 1976.

Margandant, Jo B. *Madame le professeur: Women educators in the Third Republic*. Princeton, 1990.

Marrus, M. R., and Paxton, R. O. *Vichy France and the Jews*. New York, 1981.

Martin, David. *A general theory of secularisation*. Oxford, 1978.

The religious and the secular. London, 1969.

Martin, Roger. *Les Instituteurs de l'entre-deux guerres*. Lyon, 1982.

Mayeur, Françoise. *L'Enseignement secondaire des jeunes filles sous la Troisième République*. Paris, 1977.

Histoire générale de l'enseignement et de l'éducation en France. Vol. III: *De la Révolution à l'école républicaine*. Paris, 1981.

Mayeur, Jean-Marie. *Des partis catholiques à la démocratie chrétienne*. Paris, 1980.

'De Gaulle as politician and Christian' in Hugh Gough and John Horne (eds.), *De Gaulle and twentieth-century France*. London, 1994, pp. 95–107.

Mazey, Sonia, and Wright, Vincent. 'Les Préfets', in J.-P. Azéma and F. Bédarida (eds.), *Le Régime de Vichy et les français*. Paris, 1992, pp. 267–86.

Michelat, Guy, et al. *Les Français sont-ils encore catholiques?* Paris, 1991.

Michelat, Guy, and Simon, Michel. *Classe, religion et comportement politique*. Paris, 1977.

Ministère de l'Intérieur. *Annuaire du Corps préfectoral et de l'administration centrale*. Paris, 1943 and 1947.

Montclos, Xavier de (ed.). *Eglises et chrétiens dans la deuxième guerre mondiale: La France*. Lyon, 1982.

Mugnier, Arthur. *Journal de l'Abbé Mugnier (1879–1939)*. Paris, 1985.

Novick, Peter. *The Resistance versus Vichy: The purge of collaborators in liberated France*. London, 1968.

Osborne, Thomas R. *A Grande Ecole for the Grands Corps: The recruitment and training of the French administrative élite in the XIXth century*. New York, 1983.

Osgood, Samuel M. *French Royalism under the Third and Fourth Republics*. Hague, 1960.

Ozouf, Jacques and Mona. *La République des instituteurs*. Paris, 1992.

Paul, Harry W. *The Second Ralliement: The rapprochement between Church and State in France in the twentieth century*. Washington, 1967.

Paxton, Robert O. *Vichy France: Old guard and new order, 1940–1944*. London, 1972.

Pierre-Henry. *Histoire des préfets: Cent cinquante ans d'administration provinciale, 1800–1950*. Paris, 1950.

Pinaud, Pierre-François. *Les Trésoriers-payeurs généraux au XIXe siècle (1865–1914)*. Paris, 1983.

Porch, Douglas. *The march to the Marne: The French Army, 1871–1914*. Cambridge, 1981.

Poulat, Emile. *Eglise contre bourgeoisie: Introduction au devenir du catholicisme actuel*. Paris, 1977.

Une Eglise ébranlée: Changement, conflit et continuité de Pie XII à Jean-Paul II Paris, 1980.

Prost, Antoine. *Histoire de l'enseignement en France 1800–1967*. Paris, 1968.

Education, société et politiques: Une histoire de l'enseignement en France de 1945 à nos jours. Paris, 1992.

Reinach, Joseph. *Histoire de l'Affaire Dreyfus*. 7 vols. Paris, 1901–8.

Rémond, René. *Forces religieuses et attitudes politiques dans la France contemporaine*. Paris, 1965.

Les Catholiques dans la France des années trente. Paris, 1979.

L'Anticléricalisme en France de 1815 à nos jours. Brussels, 1985.

'Un chapitre inachevé (1958–1990)', in *Histoire de la France religieuse*. Vol. IV. Paris, 1992, pp. 349–459.

Rochefort-Turquin, Agnès. *Front Populaire: 'Socialistes parce que chrétiens'*. Paris, 1986.

Rossignol, Dominique. *Vichy et les francs-maçons: La liquidation des sociétés secrètes, 1940–1944*. Paris, 1981.

Rutkoff, Peter. *Revanche and revision: The Ligue des Patriotes and the origins of the radical right in France, 1882–1900*. Athens, Ohio, 1981.

Sedgwick, Alexander. *The Ralliement in French politics, 1890–1898*. Cambridge, Mass., 1965.

Serman, William. *Les Officiers français dans la nation (1848–1914)*. Paris, 1982.

Shinn, Terry. *Savoir scientifique et pouvoir social: L'Ecole Polytechnique*. Paris, 1980.

Sirinelli, Jean-François. *Génération intellectuelle: Khâgneux et Normaliens dans l'entre-deux guerres*. Paris, 1988.

Siwek-Pouydesseau, Jeanne. *Le Corps préfectoral sous la Troisième et la Quatrième République*. Paris, 1969.

Le Syndicalisme des fonctionnaires jusqu'à la guerre froide. Lille, 1989.

Smith, Robert J. *The Ecole Normale Supérieure and the Third Republic*. Albany, 1982.

Sorlin, Pierre. *Waldeck-Rousseau*. Paris, 1966.

'La Croix' et les juifs, 1880–1899. Paris, 1967.

Sternhell, Zeev. *La Droite révolutionnaire, 1885–1914: Les origines françaises du fascisme*. Paris, 1978.

Suleiman, Ezra N. *Politics, power and bureaucracy in France: The administrative elite*. Princeton, 1974.

Elites in French society: The politics of survival. Princeton, 1978.

Sutter, Jacques. *La Vie religieuse des français à travers les sondages d'opinion (1944–1976)*. 2 vols. Paris, 1984.

Szafran, Maurice. *Les Juifs dans la politique française de 1945 à nos jours*. Paris, 1990.

Tannenbaum, J.K. *General Maurice Sarrail, 1856–1929*. Chapel Hill, 1974.

Thuillier, Guy. *Bureaucratie et bureaucrates en France au XIXe siècle*. Geneva, 1980.

La Bureaucratie en France aux XIXe et XXe siècles. Paris, 1987.

Les Femmes dans l'administration depuis 1900. Paris, 1988.

Tombs, Robert (ed.). *Nationhood and nationalism in France from Boulangism to the Great War, 1889–1918*. London, 1991.

Vassort-Rousset, Brigitte. *Les Evêques de France en politique*. Paris, 1986.

Vindé, François. *L'Affaire des Fiches, 1900–1904: Chronique d'un scandale*. Paris, 1989.

Walton, Timothy Ronald. *The French ambassadors, 1814–1914: The transition from patronage to professionalism*. Ann Arbor, 1984.

Weber, Eugen. *Action Française: Royalism and reaction in twentieth-century France*. Stanford, 1962.

Weinberg, D.H. *A Community on trial: The Jews of Paris in the 1930s*. Chicago, 1977.

Williams, Philip. *Crisis and compromise: Politics in the Fourth Republic*. 4th edn. London, 1972.

Wilson, Stephen. *Ideology and experience: Antisemitism in France at the time of the Dreyfus Affair*. London, 1982.

Wright, Vincent. 'L'Epuration du Conseil d'Etat en juillet 1879', *Revue d'histoire moderne et contemporaine*, XIX (1972), 620–53.

Index

Public institutions and occupations are normally listed in this index under their French titles.